D_ESIGN SCIENCE

IN THE NEW PARADIGM AGE

Herbert Glenauldbin Bennett RA,DS

VOLUME I OF III

DᴇSIGN SCIENCE

IN THE NEW PARADIGM AGE: VOLUME I OF III

Copyright © 2023 By **Herbert Glenauldbin Bennett RA**

All rights reserved. No part of this book may be reproduced or transmitted, downloaded, distributed, reverse engineered, or stored in or introduced into any information storage and retrieval system, in any form or by any means, including photocopying and recording, whether electronic or mechanical, now known or hereinafter invented without permission in writing from the publisher.

DISCLAIMER: The contents of this work, including, but not limited to, the accuracy of events, people, and places depicted; opinions expressed; permission to use previously published materials included; and any advice given or actions advocated are solely the responsibility of the author, who assumes all liability for said work and indemnifies the publisher against any claims stemming from publication of the work.

To order additional copies of this book, please contact:

eComRocket
www.ecomrocket.net

General Inquiries & Customer Service
Phone: 1-(403)-755-8677
Email: info@ecomrocket.net

ISBN Paperback: 978-1-77419-208-5
ISBN eBook: 978-1-77419-207-8

The main categories of the book are: 0. Spiritual and Creative Development 1. Architecture 2. Art 3. Business 4. Design 5. Geometry 6. Mathematics 7. Metaphysics 8. Morphology 9. Philosophy 10. The Physical Sciences 11. Synthesis 12. Symmetry.

Description: DᴇSign Science: In the New Paradigm Age

The process of synthesizing the Body, Mind, and Spirit dimensions of consciousness into natural and creative expressions to align with the highest and best use of space, time, energy, and thought to preserve and promote the genius of human life, environments, and our legacy with the most advanced harmonized Wisdom, Intelligence, Knowledge, and Information to create the most highly effective and rich aesthetic life support systems that obey natural laws, into the distant future.

Any people depicted in stock imagery provided by Getty Images are models, and such images are being used for illustrative purposes only. Certain stock imagery © Getty Images.

 *" You get told that the world is the way it is, but life can be much broader once you discover one simple fact; and that is that everything around you that you call life was made up by people no smarter than you. Once you learn (experience and internalize) that, you'll never be the same again." — Steve Jobs*

CONTENTS

Acknowledgments viii
Disclaimer ix
The Author's Thoughts xi
The "Prologue": The Grand Vision xii

Chapter 1   Hexahedron H_AH 1
    TRINE A: The Discipline 2
    TRINE B: 'SOURCE': is ALL the same by any other name 21
    TRINE C: D_ESign Science 30

Chapter 2   Icosahedron I_CH 37
    TRINE A: A New Paradigm Age is Upon Us 38
    TRINE B: 'Aesthetix' III New Paradigm-Value Systems 48
    TRINE C: Creativity: The D_ESign Process 57

Chapter 3   Tetrahedron T_RH 86
    TRINE A: Creative Potential 87
    TRINE B: Think Bank™ the Core Knowledge 105
    TRINE C: The Consciousness Story 118

Chapter 4   Cubeoctahedron H_AO_TH 135
    TRINE A: The Praxis of Consciousness 136
    TRINE B: Order 145
    TRINE C: Mind: The Command Center 181

The Afterword 198
Notes on the Canons 200
References 202
Career Resource Guide 208
Collaboration Opportunities 215
Addendum 254

D_ESIGN SCIENCE IN THE NEW PARADIGM AGE

THE "GRAND PERIODIC QUALITATIVE MATRIX"   COMPANION WORKBOOK CONTAINS THE ILLUSTRATION GALLERY, THE FRONT, BODY AND BACK MATTER, REFERENCES, AND NOTE PAGES. BECOME PART OF THE DIALOG.

 *Simple methods create complex, innovative solutions that can then be used in various fields of design,engineering, and the art of making (Everything). H.G.B.*

'What Herb's admirers are saying'

 The story of an Artist is one best told by surrendering to the deeply felt urge to make sense of many fleeting moments that connect us to source to find purpose. By seeking and tapping into SOURCE, we can apply direct knowledge to reach our higher selves. It is a phenomenal journey of discoveries and gratitude for all who helped along the way. All that's been before paves the way back to the SOURCE to which we must all return. SOURCE, by any other name, is all the same.

I agree with the axiom: "Self-praise is no recommendation." I prefer to let my story be told via shared experiences with friends, colleagues and others I have known and collaborated with on social and professional occasions working on projects; celebrating events and minor victories offered to me and those I love, on my travels around the world.

In 212 BC the Greek mathematician, philosopher, scientist and engineer
Archimedes said... *"Give me a lever and a place to stand and I will move the earth."*

2500 years later *DeSign Science* is the new lever that lifts and shifts mindsets in the new world to enhance human life and empower all creative endeavors in the spirit of constant creation in all our life support systems, technologies and solutions.

 "Any lean system is not an explosion of things but an implosion of things, a coming together (harmonizing) of things or better yet a Synthesis. We are not beginning to accept this notion, really, of life being totally dependent on the coming together of things" Paolo Soleri (1919-2013), the founder of Arcosanti.

ACKNOWLEDGMENTS

 **ALL LIVING CREATURES HAVE BUILT** in directional systems. Movement, position, destination, and mapping are key elements in knowing ourselves, where we are and where we are going. Our egos and "shegos" tell us we are in charge and are doing it alone. What amazes me is our total disregard for being truly aware of the dynamic principles and laws that govern our lives. We find 'GOD particles' in force fields with complex directional systems displacing ourselves from the source-goodness in celebration of our greatness, recognition and fame.

Having a multidimensional and directional compass is essential to navigating the currents of a new consciousness we need. We can map our own destinations to get beyond self, time and space with a healthy energy to inspire us.

I will take a different approach to my acknowledgments and apply a 'shifted paradigm form' of recognition with the most profound gratitude I know as 'Grammercy' (profound thanks). This is based on the notion of humans 'being spirits having a bodily experience' as a definition of life; that the connections, interactions we share form our worlds from birth 'back to forever'; that we come from source and we return to source. For our bubbles of nurturing, guidance and direction-finding to be in harmony with the Body- Mind-Spirit continuum we must shape our lives and connect in universal consciousness. The love and healing energies that are transmitted throughout the bubbles of me and you, places we have been and where we are going, help us make our contributions to eliminating all troubles using our creative talents, resources and gifts. Transform freeze, flight or fight with being fearless, focused and free.

The tradition of listing names of relatives, people, places and all who have been my compass by name would be another book. I would like to invite you into my bubble. To me the word 'compass' does say 'come-pass' which I interpret as an invitation for every part of my bubble to resonate to my love and Grammercy for all the goodness and kindness in it that we all share.

DISCLAIMER

THIS BOOK PROVIDES INSPIRATION AND knowledge meant to inform readers in the current era of transformations impacting many creative industries. With this knowledge we take advantage of the unique opportunities this 'new paradigm age' offers. The Publisher and author are not rendering legal, accounting or professional advice. Intellectual properties and ideas are available for development by innovators, early adopters, game changers, artists and designers.

Every effort has been made for this book to be as complete and accurate as possible at press time. The author and publisher do not assume and hereby disclaim any liability to any party for any loss, damage, or disruption caused by errors or omissions, whether such errors or omissions result from negligence, accident, or any other cause related to using its content. The book speaks directly to visual professionals who realize great value by applying the innovative, timeless BMS-WIKI Formulae; (Body, Mind, Spirit)-(Wisdom, Intelligence, Knowledge and Information) to their 'cultural economic business systems, their clientele and the audiences they serve'.

The book is a distillation of the author's life experiences, searches and travels on his 'Dao D$_E$Sign' journey, activating 'creative license from source' to explore and express creative horizons, found in creative fields where traditional knowledge, methods and technologies are being transformed. By synthesizing the 'abstract, the real, the new direct knowledge, and information into an identity, with a rich aesthetic, a language is invented in the flow of most powerful constant creation dynamic, with a coherent and unfamiliar vision not found now in our design professions. This is the book's contribution to this movement and to the ancestors.

The goal is to awaken our creative genius and to step up to new levels of visual intelligence needed in all design fields by formulating art, science and mathematics theories, skills and new symmetry principles into a 'MN Science™'. This is the key to embracing shifts charged with the potential for enhanced lifestyle solutions we can pursue with new passions and desires for design excellence, creative freedom, wellness, peace and prosperity.

Permission must be granted prior to using the content and/or ideas in the book. Please use competent professional representation when making inquiries related to the book's content. All rules, international conventions and intellectual property laws apply.

If you do not wish to adhere to the above, you may return the book to the publisher for a full refund to be followed by cancellation of your lifetime membership and benefits in the 'New Paradigm Movement' with all its opportunities, services and events.

DᴇSIGN SCIENCE IN THE NEW PARADIGM AGE

When there is realization, the same paradigms that limit us become portals of transformation to our creative freedom.

 *"Our consciousness will rise when we minimize material needs and maximize spiritual knowledge to positively impact human psychological behavior for a more efficient harmonious environment and planet; the real struggle is between quality and quantity". Herb G. Bennett.*

THE AUTHOR'S THOUGHTS

'In fields of 'nu' living vibrant forms'.
Thoughts are waves or energies of specific vibrations. All expressions like words are particles and sensations.
In the thought wave quantum in the dynamics of all energy fields.
Thoughts are and create energies in all forms of expressions. Words or descriptions are used to decode the symbols;
'Quanta, Qualia and 'Spiritua' for understanding and meaning to become The glue of Cohesion in the infinite possibilities of thought fields, Infinite consciousness, mental equilibrium and spiritual harmony. Thoughts are particles or states of specific vibrations.

All expressions, like physical particles too, are sensations.

In the particle wave quantum all is in the fields of 'nu' living forms'. Thoughts are energy constantly created in perpetual expressions. Where ideas or descriptions symbolically represent natural laws For understanding and meaning to become the glue for the Cohesion that mirrors the field of infinite possibilities and of Normal consciousness, with body, mind and spirit in harmony. Thought waves are enneaves of distinct vibrations of life manifested.

Densities of intensities, expressed in sound and profane geometries. The packets of sense data; particles of self-realization integrated. Sensations of higher energy flavors order our thought forms.

All in our thought sense quantum dynamic field of inter-ill-igence.

Various forms and thoughts create energy in return to source with little evidence of fulfillment and joy.

Words of description used to recycle the symbols of force on course towards understanding and 'nu' meaning to become the inherent glue: Cohesion in me and you in one field of infinite possibilities with true understanding 'all in' with the roll of Einstein's dice in the right action of a mental equilibrium in spiritual harmony. Though the realigning did not hold the way the truth was told a peaceful and prosperous world to behold is our resolution, once solved and incomplete to be resolved in much less stress and pain. Poetry expands associations, perceptions, mental constructs new Paradigms windows and consciousness...

THE "PROLOGUE": THE GRAND VISION

THE SCIENCE OF DESIGN IS a 'D$_E$Sign Science'. Managing complexity and technology in disciplines that share ubiquitous architecto-nic principles can be 'simple-fi-ed' and made exciting and enjoyable as ART. Scientists, artists, designers and others try to create systems and tools to understand "everything" with linear equations that are mired in needless complexity that defeats their purpose. Keeping within the strict Western paradigms and cultural traditions, limits, outcomes and eventually human growth.

D$_E$Sign Science: in the New Paradigm Age" suggests looking at the world from a wider, more inclusive, and open-minded, holistic, and spiritual perspective. We 'Simple-Fi' 'Spirit' here as creative spirit — that life force that holds everything together that we are not expressing or using effectively to enhance our lives. This is a "mindset shifter" or a New paradigm that is not really that new at all. Design Science is a human story. It takes us on a creative journey, not of survival but, to reconnect with our 'WIKI'™. This is the key to elevate our consciousness to live the lives we design for ourselves. The method or 'science' gives us the **W**isdom that is not generally applied to the world of things we focus on, the **I**ntelligence that is natural and more common sense than we make it, the **K**nowledge that we synthesize with the habits and experiences we all create, Ideas, and **I**nformation with Inspiration to live by. This is the *'WIKI'*. They are the four natural universal forces that hold everything together as 'one'.

The language of design expresses ideas about space, time, and energy in an aesthetic form. No one aspect or faculty of this triad works alone. This is the form of communication we use to connect to source, ourselves, and others. They are blended into a holistic adventure that takes us into the magic of Physiology, psychology and spirituality thus empowering us to create. The elements, words and energies we use are space, numbers, time, and e-motion with our creative energy. Organizing them into useful form, with our Wisdom Intelligence Knowledge and Information, (WIKI) raises the consciousness of the life force, creative spirit or any other name we use to describe it, to create the life support systems we need.

We are all part of the grand creative ubiquitous process taking place in the oneness of the verse we call our uni-verse. With our Body, Mind and Spirit as the finely tuned instruments, faculties and thought 'fuels' we were born to be about, we create forms of expression, beauty and love that flow through us, connecting to source through the works we create. Art, in patent and trademark parlance, is ubiquitous and magnetic. It enhances the skills needed to bring original and paradigm-changing ideas into 'being'. There is 'prior art' which is the state of the art and original or patentable art which is innovative. We can expand our creative skills with D$_E$Sign Science to go deeper, to unveil the 'hidden secrets', to bring new, innovative lifestyles into harmony with creative excellence and pure imagination for "*Making the abstract real*". A new vision is in the making and it will be facilitated by this new creative discipline in a new paradigm.

"Better to write for yourself and have no public, than to write for the public and have no self." — Cyril Connolly

CHAPTER ONE   HEXAHEDRON H$_A$H

1. Spiritual Principle:

Mastery over the Muladhara (root) chakra, controls the will and truth. To conquer dis-eases, knowing whatever one wants to know or to discover the innocence one wants to recover. Or we may discover HIMHERIT's compassion, in the Light and might and Love.

'HIMHERIT' is a transcendental metaphor that cuts through all conditioning's and corruptions with our references to whatever is greater than us. It is the 'GOD' placebo.

This power can be misused when he cannot do so often in mistaking.

Clairsentience, Body or physiological Intelligence, Survival instinct, find the way in the physical world cause and effect forgiving the earth, the periodic table of elements, the root, material matrix; tools for The Dao D$_E$Sign.

The behavior of mechanical and dynamic correspondences with parts, elements and geometry to operate as movement in all the multiplicities of dimensions.

CHAPTER 1 TRINE A
THE DISCIPLINE

De**SIGN SCIENCE IS A DISCIPLINE** that blends the theoretical, soul searching that empowers designers to obtain a "new paradigm" — Wisdom, Intelligence, Knowledge and Information (WIKI) — to understand and apply subtle energy dynamics to enhance our environments, our lives (culturally, socially and economically) and to define our life's purpose. This is realized through (an evolving praxis) for a "new paradigm movement" to synthesize the principles, knowledge, information, (creative)energies, passion, and inspiration from our new understanding of Man's Physical being. Nature's Psychological creative processes and the Spirit are the essence of consciousness in "DESIGN SCIENCE™".

The threefold expressions, flavors and essences of the physical, the psychological and the spiritual worlds correspond with Body, Mind and Spirit and are manifested through man, nature and conscious-ness as ancient wisdom traditions and in western science, lately.

This is the premise for a quantum dynamic system to harmonize the east-west dichotomy into 'one' infinite, normal and sub-conscious awareness we need to embrace. This creative process imbues all we do, feel and think, what we observe, experience and manifest through our ideas, thoughts and desires. With all other value systems aligned, this powerful universal MIND energy described in the Hindu tradition, is known and art-iculated as the 'kundalini energy'. With its 7-14 of many more chakras*, this becomes an essential part of the quantum dynamics for creating, harmonizing and perpetuating new paradigms for the world. We are being introduced to finer forces.

Paradigm shifts r-evolve in thousand-year cycles and are aligned with celestial dynamics and changing configurations in our universe.

These changes inspire new scientific discoveries and teach us about the world. New ideas and thoughts demand that we recalibrate our entire set of habits and perceptions or Paradigms. With shifts occurring in many disciplines, this is the age in which we now live.

'Design', one of the central elements, combined with science is needed, as one of the 'ubiquitous' tools for many of the emerging 'trades', to redefine, transform and create new growth opportunities for our new economy.

Through design science, we can create processes to correspond with the electrical, magnetic and energetic creative (or spiritual) principles (of the kundalini, for example) to manifest or create (more accurately co-create) our destiny. We continue to pay no attention to the 'complementary' knowledge shared among cultures around the world and persist in making hurdles of social, cultural and political differences when on the infinite level of oneness none exist. The kundalini has its equivalent system in the endocrine glands, the central nervous system, and all the plexes and complexes in the human body, mind, and spirit or energy.

This work's premise rests on a very common-sense definition of CONSCIOUSNESS. Here, Body, Mind, and Spirit correlate with every natural expression of nature in Space, Time, and Energy, which is in everything, form or place, what we do and say, how we feel and think. This synthesis of these three fundamental and universal laws is the core logic of this work. It is integrated for the realization and manifestation of the WIKI as the map we use for our journey.

B.M.S™ body, mind spirit and the S.T.E.P™ space, time energy (Paradigm) become systems guiding the discussion and exploration you are invited to as we adventure into the unfolding of a New Paradigm Age.

It invites and empowers us to Design our lives through self-discovery and self-realization using the science of synthesizing our own aesthetic flavor we share with the world, on the way or 'Dao'.

There is a Dao Design similar to the Dao De Jing that brings LOVE to our higher selves, not just to or for things. There are 7 (seven) Cores with their unique components and qualities to the structure of the Book. This builds the foundation where the ken of the WIKI grows to nurture human nature. It traces the patterns of every dynamic principle that we can embrace to access the necessary information we all have in us.

THE SEVEN CORES

CORE 1: SPIRIT-S	THE FOCUS, MAXIM or TOPIC
Ancient Wisdom Traditions and their KEN	Yesterday's mysteries become today sciences and technologies to add to the (internalization) of the WIKI.
Hermetic Philosophy in Egypt	The 7 Symmetry principles of Hermes Trismegistus; The Law of 7 that correlates with other paradigms.
Hinduism demystifying its spiritual materialism for real applications	The Kundalini and the 7 chakras is a valid universal creative process with a praxis for design applications across the span of consciousness, infinitely and definitely. There is evidence for this.
Artifacts and Evidence	Monumental and celestial architecture based on spiritual principles.

THE DISCIPLINE

D_ESIGN SCIENCE IN THE NEW PARADIGM AGE

CORE 2: MIND	THE FOCUS, MAXIM or TOPIC
The East-West dichotomy: expanding the universal KEN	Spirituality is real HOCUS-POCUS; magic objects, feeling, spoken words expressing thoughts to create transformations. It is natural LAW that is based on intuitive science and design, hence D_ESIGN SCIENCE.
The Western Paradigm	It creates values, obeys principles, applies to life, and promotes human development, growth, and abundance.
	Physiology, Psychology and Energy paradigms are being transformed by expanding paradigms that described nature in earlier stages of man's knowledge and the constant expansion of the universe, consciousness, and our creative abilities.
Cross cultural knowledge correlations of the quest, the questions and the requests we seek	The subatomic, quantum, and other models presented since the big bang continue to evolve and correlate more accurately with oriental philosophical, and scientific evidence and 'truth'. The more we resist collaboration, the slower will be our journey to understanding who, why and what we seek.
The Specific focus is to Harmonize lasting peace through a Global WIKI	The Kundalini and the 7 Chakras exist in all consciousness dimensions, the connection to the Central Nervous System, the Electromagnetic fields or Aura, the subtle bodies and their link to the Quantum fields, and their theories and concepts that can harmonize the dichotomy.

NOTE: The evolution of paradigms of Science (in the space, time, and energy paradigm) in their most coherent form operate behind a veil (of compounded irrationality and an aversion to spirituality) we are unable to penetrate or mitigate. Maybe this world view can get us closer to where answers lie.

Hocus-Pocus. 1620s, Hocas Pocas, common name of a magician or juggler, a sham-Latin invocation used in tricks, probably based on a perversion of the sacramental blessing from the Mass, Hoc est corpus meum "This is my body." "This is my Son (Creation), whom I love; with him (it) I am well pleased."

CORE 3: BODY-B	THE FOCUS, MAXIM	TOPIC
Mathematics: Geometry; Matrices, Logic Structures, Numbers and their encoding functions.	As paradigms emerge, they are described by forms and shapes using the processes that are aligned with the B.M.S. and S.T.E.P, they change to the new tools to update the new descriptions. Simple-fi complexity has always been the goal, we were told. It engages us in a playful 'inventigative' (derived from invention and investigation) mindset. Play is critical thinking and learning.	Visual mathematics is the synthesis of Art, Science and Mathematics used to enhance the powers and fidelity of life. Rational thinking has limits. The only way to continue is to go beyond them with non-traditional methods like D_ESIGN SCIENCE which is inspired by the courage and passion of the seeker not the weaker observers who do not participate. New shapes and forms express new paradigms.
Form generation: using Euclidean and Non-Euclidean Polyhedra and their descriptors.	Periodicity is critical to managing diversity in or from minimum inventories. Nature loves small numbers and very neat, simplefied arrangements.	Visual Intelligent systems are used as "Thought Experiments", Thinking, Feeling and Imagining, synthesized into a guided meditation directed from source with you not as the thoughtless nothing and no one, and in no NOW.
Qualitative and Quantitative Systems		

CORE 4 HEART	CREDIT AND REFERENCES	THE FOCUS, MAXIM or TOPIC
Core Components	The first three B.M.S cores are synthesized into a creative formula used to forecast, accommodate, and anticipate the paradigm shifts.	The consumption of the current cultural 'capital and creative energy' is in stasis, even though there is evidence of abundance.
Heart Centered Mindset	Where are the models for this transformation and centeredness?	Who are the thought leaders in this space? Avatars - Jobs, Fuller, Gandhi
Synthesis	Optimize the B.M.S and S.T.E.P formulae. This is the *nucleus* of the centers where positive habits transform lives.	Create applications to enhance the Physiological, Psychological, Mental, and Spiritual Habits/individual and collective Paradigms with the proper disciplines, processes and energies.

THE DISCIPLINE   _D_SIGN SCIENCE IN THE NEW PARADIGM AGE

New Paradigms are removing the veils, beams and motes from our eyes. The inner eye is Stephen Covey's 'sharpened saw' we need to see without doubt or fear; (False Evidence Appearing to be real).

The Lower three registers represent the physical world where creativity, work and matter are blended into form using the primary energy for getting things done.

THE DESIGN PROCESS

CORE 5 SKILLS	UBIQUITY	THE FOCUS, MAXIM or TOPIC
Applications and Disciplines	D$_E$sign Science, Architecture, Industrial Design, Art, Traditional Science, Visual Mathematics, Philosophy, Problem Solving, Holism Theory and Community Building, Synthesis.	Credit to R.B. Fuller for his D$_E$sign Science suggestion in 1957, that's still idling in our brains. This stops NOW.
Application	The art and science principles are everywhere and are forming our design vocabularies as we express our creativity.	The Core areas are Symmetry, Logic Structures, Synthesis, Non-Euclidean Geometry and other methods.
A-Empowerment	B-Self-discovery	C-Self realization

CORE 6 COLLABORATION	EDITORS, REVIEWERS, SALES	THE FOCUS, MAXIM or TOPIC
Suppliers, vendors	Send content to professional editors and reviewers.	Sales strategies using email with JV and affiliate partners.
The Peace & Love Campaign	The Products: book/s, info products and other swag.	Social Network Platforms, media: radio, TV interviews.
	Communication: Word of Mouth-WOM, email campaigns, Audience Development.	The New Paradigm Movement.

CORE 7 CREATIVITY & SELF SUFFICIENCY	SELF-PUBLISHING: Production and Distribution	THE FOCUS, MAXIM or TOPIC:
Books, Forms, Info products	Production/Manufacturing (Generic) Mgmt. Systems.	Feedback and follow up Customer Care.
Design Solutions	The ideal Clientele, IP Licensing R&D.	Art Exhibitions and Events: Book Readings and Parties, Sales

NOTES: Transformation is the goal the designer chooses and determines what form it needs.

These 7 Modules correspond with all expressions of the Law of 7 in the three (3) registers or levels of vibration, each with its frequency.

THE CORRELATION MATRIX

OLD PARADIGM	NEW PARADIGM	B.M.S/ S.T.E.P FORMULA
From an over-done work and competition ethos (Prone to burnout)	To a growing recognition of the humanizing powers of play and fantasy, cultivating imagination, visualization and dreams.	Flavors of expression of consciousness can be harmonized to make life effortless and fun.
From an over-focus on language and reason, history and basic subjects.	To a re appreciation of the need for using the arts to develop a more balanced mind and life	The synthesis of body, mind and spirit creates harmony beyond logic.
From thinking about things to begin creating them.	To think about the way we think about things, questioning assumptions and fostering a more flexible philosophy of mind: i.e. meta-meta cognition, critical thinking.	Things are material and need to be balanced with psychology and spirituality in all space, time and energy.
From an over-controlling and unrealistic estimate of what we can and cannot do.	To a more realistic understanding of the limits of our power– humility and surrender.	To the recognition of SOURCE as the infinite consciousness that knows all and is all ONE.
From thinking that cheerfulness is something that reflects inner mood.	To realizing that it involves a mixture of positive attitudes, willed intentions, and skills that must be implemented even in the face of negative circumstances or inner sadness or fear. It's not denial, covering-up or disguising, but rather a turning away from the dark into the light, an act of faith.	To recognizing that the Kundalini and its 7 chakras act as one spiritual energy field that correlates with the physiological and endocrine or psychological knowledge we think of as our privyl(e)(i) dge / lidge and ledge mean the same.
Similarly, from thinking that wisdom is something that one attains and then possesses	To a more process-oriented idea that wisdom-ing is how we use all our skills along with our highest values to respond to changing all/our circumstances. Like love-ing or faith-ing, be-ing, becoming an activity, not a static quality.	There is ONE source of wisdom to which we are all connected. Life is a quantum dynamic.

From accepting the authority of past "experts," recognizing that emerging knowledge and changing circumstances affect and modify even the most seemingly wise pronounce-ments made in the past.	The need then becomes the recognition of the need to re-think in the here-and-now, weaving together best judgment, highest values, the needs of the situation, and most current information. There is no guarantee that the product—the final response—will be effective, so also one becomes open to feedback about what doesn't work and re-thinks, modifies, and tries again. The illusion of "being right" is recognized as a type of non-productive egoism and vanity.	NOW is all that matters. All else past and future are illusions.

The essence of the Science of Design is a D$_E$Sign Science.

It heals all. It creates. It repairs. It restores and transforms all tangible material objects, physical places, and spaces — from the Nano to the macro. It conducts behavior and forms Habits and attitudes. Essences, flavors and qualities of expressions of and to all degrees of the infinite, the normal awareness and the sub consciousness, energies and thought (singular) are all subject to laws, symmetry principles, and LAWS.

Concepts mentioned in the singular form are principles. When they are in the plural form, they represent their expressions. Example

Form is the phenomenon. Forms (phenomena) are expressions of the phenomenon.

"The Ray of Creation"

There are three registers or realms of the design process that correspond to the infinite order of what I call the "Ray of Creation".

It is the spectrum of all living vibrations operating the universe and is operating in it. It governs all manifestation. Design is a ubiquitous dynamic. It is the science of all forms of manifestation, not aimless conjuring with misguided emotions and 'guts'. Design is living in constant creation at the core of humanity and at articulations and expressions of the human Body, Mind, and Spirit — the elements of the synthesis that simulate consciousness and stimulate imagination, desire, and will to fulfill needs.

It obeys the Space, Time Energy continuum and natural laws. Why do man's laws change when paradigms shift and natural LAWS do not?

The universe, Life and Man are interactive, dynamic, creative processes with powerful correspondences of all consciousness that is above and below. There is a ray of light (an umbilical) connecting us to the *SOURCE* of creation. Our inspirations, thoughts, and ideas reside 'above' and are transformed into reality 'below'. Using our imagination, creativity, and resources and creating life support systems to satisfy our physical, mental and spiritual needs, we are the 'mediators' travelling along 'THE RAY OF CREATION'. Different traditions throughout time have defined this source of energy in a multitude of 'frameworks', within the limits of their perception, their vision and their language. The most inclusive 'gauge' I am aware of is known as the 'Kundalini' with seven energy centers known as 'Chakras' or wheels in Sanskrit, as it is a source of devotion in the Hindu tradition. The western philosophical traditions' interpretation of this dynamic and electrical process is found in the endocrine system of the ductless glands. The most subtle systems we now know exist in the new world of physics. The 'gauges' of interpretation and communication that support the visualization and imagination in this creative process come from source.

We also use this ray to elevate our consciousness to tap into the sources of inspiration and stimuli that transform into sense data, thoughts, concepts, and ideas to design our lives and worlds. The human mind reflects the universal Mind and connects to the ALL of ALL. Natural creative principles reveal structural logic, myths, and mysteries to us, creating value systems that enable us to synthesize knowledge within constantly changing thought form frameworks and paradigms. Physical expressions use symmetry principles that obey natural laws. The fundamental law is the *Law of Three* (3). Every thought, idea, expression or being is a corresponding vibration with flavors defining its form. Mind, Body and Spirit form a 'triad' of 'flavors' composed of subtle (above) and gross (below) expressions.

They are synthesized using symmetry laws and principles that transport flavors, qualities and gauges of matter into reality. Abstraction is essential to 'transformative thinking' for clarity and true understanding. Using concepts like 'suchness' and 'muchness' instead of names help creative thoughts, feelings and emotions flow.

Abstraction keeps our mind open and full of possibilities up to the moment of 'cision'. Decision, incision, and precision come before creation in the world of design.

Understanding correspondences with Body, Mind and Spirit, Space, Time Energy and Paradigms, 'above and below', and the Hermetic symmetry principles transforms electrical stimuli into sense data mentally. 'Mentalism' is being true to form. All things are mental.

The 'ray of creation' leads to pure principles. Pure extension is Space. Pure duration is Time, and pure thought is Spirit. All consciousness and its expressions of reality are governed by 'three principles' – physiology, psychology and spirituality. The word 'spirituality' used here means creative spirit or work-energy. The finest fuel of all we know is thought. All expressions of nature are made of three basic elements. The universal codes are physiology, psychology and spirituality. These are the instructions that created us with our qualitative and quantitative, gauges, behaviors and strength. They work with every Body, Mind, and Spirit vibrational level we think of as reality. This is creation's code. We use it to create our worlds.

THE DISCIPLINE

D_ESIGN SCIENCE IN THE NEW PARADIGM AGE

Space, time, and energy correlate with all qualitative (suchness) definitions and quantitative (muchness) descriptions of natural phenomena and "thought forms." Stimuli are transformed into ideas based on natural phenomena, encoding functions and behaviors.

They are reduced to concepts that follow the fundamental *Law of Three* (3) becoming all regenerative symmetry principles for physical, psychological and spiritual expressions. Principles are laws or facts of nature encoded into thoughts, artificial devices, and expressions that adhere to discrete symmetrical rules with unique identities.

This symmetry is dynamic. It is not the mirror reflections we know, but "the behaviors of parts that make things work holistically." Geometric expressions have unique identities and symmetries. When rules and behaviors are understood, identities are transformed.

In addition to standard symmetry, with enantiomorphism or handedness, there are Rotational, Glide, Polygonal and Spiral symmetries. This Triad applies to periodicities of expressions in nature as light, orientation, matter, color and numbers. When the three fundamental elements are reduced and distributed, they form expanded expressions of flavors and 'phyla' of natural and artificial phenomena. When symmetries and triads are aligned, creativity is harmonized and consciousness is transformed into reality. We see the *Law of Three* (3) as being fundamental to artificial and natural processes. Are there other number laws working in nature? Could living in a three-dimensional reality be one reason why this law exists? Does this relate to the three developmental stages of the human brain?

Transformations are created and experienced by tapping into the sub, the tangible, and super consciousness. Our tangible consciousness is enriched when the sub (below) and super (above) dimensions support our normal 'RAM' minds. Attributes of the Body, Mind, Spirit (BMS) or Triad, are tuned to higher thought vibrations and correspondences. We use threefold symmetries to transform ourselves intuitively and unknowingly. We have mastered the materialistic expressions, leaving the psychological and spiritual components less developed. When we internalize this knowledge, our actions become clear and lives are transformed.

We stop rolling dice to begin living lives in total harmony. What are the factors involved in developing our psychological, spiritual, or electrical lives? Yes, my friends, life is electric and magnetic like the cosmos with the 'ALL of consciousness' we mirror.

Rene Descartes' definition of 'Man', the 'plumbing model of circulation' is replaced by Man, the complex bio, magnetic, electrical, plasmic being to reflect the new understanding of 'self'. Transformation involves becoming our highest and best self-image, and knowing who we are to develop a 'toolbox' to align with our true self. Every era has a very distinct expression, identity and flavor.

We have the opportunity, the technologies, and intelligence to identify, question, and research the relevant principles to invent new toolkits. Paradigm shifts lead the cyclical potential of transformations between changing historic periods. *Carpe diem* is the order.

Technology, philosophy, and culture (Body, Mind, and Spirit) evolve with enduring principles in tow. Recognizing that we are part of 'movements' and resulting 'consciousness shifts' is "the essence of Transformations." Transformative thinking, or 'Structural Philosophy', is the first step in understanding how to create 'thought forms'. The highest form of energy we know is thought. Ideas, new form vocabularies, technologies, and inventions tell the mankind's stories. The shift is already here. Are we ready to embrace it to 'reinvent' ourselves? What tools do we have and what knowledge do we need? Creative expressions emerge from the internal dialog using visual or qualitative and quantitative mathematical processes along with the metaphysics of energy in all its expressions. It starts by transforming electrical impulses and brain stimuli into sense data for thought form re-cognition. There is a communication rule of thumb we all use here.

When we speak to ourselves, we think. When we speak to others, we communicate. What are thoughts? Do they make us who we are or vice versa? What values do we incorporate into our thought processes and into people's lives? What is the role of culture and aesthetics in this process? How do we define them?

Culture is the blend of the artificial with the natural. 'Man' uses *natural materials* to make beautiful things. Another popular version describes it as 'art forms' – dance, music, art and food. *The Law of Three* defines consciousness and culture as harmonizing body, mind and spirit, with the 'Ray of Creation', in the Space, Time, Energy continuum.

The first definition of culture refers to the past. It is stored sub-conscious experiences in space, time, and energy as sense data and images for 'information' recall. This is the realm of universal mind.

The present popular view reflects a prevalent contemporized attitude of 'presence'. This is a vital state of consciousness where awareness, focus, and attention are its complements. The third is the future super consciousness set to inform new paradigms.

Thoughtless awareness is the transformational state that cycles through all others. These are the big-picture views of the world with newly transformed ideas that rely on proven and sustainable principles that change when paradigms shift. They modify our thought processes, impact our language and transform our lives. Where does transforming this esoteric knowledge into practical strategies for solutions lead? Languages change over time to correspond with the evolving thought forms, rituals and rhythms we create. Science and other disciplines constantly evolve. It is nature's way of revealing new sources of 'suchness and muchness' we can revisit.

The east-west dichotomy is a cultural divide and a paradox of 'globalism' with well entrenched and intact mental boundaries, dichotomies, myths, and mysteries. Oriental systems of thought are often strange and difficult to accept by western views (paradigms). Western ideas are sometimes not readily accepted by oriental cultures. These schisms lead to wars and other socio-political and religious differences with unresolved conflicts.

How can there be true 'globalism' if we cannot find common ground in philosophical and cultural traditions in the present East-West schism?

THE DISCIPLINE

DESIGN SCIENCE IN THE NEW PARADIGM AGE

'Meditation' and 'visualization' two major contributions to the West that corresponds with our endocrine system that still challenging us. The endocrine system, the brain, and the central nervous system form western medicine's triad. Eastern frameworks start much earlier with the understanding of the Body, Mind, and Spirit continuum built upon manifestation, healing, meditation and visualization practices.

Western medical science is a space-time framework without 'spirit'. It focuses on physiology, chemistry, biology and many other synthetic disciplines. It is primarily a physical science.

The law of polarity governs these orientations we do not comprehend. This knowledge helps transform concepts into practical solutions from a deeper understanding of the 'mechanics of consciousness', synthesizing and harmonizing new creative methodologies. Be the potter, mold ideas (or yourself) on the wheel of life. The material, the mental, and creative processes interact with all the creative forces you are already connected to, expressing who you are and all you make. What you want and can create reflects who you truly are deeply and passionately. The only essence you can diffuse or refuse flows through you from source into the world.

Start by looking at earlier stages of your life to find what you were curious about and enjoyed doing. Early first impressions become passions with life transforming creative skills and opportunities. I used to shape the tops of large milk tins into plates. Now I design ceramic dinnerware. I wanted to discover nature's secrets for making forms. I patent useful vocabularies of three-dimensional forms.

I love cutting and folding forms made of paperboard. There is a tactile and Zen quality to it that does not exist in cyberspace. Cutting and folding, by hand-mind coordination, is free, fluid and graceful.

I invent curved three-dimensional forms while conducting geometric experiments in this relatively new 'Non-Euclidean paradigm.' From a simple, (meditative) task, I distill knowledge through a complex process. Dancing with 'thought-forms' in my head that then leap onto stages of my life as I grow to understand the language and geometry.

Retrace your steps, find your joy and make it your theme. Explore and consume everything about it. Study, read, draw and model as many forms as possible. Drawing is a vital, spatial learning skill. Doing expands your creative and critical thinking abilities. We forget these earlier clues and lessons as adults and let the world define our needs.

Then there is crisis, loss, or pain to motivate us to find our joy again. Early play, focus, observation, and formalizing earlier passions are great experiences. I still am amazed about what causes animals to run with their herds, minutes after they are born, while humans take years to complete their brain wiring, if they ever do at all. Connect to that version of what you want to be, to do and say what the world needs to know. Gain deeper levels of understanding of natural principles and laws by being curious again. Observe, reconnect, and 'play' with what interests you the most.

Begin to focus your physical, mental, and creative spirit or energy and begin to align with the creative intelligences we are all connected to. The ability to access, freely and abundantly, the knowledge you want is in you. It is in the 95% of your 'junk DNA'. Transform metaphysical strategies and bring real ideas into the world whether they are from your past or are new.

May this creative process be your value system generator for *your* original ideas. Start with a vivid mental picture of the life you 'want' with all the things, positive feelings and power you want created by your ideas. Let the joy of that intention be your inspiration.

Recognize this as mentalism in action; the dream is being realized with focused imagination and clarity of thought. Meditate (think) and visualize (imagine) clearly and precisely. Create (with energy) the reality you want, and will to manifest with passion and ease of repetition.

Master your focus and focus your focusing mastery by paying attention with positive intention. Be open to knowledge without cultural bias or judgment. Develop your hand-mind–heart coordination to enhance your sensitivity and integrity. Apply the

'Body, Mind, and Spirit Triad' to phenomena you see clearly. Make the *Law of Three* (3) work for you. Study elements and forces of nature with your new "nanoscope." Let these principles be the cure for fear-based 'need' thinking. Conquer the freeze, flight or fight limbic conditioning by cultivating better responses like freedom, being fearless and focused.

Become compassionate with open heart-thinking. Invite positive thoughts into your work life through your life's work. Explore new values, experiences, intuitions and insights by thinking abstractly. Rethink quality and not quantity (body), change behavior (mind) to harmonize with principles.

Connect to your higher creative spirit through your creative language to communicate on the physical, psychological, and creative levels through your heart thinking. Be in control of your creative destiny and freedom, live fully, and be happy. See your future with new attitudes, design perspectives, materials, and technologies forged by the digital redefining paradigm creative expressions and designs as "Cultural education".

Culture is the environment that nurtures us along with our inner direction and connection to source from which all wisdom, intelligence, knowledge, and information flow. Develop a visual intelligence and inspiring innovative and smart technologies supported by your vision to impact the world now unlike any other time in history. Teach, share, research and design your life.

Teach yourself, research and Invent, be the author and Designer of ideas that the planet needs. Use multiple art forms to make products and accessories energy efficient with sound economic strategies to satisfy project needs and design parameters. Develop innovative and alternative systems and form vocabularies and innovative technologies in collaborative communities.

THE DISCIPLINE   D_ESIGN SCIENCE IN THE NEW PARADIGM AGE

Direct other cultural and business organizations for their product development needs as they create their corporate collateral and synthesized branding development. Participate in creative community activities: like being a curator, moderator and panelist on several community Boards or help artists with their careers. Create graphic and media assets with access to a clientele of entertainers, dignitaries, cultural institutions, galleries, and well-established and emerging businesses. Be featured in all forms of media — print, digital, video and alternative for exposure and recognition.

What are the keys to these strategies?

The law of Mentalism is the key. Hermetic philosophy teaches us that everything is mental. But what exactly is thought?

When we talk to ourselves, we think. Thought is a higher vibrational dynamic accessible through thinking. Not all thinking reaches the level of 'Thought'. When we talk to others we communicate. These are ideational skills that design depends on at the conceptual levels of creative action. Who else do we talk to?

If talking is the exchange of information and energy, is this not the same action taking place with us and the creator? I call it SOURCE.

The third-third or *upper register* is where we find 'Thought' — Polarization, Ideation and Formalization: Visualization and Imagination along with Communication and Media.

The second or 'middle third register' has three 'flavors': one where Heart links with the brain, the second Links with emotions, and the third is with the physical body. Here we find the Heart-Mind connection where Love and Compassion linked to Thought and Reason live. This Heart-Brain connection keys are courage, confidence and community. They are the main actors supported by the other centers. This also serves as a control room. Signals go out to the lower registers at the root for wisdom and innocence and rise to the sexual center for creativity and pure knowledge.

The next center is the energy center. Satisfaction and generosity are the flavors here. It makes absolute sense that this center would operate within the infinite VOID in the background acting as 'The Universal Intelligence' portal. Voids are mostly transitional phenomena. They are the places where transformations and transitions are possible.

The first third, or lower register, is the realm of effort (work) or Energy and Production, Creativity and Gender Symmetry.

This is where Form and Shape provide encoded instructions (DNA) to inform Matter, in the realm of being and becoming. The next center functions when there is detachment and community at work. Here again logic prevails. If this is the center of communication and media which is overloaded with the Ken and all other resources. It is unfathomable that we can manage all this information and not be congested with its vastness. It makes sense that allowing the flow detachment would be helpful. We can apply this to the real world of hoarding and cluttering our bodies, minds, and spirits too.

Discretion is a critical value contender. It is situated between detachment and forgiveness. On the other hand, for there to be genuine surrender before arriving at forgiveness in peace and love, forgiveness demands preparation, reflection and withdrawing from mental clutter. Self-realization is the integrator of all centers, flavors and qualities in the three dimensions of consciousness — the infinite, the normal and the sub. Since we have identified the supporting centers as the cast with their sub plots, let's look at the Heart-Brain Connection again.

Logic says Heart can live without brain but brain cannot live without heart. It would be safe to think then, that heart and brain govern the processes of life physiologically, psychologically, and spiritually. Do we really know the expressions of heart's energies we interpret as a true romantic feeling that we have conditioned ourselves to expect and experience as being pleasure? Is the heart-brain the pleasure link?

The 'mind' is an 'infinite regenerating toroidal energy field', in our longest most mysterious story never told. It defies definition or description. We all have the right 'portal finding systems' to enter this field. The scaffold for accessing this field could be 'thought'. Why thought? Because it is the finest fuel we know. We do have some ideas about it now that we never had before. We think of "the universe as the grand container of containers". Containment is the action of keeping something under control and not necessarily within limits, especially with what we do not know.

Consciousness is the next useful concept on the 'scaffold' (of being in and becoming total awareness). We can try to grasp some boundaries within to 'capture' some part of the infinite mind field of SOURCE. The Infinite-Spirit, the normal awareness-body, the sub-consciousness - mind, and thought mirror the four forces in the tangible world as the "above so below" Hermetic correspondence symmetry principle.

We have a framework for the translation of any of the analogies used thus far. Without it we cannot truly understand or describe mind.

The next Hermetic principle is 'Vibration'. All is vibration. We interpret sense data through vibrations. There are realms of silence and nondescription we are not invited to, no 'matter' how we try to get there. We are not built or are we capable of vibrating at intense levels of accessibility and possibility on that high frequency quantum level.

When we become open to the possibilities other cultures share with us, we might come into the light. Conventional knowledge informs us that mind is the element of individuals that enables them to be aware of the world and their experiences, to think, and to feel, using the faculty of consciousness and thought. Mind makes the music that the instruments, the player and the medium, play with finely tuned skills to express the cacophony of either dissonant or harmonious sounds. The entire trio in the Body-Heart-Mind connection is represented and sets the tone, the pace (timing and rhythm) for the drum and the drummer that makes the difference to perform.

THE DISCIPLINE   DESIGN SCIENCE IN THE NEW PARADIGM AGE

From the artist's view (paradigm) there are three flavors of heart at the middle register, where we believe only one heart is. The 'physical heart' connects to the physical world as in the "love of things".

Which heart are we using to go shopping? There is the personal, emotional love of self, strangers, and the intimate connections designed for human preservation or 'carnal love'.

The love of *ideas, ideals and art* is a unique philosophy that expresses the highest vibrations of each form with its own connection to source. They can be synthesized as well. This is the level at which we engage in originality. We seem to get our 'loves' all crossed up.

Technically nine (9) centers exist on the "ray of creation". For the designer 'attractive love' or beauty is the 'reality tester'— a gauge for inspiration and the quality of ideas we create. This 'everyday love' is quite different from the 'sacred love' of the Eros, Agape and Philos. Eros is a selfish kind of love related to sexual love. Agape is a special term which represents the divine-love *of the Lord towards his Son Jesus Christ,* human beings and all believers. Philos love is for a pal who is really close and dear to us. It is characterized by various shared experiences between two people.

These flavors trigger hormones that interact with an ethereal flavor machine or bank which transmits light energy to the centers or the supporting cast. There are colors, characteristics and properties associated with the centers, making their expressions unique. This becomes a qualitative periodic matrix similar to the periodic chart of elements but much more complex. In the upper register, we experience Realization(self and of other types) through paying Attention. Cognition and awareness are functions of the creative process here too. There is an energy felt and held intension that could be representative of the mentality or state of the intention in the Heart-Mind connection that is in the realm of feeling.

How we think is how we feel and vice versa. This in turn impacts what we hold on to, do, and create in our lives. The time-emotion element of anticipation and expectation and other time-sensitive dynamics are either activated as uncontrolled or directed actions. How we respond to this feeling of tension can cause stress and negation (negativity) as depleted energy, or it becomes the positive response, which is effortlessness, 'with ease' and surrender for PAIN to be transformed into pleasure and for disease to be healed.

Design, as with music and art, is definitely a 'healing' process in many forms. Knowing its value inspires us to create what we desire, want and need to serve ourselves and others with our talents. That it has evolved into a science was to be expected based on the exponential pace of innovation over the cycles of each paradigm we experienced. Each demanded from us a shift in our individual mindset with some level of creative and spiritual grounding and accepting *change*. Cultivating a strong will requires elevated emotions and awareness combined with the surgically and laser-focused attention the mind is capable of. But we have to be engaged in our empowerment.

When all the key elements are harmonized, all things are possible. Following are some of the layers of concepts involved in this complex process starting with 'realization'. From a flood of experiences, memories, and possible solutions, a designer must observe and realize what he or she is looking at. Feelings, intuitions, and deep subconscious realizations might be summoned as the first attempt at pattern recognition. Recognizing old habits and conditionings is first.

Feelings 'conjure' an idea or impression in a complex emotional state of thought as a principle triggering an energy with any of the following 'terms of experiences' — apprehension, belief, consciousness, hunch, conviction, eye, inclination, inkling, instinct, mind, notion, opinion, outlook, persuasion, point of view, paradigm, presentiment, reaction, sense, sentiment, suspicion, thought, view, and much more. These are motivators. We normally operate with a more limited tool box than this. Our binary apparatus does not like 'mind floods'. It prefers brain storms. What is needed though is a more rigorous science to decode, process and store, the vast amounts of information we have gathered, sorted and taxonomized.

We take this to our knowledge base, or resource, that's been developed, over time, by the cultures of the world. The language in ours is English. Following the same design process, these constructs took considerable time to be experienced and encoded to create the vocabulary that is still evolving.

The KEN is another resource we have. There are keys to this set that are essential to the creative process. When we get past conception and perception, we encounter other challenges we overcome.

Is there a 'traffic light' system that controls our thoughts and the outcomes we desire? I believe they are our habits, paradigms, and views of our worlds — past, present, and future.

Here are the signs from which we need to extract our attention as we encounter the red, green and yellow lights in our way. Attention, as a green light, gets us clued in and focused on the process once we have determined that it is important enough to invest our time and energy toward a desire [going from pain] or desire from the great-spirit or [SOURCE] or we feel the need. Words are codes with profound hidden meanings — an entire phenomenon altogether. Here is the tool box. Judge which color lights apply to each. Here's the legend: right gets green.

Wrong gets red, and yellow is doubt and uncertainty. Which color lights apply to each of the following? Apprehending, apprehension, attitude, awareness, cognizance, comprehension, concept, consciousness, grasp, idea, impression, insight, judgment, knowledge, light, notion, picture, realizing, recognition, sense, sight, understanding, vision. Is this all being secretly processed at the same time and we are not even aware of it?

The paradigm age we are experiencing is of a 'heightened spiritual awareness'. Our understanding of Space, Time, and Energy is being challenged. There is a definite disconnect between the schools of thought dealing with how lives and desires are created, designed, or manifested. There is the idea that past and future are subconscious and related to infinite consciousness and are dissonant to the

THE DISCIPLINE

D_ESIGN SCIENCE IN THE NEW PARADIGM AGE

process of harmonizing and manifesting desires. Designers, on the other hand, deal in the real world's (hi) story with highlights, current events, and projecting their vision of it. Is design a spiritual discipline or simply a practice for organizing information and engineering?

This is one of the many issues D_ESign Science addresses. It relies on an open mindedness we need to prepare for, embrace, and adopt.

This paradigm moment in our story is apropos for not only discussion but immediate action. What it also questions is our Knowledge which is the schema we have compiled, over time, as our 'go to' material re-source becomes available to serve us. With the Knowledge tool box we can celebrate our personal understanding — information, ability, accomplishments, acquaintance, apprehension, attainments, awareness, cognition, comprehension, consciousness, dirt, discernment, doctrine, dogma, dope, education, enlightenment, erudition, expertise, facts, familiarity, goods, grasp, inside story, insight, instruction, intelligence, judgment, know-how, learning, light, lore, observation, philosophy, picture, power, principles, proficiency, recognition, scholarship, schooling, scoop, substance, theory, tuition, (Intuition) wisdom, and the science. In this case it is the D_ESign Science.

The qualities of this phenomenon [of light and intelligence] we call consciousness comes to us as energies from the Infinite Consciousness, Normal awareness or consciousness, and the Subconscious levels of Space, Time, and Energy, through the Body, Mind, and Spirit filters we use to identify, codify, and process Wisdom, Intelligence, Knowledge, and (as) Information and data designers use. Its source is the electric universe. Infinite...

Consciousness is our future. Awareness is our NOW (which is the best state to stay in). The Subconscious is the past.

Summary:

This paradigm age of 'heightened spiritual awareness' builds on the premise of science. Like the definition of love with its three flavors, there is a physical science, a psychological or behavioral science and a spiritual science. These are the trail-blazing paradigm-building protocols. Based on their understanding of how nature works, we follow their lead and the patterns they set for creating our world views and the life support systems we trust. There is an order of validity here starting with the physical, the psychological, and the spiritual the social, cultural and spiritual fabric (in the BMS order).

Understanding the principles of the new world view is capable of balancing the sciences with more open minds to lead to expanding our awareness to positively impact our lives.

I believe (no more now, I know) D_ESign Science is the way to begin the synthesis needed. If heightened consciousness is the cause, then the effect is this synthesis of consciousness with all creative processes enhancing expressions we depend on for our evolution and civilization building. The physical elements are creatively harmonized with thought and energy blended into an aesthetic expression.

Resolution:

This is the 'design agenda', the priority and mission of our age.

Is design then a spiritual exercise or simply an organizing information ritual with engineering support to protect life? Or is it a healing method or science and art that nurtures deeper understanding of all new ideas sent to art-iculate a new era for 'kinder-man'. This is one

of the many issues D$_E$Sign Science addresses. It relies on an open mindedness we can now prepare for, embrace, and adopt. This paradigm movement is a moment in our story, opportune for not only discussion but immediate action.

Just as each guitar string corresponds to a note, each chakra corresponds to a Solfeggio Frequency. The Kundalini, the seven chakras, and their colors tune all our frequencies. Knowing the chakras and their frequencies creates synthesis and harmony.

Is design a spiritual discipline or simply a practice for organizing information and engineering? This is one of the many issues D$_E$Sign Science addresses. It relies on an open mindedness we need to prepare for, embrace and adopt. This paradigm moment in our story is the right time for not only discussion but immediate action. Love is the force behind all we do.

LOVE IS DESIGN AND DESIGN IS LOVE IN UBIQUITY (EVERYWHERE)

The Three Types of Love

Irrespective of status, race, or economics, everyone values love and recognizes that it shapes what is true and good. It is more than the emotional attraction between two or more people. The three kinds of love in the Bible include Eros, Agape and Philos.

EROS LOVE

Eros is a selfish kind of love associated with sexual love. This kind of love is based on the physical traits. This type of love can end up being possessive, since it always seeks to first conquer and then control.

Desire and longing are part of 'sexual love' which is crucial in any marriage. This love was meant to be preserved between couples in a healthy marriage. Falling out of love is the result of an unhappy union.

This is the conditional type of love that may not have enough passion in it.

AGAPE LOVE

This is a special term which represents the divine-love of the Lord towards his Son Jesus Christ, human beings, and all believers. This is the best of the three types of love in the Bible. In fact, Jesus himself showed this type of divine love for humanity.

Agape love is the love that God commanded all believers to have for everyone whether or not he/she is a believer. Agape love should never be determined by our feelings. It is more of a set of behaviors or actions. With agape, you do not have to actually feel it for you to give it, which means that you can show love without feeling anything at all. At times, feelings can follow after showing this kind of love.

PHILOS LOVE

This is a unique kind of love akin to the one you have for a companion or pal. It refers to loving another just like your brother or sister. This love is for a pal who is really close and dear to you and it is characterized by different shared experiences between two people. And although philos love is wonderful, it is not very reliable, since it can end up souring at times, as we have all experienced at some point in our lives.

Creativity: The love of Art. "Thou Art yourself".

 *Creativity is a marrying (Synthesis) of our values, which determine the field of our endeavor, with our intentions, which draw to us the people, resources, and finance. Creative genius values love and service and intends whatever is most urgently required - Wallace Huey*

CHAPTER 1 TRINE B
SOURCE: IS THE SAME BY ANY OTHER NAME

VARIOUS CULTURES USE DIFFERENT NAMES for the same dynamic omniscient, omnipresent omnipotent, ever present and creative vital energy such as God, Consciousness, Great Spirit, Creator and Source. There is an absolute quality in its oneness, informing, reforming and transforming itself, its natures and qualities into a matrix of vibrations that makes up the uni- or multi-verse/s and who we are as its expressions, making us 'conscious'. This takes place in a 'micro-conscious' state we possess as humans called life where we reflect and project the creative effects the 'eternal electric Source'.

There are three states of consciousness in this process. There is the normal (conscious) awareness experienced in our awakening. There is the super-consciousness Source we are linked to and there is the subconscious state. Can you Intuit, Imagine, or think of synthesizing these three states into a hyper-dimensional state? This creates the intersection of all three rising to higher levels that these individual states cannot achieve individually. Maybe this intersection is what we could call MIND. The hyper-synthesized mind is the Source.

It becomes individual expressions of body, mind (mental and emotional), energy and spirit as the three dimensions of consciousness into infinite expressions on all levels of vibration. Life is an internal and external dynamic we experience in all these states, projected through the lenses of the threefold prism of Source to generate reality, as it is again interpreted or 'refracted', into a seven-fold symmetry by the Source dynamic with other parts, faculties, and energies added to the orchestration of its appropriate and coherent expressions we experience as natural phenomena and form.

We develop abilities to think, to sense, and to feel along with all our human functions when they are harmonized. Some states are 'alive', organic, and conscious. Others are inanimate and inorganic, not operating with the same human conscious vibrations but nonetheless very energetic and 'vital'. Humans are one of the many phyla of living conscious expressions 'made in the likeness of Source'. Source implants its eternal flame to fuel our creativity and passions that link us to it to be and to 'become' one with it before or after our transition. We are extensions and reflections of Source.

Now let's explore some scenarios about creation:

First, there can be but one source from 'outside or beyond' all other things known and unknown but knowable operating as the creator. This can be called "Adherent". "Exherent can be a new term for this dynamic. Second, within all that is known and unknown, but yet knowable, resides an internal dynamic as Source. This can be called "Inherent". The third option is that there can be an interactive combination of the first and second in the adherent or expanding phase that relates to the inherent state that becomes a breathing, interactive dynamic. This implies that the adherent and inherent states are alternately reciprocating or operating as a simultaneous dynamic. How does this relate to the expanding universe we observe? The expansion is one of consciousness or events of contraction and implosion. Is this wave-particle like?

Other correlations we need to consider about consciousness deal with definitions of the three phases of consciousness correlated with time. Subconscious is past or the Ida Nadi. Being conscious is present, now, or Sushumna Nadi. Superconscious or Pingala Nadi is future. Past experiences are stored in the subconscious as memory. The conscious is present and the superconscious is the state we 'Will' experience in our future when all the elements of manifestation are "present in a future now".

The Nadis are the meridians of the Central Nervous System, the Brain, and the Kundalini with the seven Chakras.

Are there modes of time that can be gauged or measured without involving "change"? In any event involving movement, Time, Space, and Energy are interacting in very logical ways. It takes thought, energy, and effort or work to move from a point in space with its potential energy and sense of direction to become a vector. Time is spent along the path to get from the point of origin to the destination. Space is displaced between the origin and the destination. These three experiences are occurring (or taking) place simultaneously. This is objective time. The time or inner experience that complements this objective event is basically emotional and spiritual. There is no objective displacement with spiritual or psychological movement in subjective reality. Space is pure extension. Time is pure duration. Energy is pure effort or work. The purest form of work is thought. Grosser forms of energy are mechanical, electrical, chemical, magnetic, and plasma. They operate in combinatorial sequences as functions require.

Does subjective and objective time relate to the idea of change, displacement and motion? Can emotional and spiritual essences found in the range from finer thought to gross work and energy needed for transformations be considered temporal? Does subjective time relate to an internal, emotional dynamic that moves the human spirit? Can that movement be measured in 'real' time, space, and energy? That movement is unmeasurable in terms of physical displacement. Movement without change is an emotional dynamic that is internal and therefore subjective. There are two terms we now need to consider. One is motion and the other emotion. They both involve movement. Motion is objective or quantitative. Emotion is subjective or qualitative. Rest is inertial, 'zero pointal' and fulcrum like.

THE ENERGY MATRIX

KINETIC	POTENTIAL
Electrical and Magnetic radiation - LIGHT	Magnetic
Electricity	Gravity
Heat/Thermal / Solar	Chemical
Sound	Elastic
Rotation / Movement	Nuclear
Wind	Mass

Transduction is the Key to all the Senses and higher faculties. Here is probably the most basic question in all of sensory neuroscience (the study of the senses). How does a ray of light enter our nervous system, to eventually become something that we see, feel, taste, touch, hear, and then 'know'?

How, in fact, does anything external (anything we touch, smell, taste, hear, or see) get turned into something internal (some kind of signal in the brain that tells us to sense something)? The answer is simple, so simple in fact that it is one word: Transduction. In a sentence, transduction is the conversion of one form of energy into another.

Try to think back and remember the different types of energy:

Kinetic - Sound - Chemical - Electrical - Light - Heat - Nuclear - Magnetic - Gravitational potential - Elastic Potential and Toroidal.

These are all the main types of energy that we can sense.

Touch	Kinetic	Heat	Gravitational	Elastic Potential
Taste & Smell	Chemical		Potential	
Sight	Light			
Hearing	Sound			
Conscious-ness	Thought	Knowledge	Intelligence	Creative Spirit-Genius

Self (awareness of where our bodies are): CONSCIOUSNESS is (the synthesis of all the senses). The nervous system only uses one type of energy and that is electrical; therefore, if the brain is what allows us to sense the outside world, all of these energies we mentioned previously have to be converted into electrical energy so they can enter the brain. That is where we know transduction comes in. This model expands

SOURCE: IS THE SAME BY ANY OTHER NAME

DESIGN SCIENCE IN THE NEW PARADIGM AGE

to include the Kundalini, the three 'Nadi Meridians', the chakras, and the endocrinal system — all allowing energy to enter the organs, the nervous system and the brain. Here subtler energies are at work. One of the complementary energies is magnetism — the force that is activated by intention, focus, and desire in our electric universe. Do these have their corresponding expressions in other realms as well?

In all of our sense organs (eyes/ears/tongue etc.) there are nerve endings which contain hundreds and thousands of receptors. Each organ will have different types of receptors that will react differently to each type of energy. Recent discoveries of dark matter and knowledge of the endocrinal system correspond to the Chakras. We can resolve cultural definitions to arrive at the common understanding and say that the chakras are in fact the Hindu expressions of the Endocrinal system. The centers or ductless glands and plexi (the plural of plexus) have specific functions that take transduction to subtle and higher functional levels.

Melanin has been found to be involved with the transduction of chemical to light energy in the endocrinal system, and by extension, the entire system of the body. Is this considered part of our evolution when this knowledge has been around for ages and available to other cultures or even buried deeply in the esoteric and mystical traditions of our own culture?

In the eye there are 'photoreceptors'. When light touches them they generate electrical energy. 'Chemoreceptors' in the tongue and nose react to chemicals and generate *electrical energy*.

The skin and ears use 'mechanoreceptors', which are physically moved, either by our touching something or by our hearing something. Receptors open up, allowing electricity to enter. By transduction, receptors convert one form of energy into electrical energy. The electrical triggers in the endocrinal system are the chemical receptors known as hormones. They have the capacity to exert specific types of forces with specific codes and programmed 'bits' of information to vitalize the organs that support life.

The sense organs, the vital organs, the central nervous system, the endocrinal system, and the brain are the 'gross' or dense matter components of the bio electrical, magnetic plasma complex that is human. The complement to this is in the realm of the subtle forces and energies, with their own versions of transducing and transforming energies that cannot be measured, but are essential to creating the harmony of our body, mind, spirit continuum.

That we do not recognize or use this knowledge to create fundamental frameworks for the growth and development of our culture, in all of the aspects that this knowledge can support, is unfortunate. Whether this is by design or by some strange accident of philosophical misdirection, has yet to be sorted out. In my opinion 'cultural arrogance' is the culprit here.

"My favorite things in life don't cost any money. It's really clear that the most precious resource we all have is time."
Steve Jobs

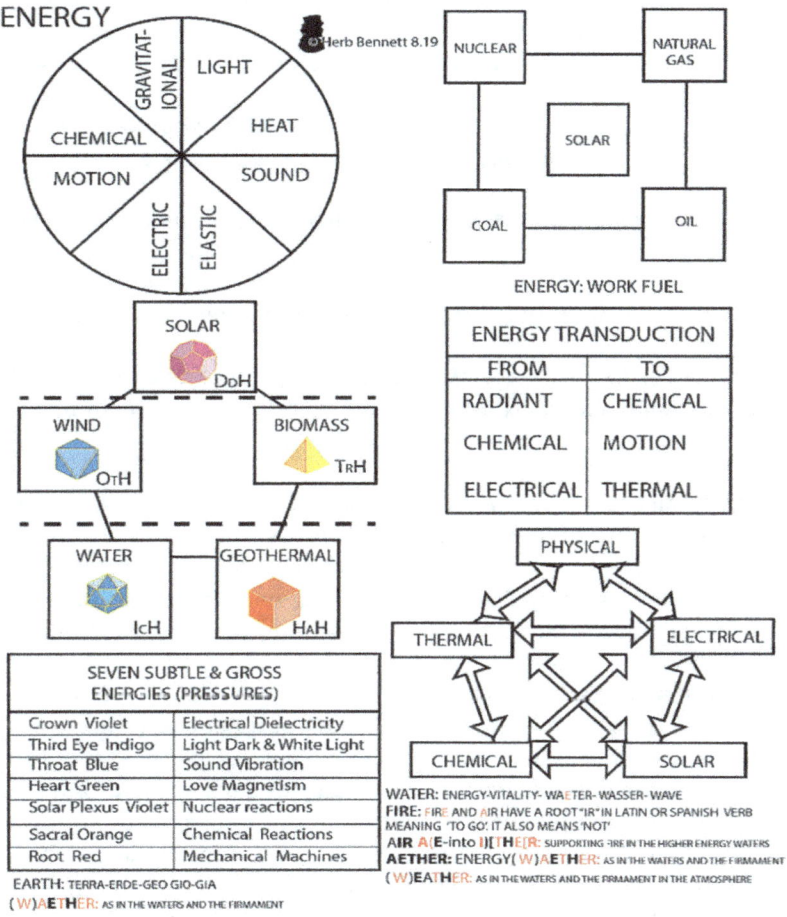

Fig 1.

Our *'illuminartsy'* expressions of creative genius are founded on the principles of new CONSCIOUSNESS theories derived from various cultures and the emerging paradigm shifts we are experiencing as syncretism. Though their languages vary, their 'paradigms' are surely connected. The designer receives external electro-magnetic impulses, and transforms them into sense data and information to manifest designs. Electrical transduction takes place through the various essences and energies regulated by senses using the IDA Nadi, the Pingala Nadi, Shushumna, the Kundalini and Chakras.

The endocrine system — comprises the ductless glands, organs and plexes, the Central nervous system and the brain. This complex of energies, organs and processes (MIND), transforms impulses into sense data and information. They correspond to the appropriate flavors; forms and images with the quantitative properties and qualities that focus the light of the basic energy systems of the inner light of the Shushumna Nadi. The new reality then aligns with the proper vibration, the quantitative, qualitative, and energy aspects of the form to make it *internally visible* as the impulses are transformed into a clear and well-defined thought. The external light of reality is transduced into the flavors that are processed to illuminate the inner light through thought at the crown, imagination and visualization at the third eye, communication at the throat. The heart is the reality tester of the idea. This is truth science. It is great to have the 'p-RA-ct-ical' knowledge, but the 'artist or designer' needs to know and internalize the other subtle energies involved in the creative process.

The next level down is the subtle energy-work center. We then go down to the sex-gender level and then to the root for the materials needed to produce the thought-form conceived earlier as the manifested thing. Expressions of light and consciousness are aligned and manifested. Engaging the IDA (idea) Nadi awakens the will or desire to activate an "upward or higher level" of consciousness, desire and need that registers with the universal consciousness. There are psychological and spiritual paradigms that activate the Visual intelligence and other internal energetic processes, working through the Pingala Nadi, where the quality or state of 'Future' and manifestation are defined by the event's time frame.

Structural integrity is harmonized with the Body-Space, Mind-Time, and Work-Energy continuum operating with the 'cause and effect' dynamic and with all the other symmetry principles and laws in harmony.

THE-ology: the study of religious faith, practice, and experience; especially: the study of God and of God's relation to the world. Theosophy: the teaching about God and the world based on mystical insight or Science.

1a: the state of knowing: knowledge as distinguished from ignorance or misunderstanding.

*2 a: a department of systematized knowledge as an object of study *the science of theology* b: something (as a sport or technique) that may be studied or learned like systematized knowledge.*

The Phrase found in Genesis *(The Genes of Isis)*, "Let there be light" (activated) is interpreted as 'Universal Consciousness'. This implies that there was darkness or 'dark matter' before. Expressions of this Universal Light are the 'Alpha and Omega' of ALL reality past, present, and future. All is light. The UC Light is the source of intelligence which is extracted by faculties, processes and energies operating as the inner dynamic of life itself. Transduction of energies generate vibrations at various frequencies that determine the nature of the expressions we create. Humans mimic the universal creative process on deeper levels than we are aware of. If we were aware, we would be able to connect to it more regularly.

What blocks this 'communication or transduction' is the polarity of the charge. Electrically charged systems and elements ignite our inner conscious light that corresponds with and reflects the Universal Light of Consciousness, we now call 'mind' and its intelligence.

We use many words related to 'light as our source' to describe our relationships to being, awareness, knowing, and becoming, but on this 3D realm consciousness embraces all of what we are about. Exploring the nature of Mentalism, thought, thought forms, and expressions is becoming a rewarding endeavor in science.

At some point our space, time, spirit, and energy continuum will be challenged again.

THE CURRENT PARADIGM SHIFT:

Epigenetics is painting a different picture for us now. (Epi as in beyond) It is the science that studies how the development, functioning, and evolution of biological systems is influenced by forces operating outside the DNA sequence, including intracellular, environmental and energetic influences and interactions.

The language of the body is vibration and sound. Invisible sound waves or vibrations are the body's secret communication system. Understanding the subtle "body language" with the Kundalini and the endocrine system as the primer, will unlock untold breakthroughs for health.

The life force is an electro-dynamic phenomenon that is beyond the traditional paradigm perspectives we still embrace. Science maintains that nerves communicate information to the far reaches of the body through electrical impulses. We equate theories with "physical laws of thermodynamics and electrical impulses that produce heat as they travel along the nerve, but experiments find no heat. We need to reevaluate standard thinking about inter body communications via the nervous, Kundalini, system. At this point, the east-west dichotomy becomes critical to our new paradigm view of how things work in our creative processes.

Paradigm Shifts and disruptions that we are unaware of, are taking place throughout many disciplines. They are transforming our lives and our reality, profoundly. We continue to resist the call to elevate our own consciousness that, interestingly enough, we pray and have asked for. The discipline of epigenetics itself is guilty of not recognizing or attempting to embrace the cultural information and knowledge contributions of other people in the world who have been around much longer than we have.

Globalization is not just directed at feeding our insatiable desires for material things made by low-paid workers in oriental and foreign cultures that are much better grounded in the spiritual traditions that western societies, with their philosophical materialism, ignore. It is only a matter of time before they demand their equitable rewards for their work and the ability to afford the quality of life others are enjoying at their expense. It's human nature at work only in reverse.

Thought is the highest form of energy that humans use as the fuel of consciousness that in-forms our bodies, minds and spirits. Thought is the Illumination of LIGHT, the force that also obeys the threefold symmetry dynamic of Consciousness namely the Body, Mind and Spirit. Every expression of nature or MAN follows this LAW of Three which generates a MATRIX with each dimension and its unique qualitative and quantitative aspects, arranged in a hierarchical order, according to the vibrations that define them. Light is no exception to this Law. There is the Physiological aspect of light which is the external radiation we interact with that also provides thermal energy or heat. To interact with our world, light is critical to our 'seeing' it. The information we process with our senses involves our Psychological paradigms, our biological and spiritual and energy characteristics, parts and attributes that defined us as being human, and behaving as humans with the potential to elevate our consciousness to be harmonized into what we call our HUMANITY. All is light. All is thought. All is Energy or Spirit. All operating in space, time, and energy, interacting with the corresponding triadic BMS aspects of human beings to achieve higher states of creativity and consciousness. The light that is external is composed of, or refracted to reveal the various levels of 'color' vibrations as the force that is transducing the energy into electrical impulses with which the senses interact. Light is the cause. Vision is its effect.

This external light energy is transformed into vibrations of various frequencies and qualities, creating 'reflections' of the clear objective stimuli impressions or visions of our external world as thought forms.

How they are interpreted is subject to evaluation by being familiar or by complex differentiation.

Is what we are seeing registered in our memory as familiar or strange, the initial response? There is an internal and subjectively psychological light that corresponds with what we then see or imagine. The Effect of the external and internal processing of this light is fueled by and in return enhances the thought process as it creates the conscious and intelligent information that is generated and regenerated. A 'mnemonic light', stored in our memory, is part of our learning process and is designed to protect us and to support our development. Thought is light and Light is thought. When they are focused, intensity grows to power and illuminate the body, the mind, and the spirit. The imagination, emotions and the senses are excited in their dualistic absorption and emission cycles to translate their power into action, movement, and/or creative expressions. Light is intelligence that we process with our physical, physiological, and spiritual consciousness to create knowledge, wisdom, and understanding. The mind's light is the synthesis of all the forms of light harmonized and balanced to resonate with the forces with which we are constantly interacting. The mind's eye (the third eye) is the portal for the internal and subjective light that results from the process of other forms of light we interact with.

Eventually, the expressions are charged with flavors of 'aesthetic', qualitative vibrations to stimulate the senses of others who are experiencing perceptions and communications, to stimulate the senses, and move our souls as we resonate (reason) with ourselves, the information, others, and the world. Human beings, our paradigms, and our Thoughts obey the symmetry laws which dictate that consciousness compels us to be human beings on our path to becoming our higher and better selves.

The New Paradigm suggests: *scientific minds need to trust that we are not victims, but masters of our genes, and that according to Epigenetics, this gives us control of all our bodily functions and the knowledge of how the development, functioning, and evolution of biological systems are influenced by forces operating outside the DNA sequence, including intracellular, environmental and energetic influences.*

We are learning that the language (of the body) is not only sound and words. In it are the vibrational dynamic faculties and functions of the human bio, electrical and magnetic complex. Invisible vibrations, spiritual or energetic, are the body's covert communication systems. The major system is the Kundalini with the seven chakras, the central nervous and/or the endocrinal systems with the brain as the control center. There is a practical method to this process, one of realization.

Science still maintains that nerves communicate information to the far reaches of the body through electrical impulses. It does not know the role of the senses and how they are used in the transduction of the external energy into subtle electrical impulses. The transformed sense data becomes psychological intelligence, vitalizing the spiritual energy of information as the outcome. Alignments with the Mind, Body, and Spirit continuum of human consciousness cascades into the space, time energy continuum. Expressions begin traveling along an infinite path to a considerably lower realm, in the process of constant creation applying symmetry laws to synthesis. The ductless endocrine complex is one system that operates this way.

"New Consciousness Frontier and Spiritual Adventurers now see their higher selves as 'Spiritual Beings' having physical experiences. This is "a major shift" for man and a grand and accurate transformative step for kind-man" in our evolving spiritual frontier on our mission back to the source of our arising, or SOURCE.

On this journey there are logical but still unexplained principles and natural laws that 'ALL' expressions, emotions and flavors obey such as: mentalism, correspondence, vibration, rhythm, polarity, gender, cause and effect as the symmetry principles of consciousness we are clueless about yet they are the flavors of 'the nectar of life' itself. Design Philosophy complements a D_Esign Science Praxis to help "Make the abstract real."

The numbers 3, 4 and 7 are no longer used to keep score. They become much more for us to explore the eternal store. Number, color and form systems become art and magic used to decode the mystery of the universe. HGB

The connection to Source creates a flow of Wisdom, Intelligence, Knowledge and Information in a Constant Creation process we connect to that's beyond life itself. H.G. Bennett

CHAPTER 1 TRINE C
D_ESIGN SCIENCE:

THE COMPOUNDED FORM OF THE words design and science becomes 'designscience' [conscience] defined as an inner feeling or voice, viewed as acting as a guide that flavors creative habits, emotions and behaviors. Sentience is the ability to perceive or feel things. Consciousness is the state of being awake and aware of one's surroundings. Design is much more profound than we know and think. The language used to interpret concepts with which we define our 'reality' are inherently materialistic. Excuse me for getting off topic here, but I believe this is a profound level of conditioning by "design". If language responsible for the quickening of human consciousness is as inadequate as it is, do we have to wonder why it is in its current state? One of the key definitions of the 'coveting materialistic dynamic' with which we are obsessed and plagued, is the intangible, ephemeral and ubiquitous scarcity, or lack of the abundance, and "CLARITY" or in this case, manipulation.

Here is a new paradigm equation of everything we need to consider now. It is E= $\sum$ (Everything) no coefficients needed. Consciousness is to Creation as the newly art-iculated compound 'Designscience' is to the totally imbued ('WIKI of the 'Human, Natural and Spiritual') or Ken: the space, time and energy continuum frame-work operating within the three-dimensional symmetry principles of the threefold Body (matter), Mind (time) and Spirit (energy) which are all forms of light. This is manifested in the fourfold Space, Time, Spirit, Energy to synthesize the sevenfold principles of all sources and their expressions. This self-regulating dynamic needs no coefficients to harmonize itself or this equation. Even in the realm of whole numbers there is an elegance that man is not capable of. The formula is written symbolically as: '$C_S : C_N = D_S : K_N$ space, time and energy-continuum'.

This supports the notion that there is a higher, conscious dynamic, involved with 'Designscience' and all its meaningful correlations in the oneness of consciousness (ipse) to guide this newly synthesized discipline of 'D_ESign Science' and the D_ESign scientists to attain higher levels of excellence in all creative ways. This is exciting. There is universal precedence to support D_ESign Science, giving us keys to its Unfolding, The Quickening, The Awakening and Trans-forming into the New Paradigm Movement and a new reality. For this we are profoundly grateful.

D_ESign Science, the grand synthesizer of all arts, sciences, wisdom, intelligence, knowledge and information evolved from the infinite consciousness or source now being art-iculated as an epochal shift of human consciousness and mind in and through our space, time and energy continuum. It is abundantly clear that architecture, once considered the mother of the arts, has definitely evolved. It gives us our understanding of "CONSCIOUSNESS". Our creative expressions of it teach us how to attain higher states of being, and becoming in harmony with all principles and laws we seek to create our lives, support systems for life and necessary sustainable processes.

Where does it apply and what is its 'Gene-of-Isis? [A meaningful but critical digression] Here we find ISIS of Egypt when we *wordsmith*.

EXOGENISIS (or EPIGENESIS)

In the Egyptian wisdom tradition, "Genesis" could be the 'Genes of Isis' or Generation of Isis. The Egyptian tale, taught to initiates in the Great Nile temples bestowed the title, "The Christ," on successful graduates who achieved 'The Christ Consciousness.' The syllable 'Gen' means "woman" or "queen." Isis was the Egyptian goddess of the moon and the wife of Osiris.

Wordsmithing reveals to us the aspects of the 'primal female parent' elevated to the esoteric status of womanhood with man as the cocreators of life as in the laboratory of 'gen' meaning woman, hence, gynecology and eventually genealogy. The words Genes (passed down from the mother), Jini, Genealogy also came from it. "Genius," is someone who was infused with the Muses; the female creative forces (plural). Let's take a quantum leap here and say that Isis is the ultimate 'designer'; the primal synthesizer of energies beyond normal human comprehension, and creation capabilities who understood space, time, spirit and energy, inherently, as the threefold dynamic of Body, Mind and Spirit that we now decipher from the Egyptian Canons — another topic altogether for later or for you to pursue.

A Hymn to Osiris from Dynasty 18 (stela Louvre C 286) narrates her actions in the form of two scenes: (1) Isis' search and her care for the body and (2) the conception, birth, and childhood of Horus. I propose that these names are the names of forces.

The Ennead (9 GODS of Egypt are the extrapolated forces of the three 3 or Trinity) rejoiced: "Welcome, Osiris' son, Horus, (Jesus?) stout of heart, justified, son of Isis, heir of Osiris." (Hymn to Osiris, Dynasty 18, stela Louvre C 286; from Jan Assmann, p. 24-25)

Quickening happens in a flash of insight we call intuition, etc. and all of a sudden it connects one to source. The power says, "See this. Listen to this. I'm talking to you!" Visions are like pieces of a puzzle that perfectly fit the shape and form of life to be purposeful. We could rewrite our life stories and manifest them when we align and operate with natural laws. Are we just (relationally) connected to this 'force or source of energy or are we the same imbued with the power and all its gifts as well? How do we come to this realization and attain our birthright of Christ Consciousness? Is this the ego speaking or source?

Is science so bold as to make this claim and help the world attain its self-realization without its own? Of all the disciplines and sciences D$_E$Sign Science touches, its most important quality beyond 'ubiquity,' is the multiple 'degrees of creative freedom' it affords every quanta, qualia and spiritua of energy and thought. Spiritua is the active agent in the BMS interactions or force.

D_ESIGN SCIENCE: D_ESIGN SCIENCE IN THE NEW PARADIGM AGE

It is more than the harbinger and deliverer of true freedom in many more dimensions than any other art form I know. All else is brought into corruption.

I use the concept of corruption in its clinical and strictest philosophical context here, as the process by which something, typically a 'word or expression,' is changed from its original, function, in-tention, use, purpose or meaning to one that is regarded as erroneous or debased. Design as we have known and still do fits this description. It has lost its charm and passion. Creativity and the Design Process - Art, Design, and Visual Thinking are all correlated. They are expressions of consciousness.

D_ESign Science involves applying multidimensional thinking to use the existing or to 'create' original Ideas, Wisdom, Intelligence, Knowledge and Information (WIKI) that aligns with universal laws, strategies and principles of Body, Mind and Spirit to synthesize holistic solutions, expressions and flavors of space, time and energy — the faculties of consciousness.

D_ESign Science allows us to access and harmonize the three states of the normal awareness, ill-defined sub-conscious portal to source, and cosmic or infinite consciousness which we extrapolate into the physiology of matter, the psychology of all dynamic behaviors and the spirituality of thought, energy and (work) effort, with natural forces and principles aligned.

D_ESign Science involves a totally harmonized and balanced praxis that manifests, articulates and expresses solutions, ideas and thoughts through the use of the materials, the application of creative disciplines and the correspondences of spiritual Laws to create, support and attain higher states of creative excellence, optimized living and self-realization in the freedoms we enjoy; of safe space, abundant resources, free expressions for all right actions, thought, energy and lasting unconditional love in peace.

D_ESign Science uses all media, technologies and creative processes in the manifestation of all of the above that we bring below as true Scientists. The oneness of our vision and purpose from now makes this our sole profession. All titles of the old paradigm definitions disappear. Who am I? I am a D_ESign Scientist AXE! There are other interpretations of D_ESign Science used in the old paradigm that are as follows: Standard Definition: D_ESign science is an outcome (not input or inspired) based information technology research methodology, which offers specific guidelines for evaluation and iteration within research projects.

D_ESign Science was introduced in 1957 by R. Buckminster Fuller (homage) who defined it as a systematic form of designing (not defining consciousness itself). It now evolves to do exactly that.

D_ESign Science is an outcome-based (knowledge creation), information and technology research methodology, which offers specific guidelines for evaluation and iteration (e.g. matrix sequencing) within research projects (art, science & creative processes & performances). Very intellectual and rational without emotion and spirit. Our "world view" is expanding, our consciousness is heightening. For most creative people changing their personal paradigm could be frightening.

We can be grounded in the spiritual principles of the life force that governs all natural expressions for us to be aligned with it to empower ourselves and maximize our creative potential.

The question is — How? We need a Praxis for applying new theories and technologies to evolving creative disciplines to manifest our visions in efficient and aesthetic ways. Self-development needs to be practical. The "world view" will continue to expand and be embraced, for creative people to change their personal paradigm to elevate their consciousness. We can be grounded in the three principles of body, mind and spirit as the fundamental elements of everything in the life force that governs natural expressions, including 'MAN,' to align with and empower ourselves to maximize our creative potential using our D$_E$Sign Science intelligence, knowledge, information and skills.

Following are some of the ideas we can familiarize ourselves with as we internalize new concepts, attitudes and our consciousness for Lasting Optimized Living ('LOL'). Who's laughing now?

0. INFINITE CONSCIOUSNESS-GOD-SOURCE: AKASHA
1. THE TRIAD: CONSCIOUSNESS BMS/STE/123/ PHYSIOLOGY, PSYCHOLOGY, SPIRITUALITY AND ALL OTHER EXPRESSIONS.
2. FORM: GEOMETRY, DESCRIPTIONS OF THOUGHT, EXPRESSIONS & REALITY THOUGHTS CREATE REALITY: MENTAL-ISM (HERMETIC LAWS) SYSTEMS OF GEOMETRY – EUCLIDEAN, NON-EUCLIDEAN AND BENNETT EXPRESSIONS
3. LOGIC STRUCTURES: THE FLAVOR MACHINE, THE SYNTHESIS MODEL, THE THREEFOLDMATRIX, THE THIRD ELEMENT AND OPERATING SYSTEM/S, PREDICTABLE CREATION, QUANTUM PHYSICS, POSSIBILITIES.
4. THE BIO ENERGETIC ELECTROMAGNETIC QUANTUM MODEL-THE EAST- WEST DICHOTOMY.
5. THE KUNDALINI AND CHAKRAS IN ALL FORM SYSTEMS INCLUDING HUMANS
6. ESOTERIC KNOWLEDGE, METAPHYSICS OF WISDOM TRADITIONS.
7. QUANTUM PHYSICS: THOUGHTS CREATE OUR WORLDS THROUGH MENTAL-ISM
8. HERMETIC PHILOSOPHY, SYMMETRY PRINCIPLES AND OTHER LAWS
9. NUMBERS AND SYMBOLIC COMMUNICATION
10. THE QUALITATIVE MATRIX (OTHER PERIODICITIES-ELEMENTS ETC)

We are now ready for the journey, of Innovation Diffused Internet of Things — 'IDIOT,' — through the new paradigm movement we have been experiencing for the past fifty years or more.

We have touched on the spiritual, cultural and creative perspectives that govern all other human endeavors. This becomes the groundwork or foundation upon which we can build. We still need the scaffold to allow us to attain the heights that can align with our fullest potential and self-realization. We empower ourselves to design our lives in the spirit of true, constant creative freedom. We may not believe in man-made laws. Natural laws do not offer choices especially to the un-in-it-iated. If you are not in Connection with SOURCE you are not united, aligned with the creative life support principles.

CULTURES: harmonize Body, Mind and Spirit (not just singing and dancing) things made of physical 'MATTER', psychological, emotional experiences, behaviors, feelings and habits along with a vast array of gross and subtle forces and interactions with, spiritual and thought energies and processes. From this complex smorgasbord of flavors we have settled for a very narrow range in the spectrum of human potential: Belief in the things we desire give us the feelings we respond to in order to satisfy our senses that — all driven by our ego and a heavily overburdened devastatingly, directly and indirectly conditioned past that made sure that none of this could ever last as we stayed on the carousel to hell. This seemed enough. Living in fight or flight crisis and trauma is not enough nor is it healthy. It is dangerous stuff. For most of us it's not summertime and living is not easy. No more cotton-picking freedom that so many died for with the synthetic swabs we now use. Then comes the wakeup call!

Behind this rhetoric is a poetic dynamic meant to support this idea of design and all of its contemplative methodologies (sciences) becoming an empowering and compassionate principle to build our lives on, with and for. Here we look at the Dao; the way, the purpose and many ways design can be used to create and live the lives in a more pro-active way. Knowing that all things coming from SOURCE can 'simple-fi' the needless complexity and confusion of our materialistic world, we can redirect our sensibilities to much greater goals.

We start with some ancient wisdom traditions, looking for the transcendent principles that we can apply now.

Why D$_E$Sign Science?

The M7: Mental Mechanics of Meditation, Manifesting, and Miracles for Making Money and things for lifestyles is all the same physically, emotionally and spiritually. If you follow the mental purveyors; digital snake-oil sales folk to get your 'self-developed' or use meta- physics and esoteric practices along with oriental spiritual techniques, as a religious devotee dedicated to supplication and beseeching with prayer, or as a new age supplicant believing in miracles: God, Science, and Psychology in the Paranormal realms of non-reality, what is becoming abundantly clear to me is that it is all the same. The Babelian lexicon we use to describe life and the mysteries of it mean nothing. The difference is the methods used for implementation.

'Science' and its related disciplines define reality for us in terms of the measurable; See, Touch, Estimate and Measure or (STEM) 'thingification' dynamic we all have bought into. All our 'Ivory Tower' endeavors, seem to be guiding us to back 'SOURCE' with our internal and inherently natural 'spiritual science' compasses. Pretty ironic I say!

However in the context of the oneness of all things we are now realizing about our true nature; why should this be different or even surprising to us? Some fundamental fields of science are in 'flux' now. They are causing some awakened souls to rethink many of the concepts we accepted in the Newtonian paradigm as 'reality'. There is a fringe group that may have always had a clue, about where this is all going, but were not communicating it for a host of reasons. If we paid attention we would know that science is the true 'Flux M7 progenitor' disguised with all its powerful S.T.E.M systems, hocus pocus and Babel-speak with all their constantly evolving and shifting gauge theories that are not reaching nor teaching us. Who is breaking down this knowledge to us so we can apply it to our lives; down to the proverbial 'man on the street' levels of society? The purveyors have seized the day and are packaging our reality for us. Self-empowerment is not on their menu though. It does not $ell.

If 'as above' was meant to be 'so below' we still have light years of pain and tears to point the way to go in a new direction! It's all by Design and only Design can fix us and it with this inclusive and ubiquitous D$_E$Sign Science. The moniker 'architecture' has been appropriated by many other disciplines.

If we think we know, feel or understand the levels of stress along this 'spectrum of wisdom, Intelligence, knowledge and Information' the (WIKI) that divides us we are deluding ourselves. This gap has the greatest set of pain points we suffer from. Between the isms and schisms we are caught up living lies and not being in our natural state of abundance. Of the four elements of the WIKI that all work together we seem to have focused on one...knowledge. Now if this is 'by design', which is very often the kind of 'third hand dynamic' in economics or in the social schisms found in manipulating cultural differences as the 'invisible designers' often do, then the same 'design mentality' can be turned around to be the solution. At the big-inning of any new day it's a new, compassionate and responsible 'D$_E$Sign Science' that will lead the way.

Design is Ubiquitous. There are few causal elements beyond the realm of design. The forces, motions and thoughts that inspire, motivate and direct connect us to source, operating over and above the 'Flux M7 progenitor' we are engaged in now.

Regard-full of all the Flux can contribute, in any and all synthesis, design is the truest and best proactive empowering dynamic we can rely on. It mirrors consciousness and the forces operating within the transformational potential that shifts through space, time and energy from the infinite to the normal and subconscious dimension of the inner and outer worlds. Design is the driver that we use to "make the abstract real".

Let me be clear here. I take nothing away from the purveyors of development of all types. Everyone serves a purpose in the all of all needs and personalities. My (happy) calling happens to be in the *truth* of 'Design as a Science'.

It embraces the knowledge that is constantly expanding the creation story we are all acting in, making the movie and movement much more exciting, and full of possibilities for framing a new paradigm vision for a new age full of creative things to come and be done by 'design science' for humanity and the planet. This is the highest expression of the human spirit I love and will continue to enjoy and share through works I create, for the good of ALL. Here are a few new paradigm principles we can now work with to recalibrate a more inner-directed and focused mindset:

1. All is [body, mind and spirit or energy therefore] consciousness.
2. Everything comes from and connects to the source of all arising
3. We are eternal spirits, in the great race; physical, sentient energy forms at a pit stop on earth.
4. All life has meaning and purpose and is part of the plan.
5. The internality is the only true reality, externality is illusion.
6. No one thing can be whole everything is part of the All of ALL of source.
7. Nature does not judge only humans do; Judgement and humility do not align with natural law.
8. Change is the most natural attribute of consciousness and all of its vibrational expressions.
9. Quantum leaps drive change not increments nor excrements.
10. Source needs no dimensions to be it is not binary nor any other gauge we make on any level, scale or size.
11. Polarity has an inner and outer sense as extremes of oneness, they are the same.
12. We create entropic realities because we are entropic illusory reflections of vibrations.
13. No thing we create can ever be constant or eternal.
14. Ego and 'Shego' have no place in pure extension; space, pure duration; time and pure consciousness; thought.
15. Words have shadows take everything stated above with a grain of truth.
16. Thought in its purest form is light from a sun behind the sun.

"When freedom prevails, the ingenuity is the source of the natural improvement of the human condition." —Brian S. Wesbury

CHAPTER TWO   ICOSAHEDRON I$_C$H

2. Spiritual Principles:

Svadhisthana, the spleen (Sexual-Gender) chakra is the love power center. When opened, the sex forces will try to lower the seeker's consciousness. The anahata center's spiritual heart will transform impurity into purity. Purity is eventually transformed into fulfilling and everlasting divinity. Clairempathy, Emotional Intelligence, emotional intelligence for using the emotion, manifesting desires.

Gender: principle of gender that is essential to procreation.

It is the sacral or sexual center, water the gonads, ovaries, testes energy Element for the generation, creativity and the gender biology of the male & female.

There is a symmetry principle of gender that is essential to creation with the physiology and flavors along with symmetry to make parts whole according to natural laws.

CHAPTER 2 TRINE A
A NEW PARADIGM AGE IS UPON US

 **T**HE PARADIGM SHIFT ALIGNS with and brings a new consciousness replete with creative opportunities for true innovations and solutions. A radical shift of our mindset allows us to embrace this elevation of consciousness, and our understanding of our world grows. With purpose and vision, we must now collectively ART-iculate all the new express-ions for the good of all. The cycles of this evolution are historically documented in all disciplines responsible for creating the life support systems the world depends on for growth. 'Design' is the major discipline for the manifestation of new realities.

After decades of creative research and work, both in my architectural discipline, in self-study and development, I am a part of the flow of this new consciousness. The mission now is to translate principles and concepts of this intensely experimental approach into viable applications in the fields where appropriate correlations exist. There is a point in this process where principles of true understanding of how things work are revealed only to unearth that the dynamics of nature, which guide us, have very few phenomenal elements that mirror our reality, physically, psychologically and spiritually.

This threefold expression is inherently interconnected by the symmetry principles that form a qualitative periodicity as we find with that of the 'neter' or nature of matter in the periodic table of physics, chemistry et. al. (yet to unfold).

There is a qualitative periodic table of 'suchness' and one of 'muchness' — the former qualitative the latter being quantitative. We make connections with the expressions of natural forces, flavors and gauges to form a synthesis or oneness of and with the 'ALL'.

ALL that was, is, and can ever be obey the laws of nature regardless of the time, space and energy continuum we experience.

Whether we understand them or not, we are living in and within a greater consciousness that we are inherently linked to. There is a correspondence of this consciousness of body, mind and spirit that aligns with space, time and energy to begin the continuity of life. During this process we are informed by the synthesis of it ALL in ways we can apply to creating our environment with the creative life support knowledge, systems, and tools we have and need available.

As 'abstract' as this might be, we can ab-stract (take from nature, the source of ALL consciousness), what we require to create our world/s. Each era comes with its own toolkit to suit the issues that are unique to that very time and space. They too are constantly evolving as the universe expands. All else aligns with that expansion. Why should our consciousness not be expanding also, especially since we are an intricate part of its fabric? Forms of energy are unique and consistent with this alignment. The key form of energy here is that of 'thought'. After 'abstracting' the natural intelligences by using our corresponding human intelligences, of which there are a few (7), that task becomes creative, experimental and playful. By playing on this level, we learn. Observation is an essential part of this process. Thought is a pure form of energy. Space is its own pure extension and time is pure duration.

"The future is not some place we are going, but one we (imagine and) are creating. The paths are not to be found, but (invented) made. And the activity of making them changes both the maker and their destination."—John Schaar

Up to this point we are at the stage of transforming the phenomenological to be ideational. The next step is conceptual. This is the creative process that supports the formulation of expressions through the many forms of disciplines available to us humans.

We need to know, understand and create the psychology of the matter we can use with the appropriate 'sense of gauge,' or measurement, needed to manifest our ideas. It is particularly interesting when the idea is original and does not exist or never existed and is depending on (us) the creator for it to become.

The disciplines I am involved with are primarily art and architecture. They are extensive and require many other sub-disciplines to be effective. 'Design' is the intersection of both disciplines. We encode the vocabularies, and languages essential to the expression of all thought forms, concepts and ideas. The form may not always be physical. Another key element is aesthetics or the spirit of the expression of form with an internal dynamic and creative process that mirrors all universal, natural symmetry principles and encoded identities each resonating to its respective vibration, which qualifies it and makes it (real). Various frequencies of vibration are part of the periodic matrix that is qualitative and quantitative. This duality is ubiquitous until the appropriate gauge, matter and energies are aligned and the form is described, specified and then manifested.

In architecture science, engineering and mathematics are essential disciplines along with the arts. Geometry 'describes' the inner and outer worlds. It is both a qualitative and quantitative science that is considered 'sacred', hence 'sacred geometry'. This is not to be confused with religion.

Architecture in the classical sense was considered the 'mother of the arts.' All forms of art are incorporated in 'conscious' architecture. Unto itself art involves many of the subsets of architecture with one major exception.

There are many more degrees of freedom, not only of expression but as a discipline with very different or sometimes no constraints. We might qualify architecture as being objective and art as subjective.

A NEW PARADIGM AGE IS UPON US

DESIGN SCIENCE IN THE NEW PARADIGM AGE

The fundamental studies of esoteric philosophy, nature studies and logic structures, analysis and synthesis, are the foundation for the 'Design Science' (methods) and the inter-disciplinary Researchthat supports the conceptual, form and structural engineering of creative concepts that become real world solutions in 'fields of application. The universal nature of this fundamental approach transcends disciplines that are still operating in the old paradigm. There is efficiency in the oneness of creative effort and resources being applied to a diverse set of solutions with common characteristics, qualities and flavors of expression. Very often, the variations and adaptations exist in the realm of scale, types of materials, their varying psychologies and structural integrity.

Researchcontinues as the study of how forms are generated and how to classify them when they are discovered. This I call 'Philogenetics". Philo means type, as in phylum. Genetics is the creative process. Both 'Non-Euclidean' and 'Euclidean' Geometry are used to describe three dimensional forms. These forms are then applied to various disciplines and industries.

The definition of culture, once thought to be the balance of the natural with the artificial, is obsolete. In the new paradigm, culture is the synthesis of the physiological, with the psychological and the spiritual. Spiritual here relates to ALL forms of energy — from thought, to nature's forces and our creative work energies.

The old paradigm seems to have focused on the physiological and physical aspects of reality at the expense of the behavioral and creative spirit. The goal of the cultural development process is to live at the highest and best levels of human achievement.

This involves and is motivated by the inherent and internal qualities of the forms of expression which in turn 'frees and feeds the soul.' This is the realm of the 'ARTS' in this context of Cultural, Economic Development. It is the source of all expressions of solutions looking for 'problems' to satisfy them through some enterprise or endeavor formed into a business as the vehicle for delivery, distribution and reward.

The Languages we use to communicate are composed of this threefold dynamic of 'culture' and consciousness. The physical elements are our nouns. The connective, operational, or behavioral tools, if you may, are psychological. They echo all behaviors. The action words or verbs are the spiritual or energy concepts or flavors. Words are symbols and forms encoding experiences used for telling the human story of time, space and energy. They change as we evolve and as paradigms change.

Creating a workable structure for delivering these ideas, information and DESIGNSis critical. It is the essence of a business model to address the critical education, promulgation and inherent benefits and joys of these ideas and the design solutions they inspire to promote prosperity and development opportunities. On the surface it appears to be a vast undertaking. When broken down into its respective research, management and production modules, the components will be arranged in a viable production sequence for intervention. That will then lead to subsequent 'line extensions' and other products, projects with the proper relationships and participation by those engaged in the vision and mission.

All Intellectual Properties derived from the various levels of development, from concepts to information and systems, are the assets of this enterprise. They can be leveraged, licensed and used to develop variously branded technologies and products that are marketed worldwide under a holding entity registered and protected with copyright, trademarks, design and utility patent protection and filings under international treaties for foreign markets where sales and operations are targeted and established.

In light of recognizing signs and patterns of the paradigm shift, I am expecting that you, the reader, seeker as designer are experiencing or at least now open to implementing your own view of your world. A key word in this process is 'expression.' It takes on a multitude of meanings now in keeping with the Body, Mind Spirit aspects of who we are and how we grow constantly.

We begin to apply our new WIKI; (Wisdom, Intelligence, Knowledge and Information) as we continue the journey to our 'Constant Creative Freedom' in no time. Having creative freedom might need to change with other paradigm shifts that come much faster than before. Being prepared for constant change keeps us aligned with (our true) nature and with how we grow. Expressions are 'real', physical, structural things, spaces and environments made of matter. The behaviors of the matter, the creative mind that molds it with the creative work and the spiritual energy that expresses the essence of genius and consciousness are also expressions. This is the promise (*PREMISE*) of the new Paradigm Age we are in NOW.

SYNTHESIS:

Partial three dimensional 'qualitative and quantitative' matrix

ALL OR UNIVERSAL CONSCIOUSNESS	NORMAL CONSCIOUS-NESS	SUB CONSCIOUS-NESS	SUPER CONSCIOUSNESS
Consciousness	Awareness	Feelings	Thoughts Cognition
Conditioning	Physical	Emotional	Spiritual Creative
States	Physiological	Psychological	Spiritual
Affinities	Dimensions	Expressions	Flavors
Universal Expressions	Space	Time	Energy (work) Thought
Number	1 (one)	2 (two)	3 (three)
Color (pigment)	Red	Yellow	Blue

Matter	Solid	Gas	Liquid
Human beings	Body	Mind	Spirit (thought)
Orientation	Down	Side	Up
Subjective time	Present	Past	Future
Quality	Muchness	Suchness	Oneness/ Consciousness

These are the elements of synthesis used to create the blends of expressions.

THE KEY INGREDIENTS FOR MAKING EXPRESSIONS

MATRIX ELEMENTS	PHYSIOLOGY/SPACE	PSYCHOLOGY/TIME	SPIRITUALITY/ENERGY
Body/Space	The physiology (behavior) of the body /pure space	The psychology (behavior) of the body /space time continuum	The spirituality (behavior) of the body/space spirit (energy) continuum
Mind/Time	The physiology (behavior) of the mind/mind space continuum	The psychology (behavior) of the mind/pure mind [time beyond time] freedom	The spirituality (behavior) of the mind /time spirit continuum
Spirit/Energy	The physiology (behavior) of the spirit/energy space continuum	The psychology (behavior) of the spirit/spirit mind continuum	The spirituality (behavior) of the spirit/pure spirit

The time beyond time is 'spiritual' freedom? The Pure Time of time is mental? Time in time is physical, vibrational and objective time. In time, on time and beyond time are three different qualities of experiences in the space, time energy continuum.

THE DISTRIBUTION MATRIX
THE QUALITATIVE GRID WITH EXTRAPOLATIONS OF THE THREE DIMENSIONS OF CONSCIOUSNESS

7 CHAKRAS-ENDOCRINE SYSTEMS CORRELATIONS

CHAKRA	HINDU NAMES	GLAND	SECRET-ION	GOVERNS	CENTERS
Seventh Chakra	Sahasra-ra	Pineal Gland	Melatonin	Body rhythm	Crown
Sixth Chakra	Ajna	Pituitary Gland	Somato-trophin	Growth	Third Eye
Fifth Chakra	Vishuddha	Thyroid/ Parathyroid	Thyrox-ine	Metabolism	Throat
Fourth Chakra	Anahata	Thymus	Lymph-ocytes	Immunity	Heart
Third Chakra	Manipura	Spleen/Pancreas	Insulin	Digestion	Solar Plexus
Second Chakra	Svadhisth-ana	Gonads/ Ovaries Testicles	Oestrogen Testoster one Progester one	Development	Sexual
First Chakra	Mulad-hara	Adrenal Glands	Epinephri ne Thymo-sin	Actions	Root Sacral

Thymosin: One of several polypeptide hormones secreted by the thymus that control the maturation of T cells. They are derived from a polypeptide called prothymosin-alpha (PTMA) or alpha thymosin.

Here is a distribution pattern for matter, number and color

PHENOMENA	BODY	MIND	SPIRIT
Matter-Energy	SOLID	LIQUID	GAS
	SGS SLS	LSL LGL	GLG GSG
Number-Quantity & Quality	1-111-(3) 121- 4 313- 7	2-222- (6) 232- 5 212- 5	3-333-(9) 313- 7 323- 8
Color-Vibration and Frequency	RED RBR RYR	YELLOW YRY YBY	BLUE BYB BRB

43

A NEW PARADIGM AGE IS UPON US *DESIGN SCIENCE IN THE NEW PARADIGM AGE*

This is an infinite MATRIX

EXPRESSIONS:

All expressions are physical, psychological and spiritual (energy) ideas, experiences and thoughts. Those of the past, present and future form the web of our collective consciousness and our intelligence.

On the practical side these expressions create business opportunities for us to use for living and realizing our fullest potential. The metaphysics, the physics and the spiritual dynamics are keys to understanding what is needed to ART-iculate the visions that envelop and enfold or form these expressions.

Light is the transcendent element that all things use to manifest themselves on the respective levels of vibration that define the expressions — the object, the process, the energy. The highest form of all vibrations is thought. It is the creative fuel. We travel along these rays of light, along "the Ray of Creation," to return to the source of our arising.

Our consciousness expands as we travel along the rays of light since we too are light. The ability to extract all required forms of energy for thoughts and ideas in the universal source of everything is the creative force we use to manifest expressions of a collective

consciousness that has a flavor with a distinct form, quality and look. It is our 'aesthetic DNA', if you will. It changes from time to time. We are in one of these periodic shifts now.

We know this by the geometric expressions that are translated for us by those disciplines and professionals who have decoded the structural systems with which we build our reality. A system of Non-Euclidean forms is now available with consistent, repeatable symmetries to align with our needs, thoughts and energies. It is this language that will be used to build the man-made environment and all the accessories needed for our convenience along with the fuels and energies with which we ART-iculate and fashion our lifestyles. ART is the essential gift we use to support life. It is critical to the process of the extraction of subtle thought and the transformation into reality.

How do we transform this into a creative structure meant to serve our daily needs and those of the total synthesis of what is necessary for us to be human and to expand our consciousness as we grow with everything around us in harmony? The collective consciousness is the source for our collective success. Those who can journey into the realms of thought and ideas have a responsibility to 'be our brother's and sister's keeper. Together, we can also harmonize the cultural, social and economic potential of our communities.

Expressing and ART-iculating a new aesthetic with Design solutions is the goal. Through a strategy of Cultural Economics this becomes the engine for healing, success and prosperity in the spirit of 'community' — Creative community that is.

Thus, we build communities that lead to civilizations' visions and expressions.

Technologies, Infrastructure, The built environment, Architecture, Art, Design Manufacturing, financial resources and wealth creation systems are to be developed with this new form language.

There is a "generic Manufacturing" technology that applies to prototyping and creating goods, and the delivery systems needed to share them with markets.

Education, career training and jobs along with business development are essential elements of the vision and the plan of meaningful implementation. The New Paradigm is being ART-iculated as the aesthetic symbolic expression of this era for another 2,000-year cycle.

The team of experts with their special skills will put a business plan in place to guide this vision to its fullest and most efficient manifestation.

Is this a *New (North and South) American Aesthetic* in the making, with this Non-Euclidean geometric tradition, and other creative strategies? Is there a distinct and unique look to anything "Made in America "now?

Inspiring and making variations along with innovations and new applications produce products, environments, art and design objects and rhythms for living. New materials, methods and technologies help fashion our emerging aesthetic reality.

Wellness, Healing, Creative growth and development support people's lives, their communities and their homes, where they work to fulfill their physical, psychological and spiritual purpose.

Plants, facilities, and creative work places are essential to this vision.

One indication that is quite revealing as the affirmation of the timeliness of this creative process is the emergence of knowledge from our 'ancestral and wisdom traditions'.

They now occupy our minds, our media, some of our literature and the general body of the information about esoteric topics, technologies and ideas. Most of this can be thought of as being revealed from the collective resurgence of our awareness during our search for truth.

Quality is the focus in this approach. Sustainability is the other name for things that last long, are not designed or engineered to be obsolete quickly and might just become the new classic expressions of our present and future.

The development team comprises: Administrative, Technical / Design and Engineering, Architectural, Marketing, Capital and Finance, Real Estate Property acquisition and development, Public Relations, Community Development, Legal and Compliance etc. We need to identify investors, and locate grants and other forms of funding for all enterprises. Study the markets in the 'Useful Matrix of Products', services and distribution systems.

Disposability and obsolescence are replaced by the finest Quality, sustainability and provenance once again. The evolution of economics in human culture, life support and their benefits need to be reevaluated in light of the new form vocabularies. There are many more to come as well.

A culture of Creativity is our destiny. Evolving forms is a priority for research and development. The needs (Mind), Expressions (Body) and Flavors (Spirit or Flavors) of or for people, places and things inspire us to create, provide and distribute them via forms or models of business we need to explore to achieve peak efficiency.

In so doing, we add value to life. The basic needs of food, clothing and shelter can be met with an aesthetic as the inspiration for our evolution and life support systems.

CARING FOR AND SHARING THE PRAXIS

We can use Non-Euclidean geometric form vocabulary to create and design objects, our environment, art and other creative expressions. Inventions in geometry provided forms for product development; manufacturing, architecture and community development; construction. Innovative concepts employ modular units that are structurally and aesthetically pleasant for housing, consumer products etc. on all levels. Some very critical issues that impact the industrial sector of urban environments add value to the economic future with new opportunities and ideas. A lateral approach to the synthesis of systems, methods, materials and manufacturing to define new expressions in new form vocabularies is recommended to create much needed employment and other opportunities with significant values added to human experiences.

The best vehicle for finding truth is ART.

This idea is based on the historic movements like the Bauhaus which is the future presented to us as the last art and cultural moment that shaped the world we now live in. We have come full circle and are ready to define the needs for the next movement that is emerging. New form vocabularies are key to all creative development.

This also offers a philosophical, behavioral and spiritual foundation that can inspire meaningful development in many disciplines in which structure, form and ideas can now be ART-iculated with aesthetic design principles that support the creative visions of our community. We are at a critical stage in our creative 'cultural economic development'.

We, who have been working quietly behind the scenes, are now looking to align with initiatives and visions, to share information and create implementation opportunities for the good of all.

We present specific projects to organizations to explore any and all common interests and opportunities that can be of great value to our communities, its creative people (most of us are with some constructive direction and support) for our communities.

"Simpli Fi"

Simplicity, Patience, Compassion these three are your greatest treasures. Simple in actions and thoughts, you return to the source of being Patient with both friends and enemies, you accord with the way things are. Compassionate toward yourself, you reconcile all beings in the world."
– Lao Tzu, Tao Te Ching SPACE: Simplicity, Patience, Action, Compassion, Energy

CHAPTER 2 TRINE B
'AESTHETIX' III NEW PARADIGM-VALUE SYSTEMS

OUR KNOWLEDGE BASE(KEN) CONTINUES to expand as our consciousness grows. Amidst the noise and haste of an ever- consuming environment and the people and the paradigms that support it, opportunities continue to be created for a creative path towards a constructive positive future. The pattern of this expansion often reaches back, recoiling and catapulting intelligences through an eternal space time energy continuum to formulate and manifest visions of a new world and all in it as the birthright of a revitalized human spirit. We are responsible for the planet and ourselves. Synthesizing an aesthetic with a strong cultural identity is essential to our growth process. Cultural and creative expressions for all human life have at their core, aesthetic or spiritual principles that support them. Civilizations that survive have established this approach to sustainability and endurance.

'Form Consciousness' is one of these central creative and universal principles. All expressions emerge from phenomenological, three-dimensional realities of Mind, Body and Spirit in synthesis with the Space, Time Energy continuum. The multiplicity of the Chimera or Maya we get lost in distracts us from observing the simplicity of the few principles that govern all reality, man-made or natural. Design vocabularies that can help us define new environments, products and opportunities for economic and creative prosperity continue to emerge. What's needed is the dialog to begin to explore the role of the American cultural aesthetic is and how it relates to economic growth and development in our current climate.

The expanded version of our 3D Design course has a lot of room for demonstrating how an adult population of creative professionals, (in Continuing Education), can participate in an "Aesthetic Dialog".

This can inspire creative development in untappd areas. A 'Form Technology', based on new forms, with all their supporting components, can be the foundation for viable and real business development. "3D Design II" can be offered in a practical, hands-on way to design, build and set the patterns for showing how form inventions are derived and how they can be applied to our needs in various areas as we seek to respond to our creative responsibility to care for ourselves and our environment. Form and music have unique linguistic principles we engage in without knowing why or how they help us. We can be more conscious and better in-formed to understand the meaning of form in our lives and in the environment. In a Form Centered paradigm with all other principles synthesized and harmonized, a strategy for true and relevant development can begin. A Cohesive identity informs the entire inventory of interventions and applications, making the aesthetic expression viable and pleasant.

The geometric extensions of our form vocabularies continue to offer solutions as new materials and technologies are made available. We need to identify opportunities to begin the design and development process using form as the engine for our economic survival. Once this dialog begins, a system that can be reality tested and put into order for a logical sequence of activities to lead the creative development process will emerge.

Research, ideation, product creation, needs assessment, business development, sales and marketing, customer care and feedback are a few of the critical steps in making the abstract real. When this dialog starts the one unique proposition in this strategy remains the 'FORM' vocabularies that continue to grow. The new materials are next.

They both inspire new approaches to the production methods we now have available. This will in turn fuel creativity and create educational opportunities for all involved. I propose this from my own professional and personal experiences. As an architect, product developer and artist, among other disciplines I enjoy, inventing three dimensional 'Form'. The patents that protect them represent value. Sharing this is my mission; to develop a real world 'Idea and Think Bank' to inspire creative development we can all benefit from.

We have evolved to the stage of heightened consciousness or evolution as we move to higher levels of civilization creation with the need for a cultural and form vocabulary that can tell our epochal stories to future generations. Some professions have excelled at synthesizing existing knowledge, information, creative processes and expressions, doing their best with the tools they had.

With the expansion and vastness of the 'knowledge or intellectual capital' that's unfolding and the need for even more adequate processing and management systems, we would all be better served by enhancing the methodology and protocols to become 'Sciences'. Science, as the quintessential 'method maker', in the truest and most critical egalitarian context we need now, there is an open-source, 'FREEDOMGRANTING' phenomena available to ALL who are open. I can speak for the ubiquitous sectors of Design, Architecture, Art, and other visual media, disciplines and unequivocally state that this necessary 'rebranding' of disciplines can be transformed by D$_E$Sign Science. In doing so we honor the life, vision and contribution of Richard Buckminster Fuller.

We begin to establish the criteria for the new paradigm shifts of human consciousness and our recognition of the application of the essential mindset reorientations and recalibrations this synthesis affords us.

A key element for understanding the subtler forces we need to adopt is the Hindu Kundalini system and the seven chakras. Here is a wisdom tradition that defines the role of what science now calls the electro-magnetic field of energy which either is or plays a significant role in the human life force dynamic with each culture having its own name for it. The image of a parallel mirror reflection comes to mind here as the metaphor of the one in its multiple dimensions and refractions. Western medicine picks up just beyond this 'energy milestone' with its own STEM physical science model of the endocrine system of ductless glands and hormones. This is a universal system found in every culture on the planet.

The subtle systems of all life require a finer fuel to work with it if we are going to understand ourselves and be able to optimize our reason for being. My studies, experiments and exercises in this area have been my key to the knowledge and opportunities I have enjoyed on this journey. We may not be able to create the physical scaffold we use for our STEM models of how the world works. The axiom 'fighting fire with fire' comes to mind here but instead of fire we may have to use 'thought', a more intense energy. Everything is thought. It is the finest and most powerful fuel that imbues 'ubiquity'; in everything, every time and in every state of being everywhere.

The tongue, one of the smallest of all the members of the body, can do the most damage (James 3:5)-word!

THE ENDOCRINE GLANDS

GLAND	SECRETION	GOVERNING
Adrenals	Epinephrine	Actions
Ovaries/Testicles	Estrogen/Testosterone	Development
Thyroid	Thyroxine	Metabolism
Pancreas	Insulin	Digestion
Thymus	Lymphocytes	Immunity
Pituitary	Somatotrophin	Growth
Pineal	Melatonin	Body rhythm

This is where we confront the classic East-West dichotomy or better stated the language and spiritual materialism barrier. The seven centers and their attributes are described here.

HEXAHEDRON-EARTH	MULADHARA-ROOT CHAKRA [INNOCENCE]
	At the top of the kidneys are the adrenal's that produce several hormones including adrenalin, which stimulates the "fight or flight" response and ties directly to the Base Chakra's survival drive. This Chakra is related to the gonads in males.

ICOSAHEDRON-WATER 	SWADISTHANA-SACRAL CHAKRA [CREATIVITY] The ovaries control sexual development and egg creation as well as controlling the levels of estrogen and progesterone. The potential for life in the ovaries is mirrored in the drives of the Sacral Chakra. *The energies of the ovaries link with the Sacral Chakra*
TETRAHEDRON-FIRE 	MANIPURA or NABHI-STOMACH/NAVEL/ SOLAR PLEXUS CHAKRA [PEACE]. The pancreas secretes substances for the digestion of food, such as insulin. When this Chakra is over stimulated it can cause problems with excess blood sugar, the major cause of diabetes. *An under stimulated stomach Chakra can lead to ulcers.*
CUBEOCTAHEDRON-HEART 	ANAHATA-HEART CHAKRA [LOVE- COMPASSION] The thymus is located above the heart and produces lymphocytes, which form a vital part of the body's immune response. This quality relates the thymus to the healing properties of the Heart Chakra. *The healing promoted by this Chakra links it to the thymus*

OCTAHEDRON-AIR 	VISHUDDAH-THROAT CHAKRA [COLLECTIVITY-COMMUNITY] On either side of the larynx is the thyroid, producing thyroxin, which controls converting food into useful energy. This is the area over which the Throat Chakra has dominance. *The thyroid governs the rate of metabolism in the body.*
ICOSIDODECAHEDRON 	AJNA-BROW/THIRD EYE CHAKRA [FORGIVENESS] Near the base of the skull is the pituitary gland, which releases hormones influencing body chemistry. The spiritual energies of the Brow Chakra are reflected in the pituitary's influence on the whole body. *This Chakra works with the pituitary gland in the body.*
DODECAHEDRON-ENERGY 	SAHASRARA-CROWN CHAKRA [INTEGRATION-SYNTHESIS] The pineal gland lies deep within the brain and produces melatonin. This hormone affects the other glands in the endocrine system and mirrors the Crown Chakra's relationship with the other Chakra's. *This gland and Chakra hold sway over the entire body.*

By understanding the association - between the Chakra's and the glands you can see how Healing benefits a multitude of illnesses affecting one's physical, mental, emotional, and spiritual well-being. The images on the left show the chakras. Polyhedra Forms are elements: Earth, Water, Fire, Air and Ether.

Vibration is a key to the rhythm of every expression. Hermetic philosophy teaches us that nothing rests and that everything is constantly vibrating. Change, Constancy and Creativity are synthesized into a powerful dynamic man has avoided… no more! We confront ourselves and see nature in stasis, physical reality is fixed even though it vibrates constantly. Emotions cause us to be conditioned and not move to the rhythm of the universe. Our spiritual knowledge used to inspire and motivate us is stuck in corrupted and outdated languages with words, vocabularies and symbolism that fuel hate, wars and aggression.

Music is the healer of dissonance. The Chakras are encoded with the scales and harmonies of the universe. Source gave us many 'back up' systems as failsafe methods for making sure we don't blow ourselves to smithereens. Tuning Our Chakra *'Guitar Strings'*: Just as each guitar string corresponds to a note, each chakra corresponds to a Solfeggio Frequency. Here are the chakras and their colors listed with their appropriate frequencies.

Now that you know the chakras and frequencies you can begin to balance.

CENTER	COLOR	EFFECTS	NOTE	FREQUENCY
Seventh Chakra (Crown)	Violet	Awaken perfect state	Si or Ti	– 963 Hz
Sixth Chakra (Third Eye)	Indigo	Return to spiritual order	La	– 852 Hz
Fifth Chakra (Throat)	Blue	Expressions/ solutions	Sol	– 741 Hz
Fourth Chakra (Heart)	Green	Reconnecting, Relationships	Fa	– 639 Hz
Third Chakra (Solar Plexus)	Yellow	Transformation & miracles	Mi	– 528 Hz
Second Chakra (Sacral)	Orange	Facilitate change	Re	– 417 Hz
First Chakra (Root or Base)	Red	Turn grief into joy	Ut :Do	– 396 Hz

Frequencies play A major role in our diets, nutrition and health.

SECRET KEYS TO THE UNIVERSE (ONEVERSE)

What are the Solfeggio frequencies?

Solfeggio frequencies make up the ancient 6-tone scale thought to have been used in sacred music, including the beautiful and well-known Gregorian Chants. The chants and their special tones were believed to impart spiritual blessings when sung in harmony. Each Solfeggio tone is comprised of a frequency required to balance your energy and keep your body, mind and spirit in perfect harmony. They were used in over 150 Gregorian Chants.

The main six Solfeggio frequencies are:

396 Hz – Liberating Guilt and Fear
417 Hz – Undoing Situations and Facilitating Change
528 Hz – Transformation and Miracles (DNA Repair)
639 Hz – Connecting/Relationships
741 Hz – Expression/Solutions
852 Hz – Returning to Spiritual Order

Where do these tones come from?

The ancient Solfeggio scale can be traced back to a medieval hymn to John the Baptist. The first six lines of the music commenced respectively on the first six successive notes of the scale, and thus the first syllable of each line was sung to a note *one degree higher* than the first syllable of the line that preceded it. The mathematic resonance of the original frequencies were capable of spiritually inspiring mankind to be more "god-kind".

Discovering the frequencies.

Dr. Joseph Puleo was introduced, through an *open vision*, (Direct Knowledge) to the Pythagorean method of *numeral reduction*. Using this method, he discovered the pattern of six repeating codes in the Book of Numbers, Chapter 7, verses 12 through 83.

In addition to the sound vibration study the intuition experienced by *Dr. Joseph Puleo* completed the task.

This represents a type of cognition that is still not readily accessible to most and avoided by the scientists. Herein lies the critical need for establishing the authority, authenticity and credibility, not only of the content but for how it was and continues to be attained. Why be embarrassed, guilty or ashamed to relate to true 'GOD-line-ss'?

Here are the secret meanings of the ancient syllables. Did man create these tones? Each tone has its own unique potential, vibration and flavor meant to keep us aligned with goodness.

Initially written by Paolo Diacono as a hymn to Saint John the Baptist (circa 720 - 799), the Latin words "Ut queant laxis, Resonare fibris, Mira gestorum, Famuli tuorum, Solve polluti, Labii reatum," translate to *"So that your servants may sing at the top of their voices the wonders of Your acts, and absolve the fault from their stained lips."*

The syllables used to denote the tones are: *Ut, Re, Mi Fa, Sol, La.* They were taken from the first stanza of the hymn to *St. John the Baptist*:

'Ut queant laxis Resonare fibris
Mira gestorum Famuli tuorum
Solve polluti Labii reatum
Sancte Iohannes'

Another Literal translation from Latin: *"In order that the slaves might resonate (resound) the miracles (wonders) of your creations with loosened (expanded) vocal chords. Wash the guilt from (our) polluted lip. Saint John."*

In other words, *so people could live together in peace and communicate in harmony about the miracle in their lives, and how God blessed them to produce this "magic", people's true unpolluted spiritual natures required revelation.*

The above text seems to suggest that Solfeggio notes open up a channel of communication with the Divine with their frequencies aligned and vocalized as 'mantras'.

Our modern day musical scale is out of sync when compared with the original Solfeggio scale. If we want to bring harmony in our lives, we need to replace the dissonant western scale with a web of subtle and clear intervallic relationships of the Solfeggio music. Let the music once again become a tool to raise human nature and a method to connect us with SOURCE.

Giants upon whose shoulders the earth r-evolves. Tune yourself back into the perfect vibrations!

Another application of vibrations dealing with numbers is given to us by Nikola Tesla, the great genius and father of electromagnetic engineering, once said, *"If you only knew the magnificence of the 3, 6 and 9, then you would hold a key to the universe".*

The 3, 6, and 9 are the fundamental root vibrations of the Solfeggio frequencies and of the harmonic vibrations of human consciousness. Albert Einstein stated: *"Concerning matter, we have been all wrong.*

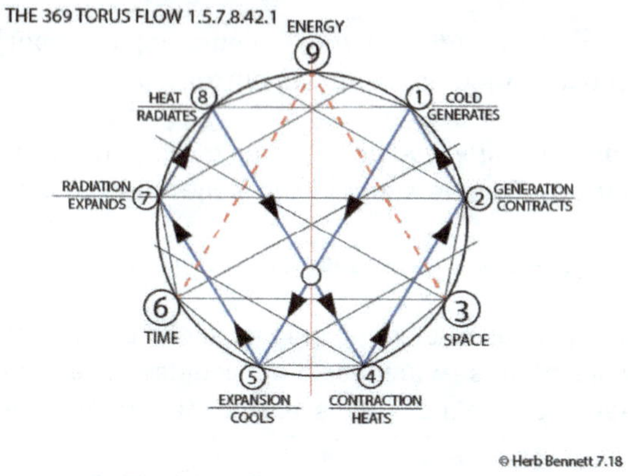

'AESTHETIX' III NEW PARADIGM - VALUE SYSTEM

D_ESIGN SCIENCE IN THE NEW PARADIGM AGE

THE 369 TORUS FLOW 1.5.7.8.42.1

ENERGY
⑨

HEAT ⑧
RADIATES

① COLD
GENERATES

RADIATION ⑦
EXPANDS

② GENERATION
CONTRACTS

⑥
TIME

③
SPACE

⑤
EXPANSION
COOLS

④
CONTRACTION
HEATS

© Herb Bennett 7.18

Fig. 2

What we have called matter is energy, whose vibration has been so lowered as to be perceptible to the senses. There is no matter."

It is all 'MAYA'. All matter (beings) vibrate at specific rates and everything has its own melody. The musical nature of nuclear matter from atoms to galaxies is now finally being recognized by science.

That is why these frequencies are so powerful. They can literally bring you back to the original tones of the heavenly spheres and put your body into a balanced resonance. *Solfeggio music is the key to the Universe.* You can either throw it away or you can use it to find healing and harmony, health and well-being. Just play the music!

"Here's to the crazy ones.
The misfits. The rebels.
The troublemakers.
The round pegs in the square holes.
The ones who see things differently.
They're not fond of rules.
And they have no respect for the status quo.
You can praise them, disagree with them, quote them, disbelieve them, glorify or vilify them.
About the only thing you can't do is ignore them. Because they change things.
They invent. They imagine. They heal. They explore. They create. They inspire. They push the human race forward.

Maybe they (are safer and) have to be 'crazy'.
How else can you stare at an empty canvas and see a work of art? Or sit in silence and hear a song that's never been written?
Or gaze at a red planet and see a laboratory on wheels? We make tools for creative people.
While some see them as the crazy ones, we see genius.
Because the people who are crazy enough to think they can change the world, are the ones who do." Steve Jobs, Apple C.E.O.

CHAPTER 2 TRINE C
CREATIVITY: THE DESIGN PROCESS

T*HERE IS BUT ONE CREATIVE process in the ALL of ALL multiverse; not universe. Multitudes we are yet to discover. We are so intricately woven into its web, unrealized yet not realizing, getting lost in nomenclature games where the shades and tones of our illusions pre-veil us from knowing we are all the same.*

The creative process followed here employs the esoteric knowledge of the chakras, subtle energies and their qualities, characteristics and potential that aligns with the natural and universal dynamic principles that govern all creative work they and their 'co-relatives' per-form.

1. The Root: WILL is the powerful dynamic here. With well-developed skills and your understanding of materials with respect for mother Earth we consistently produce high-quality original work. We achieve Inner-Direction through self-confidence and uniqueness. Artists search for and find their creative processes, interests, and rewarding experiences as they seek to impact their environments positively. This leads them to a state of Inner-direction. Originality is obtained through research, practice, and meaningful experiences including travel, networking and community involvement. Of paramount importance is the consistent search for excellence and the reward of self-fulfillment and financial rewards. Confront Challenges, think Diamonds they are created with heat and pressure as are great artists, designers and successful innovators, influencers and early adopters; all conscious and committed spirits.

2. The Sexual center relates to reproduction and symmetry gender dynamics. Here the male and female polarities complement extremes of sameness to extremes in balance.

   There is male and female in every physical, psychological-mental and spiritual expression of nature.

3. The Solar Plexus is about energy and work. Expand your Vision and Refine Your Process and Skill Set. Some artists follow some tradition, often multiple traditions. Any artwork you are inspired by might have traditions behind it; often a combination of disciplines.

4. The Heart: There are three hearts; the biological heart, the emotional and the spiritual heart that connects directly to the crown chakra and the neocortex with brain neurons all its own. The brain-heart dynamic is at work here. Do you recognize your brain heart connection? Develop Your Passion with a Unique Artistic Vision with the power of LOVE. Part of what drives us forward is our feelings, our compassion and passion. We become interested in art to fulfill our need to share our joy and love with the world.

CREATIVITY: THE DESIGN PROCESS

DESIGN SCIENCE IN THE NEW PARADIGM AGE

You will learn new skills and forms of expression as you shine you light with the world through your love of art, design and the people we share them with.

5. The Throat; Communicate with many Sources of Influence and mentors. Align your findings with your vision and identity. Synthesize multiple sources of influence to lead to more original works. Communication is a form of reality testing.

6. 3rd Eye: Experiment and Capture Random Occurrences Visualization and meditation are very effective disciplines. Creative play, experimentation and happy accidents can lead to true innovation.

7. The Crown-Mentalism: Plan for Originality of Concepts with design excellence in mind. What original thoughts or ideas can you synthesize for all your projects? What ideas move you?

To find your voice or style, explore reading, writing, sketching 3D modeling or internet research, dialog with other artists and designers with many forms of 'play' to invite your subconscious to the ideation process. The value of design as a 'subject' correlates with all other elements of its ubiquitous presence in a universe of 'discourse' that is governed by the synthesis, the symmetry rules and harmonies of all expressions; conscious or not. To understand our universe and ourselves, the observer/participator, we must first recognize the symmetry principles of Body, Mind and Spirit in correlation with Space, Time and Energy in synthesis as a law of nature.

It becomes impossible to know a subject, especially one that is as extensive and inclusive as 'design', if all its related parts are 'unknown'. Each subject is part of all others at the inclusive levels of the dynamics of "consciousness". We cannot focus on philosophical materialism alone and expect to be in harmony without all other critical parts being in place. The physical aspects of most subjects are therefore paradoxically incomplete and illusory.

There is however, one 'Grand Matrix*' that contains ALL Pure extension or Body-(Space): Pure duration or Mind-(Time): Pure Spirit-(Energy)-consciousness whose 'characteristics' and subjects are physiology, psychology and spirituality. Religiosity is 'personal' and prone to 'inversion'. What filters down from these are the tools we use to design our world. 'Thought' is the glue that holds the cosmos together. Nothing can be truly known without these principles and correlations in synthesis. Design is the method or the science that does this effectively, organically and holistically. The system then becomes multidimensional expanding our binary human modalities.

We are on a mental web; each one being a node with links we share forming the fabric of the universal and personal consciousness. Herb Bennett

THE MODELS OF SYNTHESIS

"The beginning of any 'wisdom quest' is found in doubting; by doubting we come to the question; followed by the request and desired results" — *inspired by Pierre Abela*

POLARITY

Geometry inscribes, describes and prescribes the record of our life's purpose (with words and or symbols) as we make our mark. It gives account in words, thoughts and action to be balanced. It includes all of the characteristics, qualities and flavors to live life, purposefully through our works-words!

In geometry, a point reflection or inversion is a point (or inversion through a point, or central polarity) as a type of *isometry* of Euclidean space. Isometry. ... An isometry of the plane is a *linear transformation* which preserves length. Isometries include rotation, translation, reflection, glides, and the identity map.

Two geometric figures related by an isometry are said to be geometrically congruent (Coxeter and Greitzer 1967, p. 80). Geometry aligns experiences of Body with Mind and Spirit elements. Allometric growth is when an organism grows and the proportions of body parts differ.

The word 'allometric' means different measure. ... Isometric growth is the exact opposite of allometric growth. Verse-writing arranged with a *metrical rhythm*, typically having a rhyme or speak in or compose verse; versify.

The Universe is all of *time, space*, its contents, energy and matter. It includes planets, moons, minor planets, stars and galaxies with the contents of intergalactic space, and all matter and energy. The size of the entire Universe is unknown. The definition of 'verse' as the root of the word 'universe' is arranged with a *metrical rhythm*.

Could 'uni' as the 'one' with verse offer a paradigm turn? Vegetables are good for your health, but now there's a whole new way that one veggie could help your heart: Spinach leaves can be used as a 'scaffold' for beating human heart cells, a new study finds. In several science experiments, scientists grew beating human heart cells on spinach leaves by 'perfusing' them with a detergent solution, which stripped them of their plant cells. This proof-of-concept study suggests that multiple spinach leaves could be used to grow layers of healthy heart muscle that could one day be used to treat heart attack patients, the researchers said.

CREATIVITY: THE DESIGN PROCESS

D_ESIGN SCIENCE IN THE NEW PARADIGM AGE

The dominant metaphysical idea of *any tradition* will result in its opposite effect in the society based on the principle of inversion. When social ills dovetail with the metaphysics of religion traditions as an example. They manifest on the *principle of 'inversion'*. The dominant *metaphysical idea* of any tradition will *result in its opposite effect* in the society where that religion dominates.

It seems that a religion prompts its followers, en masse, to betray its own highest ideas and ideals—that is, every religion engenders a very specific *set of* social ills causes, and the worldly or materialistic manifestations *inverting* the well imagined, thought out and intended philosophical vision.

The myths run out of 'belief power' as paradigms shift when ages change. In Pisces we go from 'I believe to I know in the Aquarian age. What do we observe when we apply this principle to 'design as a metaphysical principle'?

Does the dominant metaphysical idea of *design* result in its opposite effect on the society based on this same principle of 'inversion'? Stated another way; does the *principle of 'inversion' in the* metaphysics of *'design exacerbate or cause* social ills, poverty, and ineffective, adequate life support to prevail in all cultures when they dovetail with their design (or aesthetic) traditions?

"The dominant *metaphysical idea* of any tradition will *result in its opposite effect* in the society where that design tradition dominates".

It seems that such a condition prompts its followers, en masse, to betray its own highest ideas and ideals—that is, every design tradition attaches a specific *theme* to the social ills it causes, and the worldly manifestation *inverts* the philosophical vision. The prevailing theme in all traditions is 'economics'. The drive to provide the basic needs all humans can be satisfied with to be creative relies on 'design'.

The scarcity consciousness, of design decision makers, becomes the inversion dynamic that ART-iculates the 'inversion principle' and short changes its own reason for being. There might be conflicts of negative paradigms and egoic self-serving agendas at the root that *exacerbates* the process. How can this be reversed? Of the three faculties of consciousness we operate with which of them can we use

for the reversion of the inversion principle to be more creative? Which of our threefold Body, Mind and Spirit dynamic can we use? The body and its physicality is the result of mentalism or creative thinking. The mind and the spirit (as the creative energy and life force) are the drivers of creation.

What directs them all is the effect of the conditioning of the tradition' the environment, the culture, the family and the paradigms design submits to. Can the polarity of the mind and the spirit be reversed? We must recognize their inversion points first.

Geometry is *Poetry, versification, poetic form; 'Geometry' as a spatial (energy system alone does not describe or relate to emotions or spirit. Observe: corresponding to something else as its opposite or counterpart. Re-verse is the opportunity to say or do it again.*

In philosophy and certain models of psychology, qualia (singular form: quale) are individual instances of subjective, conscious experience. The term *qualia* derives from the Latin neuter plural form (*qualia*) of the Latin adjective *quālis* (Latin pronunciation: [ˈkʷaːlɪs]) meaning "of what sort" or "of what kind" in a specific instance like 'what is it like to taste a specific orange, this particular orange now". Examples of qualia include the pain of a headache, the taste of wine, and the perceived redness of an evening sky. As *qualitative characters of sensation*, qualia stand in contrast to "propositional attitudes".

A propositional attitude is a mental state held by an agent toward a proposition. Propositional attitudes are often assumed to be the *fundamental units of thought and their contents*, being propositions, are true or false from the perspective of the person. If we translate this into 'Body Mind Spirit' speak we arrive at models of psychology as Mind and of thought or Spirit as the qualitative elements of "qualia". The Body is the observer having the mental and emotional experiences and thoughts immersed in the 'space time energy' continuum that then becomes the physical framework with the quantitative elements with form, measurement and matter at work as "*quanta*" modules. The qualia could be wavelike with the quanta being particle-like and aligned with energy in the force field dynamic (of life that is supported by) creativity, synthesis and harmony.

The solution to this predicament demands a shift to higher levels of consciousness. Is this a passing fancy, a wish or an attainable goal? The choice is clear. We can resign from life or re-design our life. We can continue with the conditioning and status quo or raise our awareness, pay attention and rise to levels of our higher selves.

There is an equation, here where our current physical, mental and spiritual states, equate in 'balance' with the life situation directly. The qualitative and quantitative currencies are of equal value. There are three possible equations that represent 'prosperity' or 'good economics'.

The first is the status quo with equal amounts of qualia and quanta in stasis or equilibrium. The second is when qualia is in stress or crisis and much less than quanta as metastasis with scarcity attributes or others that lack '*sub-stance', integrity and pure spirit*. The third is hypostasis; the underlying reality of form and *substance*. Form and substance here are particular 'matter' with uniform but not physical properties. They can also be the real physical matter which a person or thing is made having a 'solid' presence. Solidity is now in question since vibration is now understood as the nature of the 'Body, Mind and Spirit' expressions of consciousness, man and nature. We measure 'successes with 'hypostatic' equations.

We need to build bridges between the gaps in qualia and quanta with the right type of energy, if not disconnects continue. The true connection, from my experience, is to 'SOURCE'. Here flows of energy awaken all that is already programmed in our BMS data base stored in our DNA. This internal dynamic action permeates all things. It gives us the skills, understanding, awakens our desires and passions to participate and contribute to the grand experience of living in community. That community is our humanity. The 'A-B' diagram represents the fusion or correspondence of two fundamental systems needed for the creative process of making that necessary shift. What do we do with this 'symbol'?

The metric for synthesis of Body, Mind and Spirit could be "Syntheometry' and the qualia; 'Syntheometric". There is the idea of 'Syntheometric efficiency' with the gauges and tools for the polarization, ideation and formulation or formation processes.

These will replace Geo-metry and geometric concepts for the physical properties and other energetic attributes like Tori and fractals as other continue to unfold.

ABOVE-BELOW

That depends on what cultural tradition we submit to. To do so we revisit the definition of inversion "as the dominant metaphysical idea of *any tradition* that results in its opposite effect in the society based on the principle of inversion. When social ills dovetail with the metaphysics of religion traditions as an example. They manifest on the *principle of inversion"*. We first design by desiring what we need, feel and create must be on the same levels (or higher) than our own expectations. In creation attraction is the likeness business of consciousness. Opposites might attract in the physical polarized world but mind and spirit attract each likeness. They "like' to project themselves through their great works. Applying physical principles to processes in non-physical environments do not work.

Clarity. focus and attention payed to our desires and their correspondences in energy and vibrations concentration to create (density). [(destiny-density)] Anagram: rearranging the letters of a word or phrase to produce a new word ... of a word by substituting a similar-sounding word with different meaning. Putting the three elements in synthesis can generate relationships that are not visually accessible until they are extrapolated into a MATRIX.

The Grand Matrix: A spider's cobweb isn't only its sleeping spring but also its food (for thought) trap. — African proverb

This is a partial matrix for starting any design project real or conceptual.

BODY-Space	MIND-Time	SPIRIT-Energy
Physical Matter and form	Psychological behavior of B.M.S	Analogs, Creative energy, Value, Life force systems.
Models, Objects, People, Places things Love: Philos	Properties and characteristics Form study Love: Eros	Symmetry, Beauty, Energy Love: Agape
Metrics Properties	Gauge-Fit-Proportion	Essence, Aesthetic, Style, Beauty,

The correspondences and inversions of these elements can also expand fields of information needed or the constant creative process. Three states Body, Mind and Spirit combined and inverted are represented by the symbols and their meanings: These are the six ways of combining three things as the factorial (of 3=1x2x3=6). The matrix goes to 9 combinations. This is a 'costly association' process.

THE SIXFOLD COMBINATIONS OF THE BODY, MIND AND SPIRIT ELEMENTS

Direct $B_Y : S_T$ = physical energy: The physics of energy (Source)
Inverse $S_T : B_Y$ = the spiritual body: The energy body (Source)
Direct $B_Y : M_D$ = physical or mental energy: The meta-physics (of mind's Source)
Inverse $M_D : B_Y$ = the mental body (Brain, CNS Etc.): The mental body (Source)
Direct $S_T : M_D$ = mental energy: The energetic mind (Source)
Inverse $M_D : S_T$ = the mental spirit: The mental energy (Source)

THE (3^2) 9 PLACE COMBINATION MATRIX

NULL SET	BODY	MIND	SPIRIT
BODY	**BODY/ BODY**	BODY/ MIND	BODY/SPIRIT
MIND	MIND/ BODY	**MIND/MIND**	MIND/ SPIRIT
SPIRIT	SPIRIT/ BODY	SPIRIT/ MIND	**SPIRIT/ SPIRIT**

Elements combined with themselves are their pure states.

THE SPACE, TIME, ENERGY AND THOUGHT MATRIX

NULL SET	SPACE	TIME	ENERGY	THOUGHT
SPACE	**SPACE/SPACE**	SPACE//TIME	SPACE//ENERGY	SPACE/THOUGHT
TIME	SPACE/TIME	**TIME/ TIME**	TIME/ENERGY	TIME/THOUGHT
ENERGY	ENERGY/SPACE	ENERGY/TIME	**ENERGY/ENERGY**	ENERGY/THOUGHT
THOUGHT	THOUGHT/SPACE	THOUGHT/TIME	THOUGHT/ENERGY	**THOUGHT/ THOUGHT**

A counter inversion transformation is our only option for a better world. It starts with the paradigm shift as we 'quicken and awaken' into our new age with our new D$_E$Sign Science. It is a science of consciousness, vibration, symmetry principles and laws that create synthesis and harmonies or peace and love. Which is peace and which is love depends on our passion not the measurements.

They do not exist. They are subtle and intangible and we are the medium and the gauge of and for it ALL.

HABITS AND RITUALS ARE OUR PARADIGMS

This is the kind of thinking that can build micro vascular heart muscle and blood circulation cells with spinach leaves. Popeye had it right all along.

The Ten Principles of Ancient Egyptian Mystery (Mastery) Tradition.

Symmetry Principles /Laws	Hermetism	Egyptian Religious Tradition
MENTALISM : the gods, the world and humanity are the outcome of Divine thought;	1 The mental origin of the world and of man.	Content is Atum, father of the gods.
CORRESPONDENCE: the same characteristics apply to each unity or plane of the world ;	2 Corresponding harmonics.	Content are Shu and Tefnut.
(VIBRATION) CHANGE : nothing remains the same, everything vibrates, nothing is at rest;	3 Dynamics of alternation.	Content are Geb and Nut.
POLARITY : everything has two poles, there are two sides to everything ;	4 Bi-polarity and complementarity.	Content are Osiris and [Isis].
RHYTHM : all things have their tides, rise and fall, advance and retreat, act and react ;	5 Cyclic repolarisation. Energy Conservation laws	Content are Seth and Neith.
CAUSE & EFFECT: everything happens according to law, there is no coincidence ;	6 Cause and effect.	Content are all the gods who are in the sky.
GENDER: male and female are in every body and mind, but not in the soul;	7 Gender.	Content are all the gods who are on Earth, who are in the flat-lands.
TIMING : everything happens when the time is right, everything starts (and ends) at the right time ;	8 The astrology of the Ogdoad.	Content are all the southern and northern gods.

INTENT: nature works according to a purposeful plan, pure will masters the stars;	9 The magic of the Ennead.	Content are all the western and eastern gods
TRANSFORMATION: everything can be transformed into something else, opposites meet;	10 The alchemy of the Decad.	Content are all the gods of the nomes.
INVERSION:	8, 9 and 10 are the mental Laws	Content are all the gods of the towns.

Inspired by the works of: Tolu Oladimeji. Read more at: https://www.vanguardngr.com/2017/01/englishs-language- egyptian-ancient-rulers-tolu-oladimeji

One of the classic rituals in Egyptian theology is the crossing of the crook and the flail the two most important symbols the pharaoh presented into the afterlife. By crossing these two symbols over his or her chest, it was the crossing point between the two constellations of Aries and Taurus. When rising in the east at the Vernal equinox, the Sun in this era was sitting in between these two constellations. This crossing is an 'inversion' found in many other phenomena.

In the Hindu tradition the kundalini and the sixth chakras, the Ajna, there is another inversion point at the 'third eye'. This is the center before the crown which represents the attainment of self-realization and the qualia of mentalism and divinity. Inversions are physical, psychological, emotional and spiritual. They are organic and natural appearing in many of nature and life's creative processes. It is possible for us when we know how it works.

There are paradoxes in this quotation with Intellect, divine knowledge and metaphysics. The Hermetic Divine triad of the Ancient Egyptian theology. Divine triads were used to express the divine family-unit, composed of Pharaoh (the son) and a divine couple (father & mother), legitimizing his rule as divine king. The principle of constant creation uses this construct for creation and I propose consciousness also.

The correlation then becomes Father as Spirit, Mother as creative Mind and son as the Body created by the intersection of the male and female principles in father and mother.

Pharaoh Akhenaten introduced a monotheistic triad (exclusive and against all other deities): Aten, Akhenaten and Nefertiti.

In Heliopolis, the original triad was Atum, Shu and Tefnut, in Memphis, Ptah, Sekhmet and Nefertem emerged, whereas Thebes worshipped Amun, Mut and Khonsu. The trinity naturally developed into three or one Ennead. There is a logic structure to represent this made of the distribution model shown below.

CREATIVITY: THE DESIGN PROCESS

DₑSIGN SCIENCE IN THE NEW PARADIGM AGE

The extrapolated 'Decimet' or 3 Frequency Matrix

There are nine cardinal Principles of Righteousness or being right in ancient Kemet. Now these are the paradigms or habits in the current canon. They were as follows: (1) Intentions, (2) Thought, (3) Speech, (4) Effort, (5) Action, (6) Living, (7) Reality, (8) Understanding, (9) Wisdom.

"If anyone in the earnestness of his intellect wishes to apply himself to the various branches of divine knowledge, or to the examination of the metaphysics, he will find that the whole world owes this kind of learning to Egypt"

Ammianus Marcellinus 4th Century AD

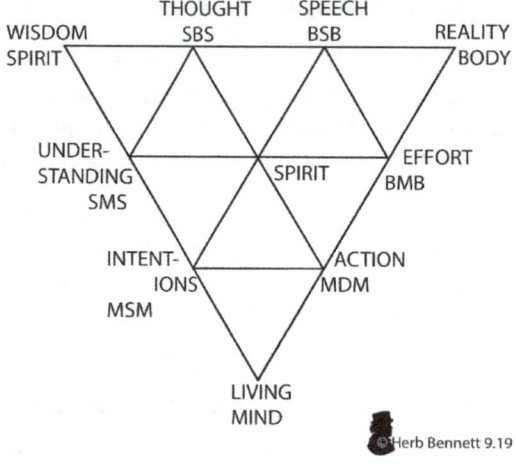

Fig. 3

"Some men see things as they are and ask why. Others invent things that never were and share them with the world to create destiny." (inspired) by George Bernard Shaw

The Hermetic Triadic elements are:

1. *God, the irreducible One, the essence of being, the Father of All - the "Decad"(10) ; The Spirit; The extrapolated decimet or 3 Frequency Matrix. There is no gender in this 'One'.*
2. *Nous, the First Intellect, the Self-Begotten One, the Mind or Light of God - the "Ennead"; The Nine elements; 9-(3^3) Mind shown in the matrix.*
3. *Logos, the "son" [sun] from "Nous" , the Begotten One above the Seven Archons - the "Ogdoad". A group or set of eight. " The eightfold way" The Body* The correlation with this knowledge can be translated directly as follows:

The nine 9 cardinal principles of righteousness are the nine expressions in the matrix when the three elements are distributed in the triangular tesseract that generates the Decad or base 10 decimal system. This is the primary cycle of constant creation or manifestation of all things. When all of these are aligned self-realization is attained. This is the Egyptian Paut Neteru.

MENTALISM:	CONSTANT CREATION
Egyptian thought	(1) Nun : everlasting, undifferentiated ocean of inertia; (2) Atum: autogenous origin of the totality of order ; (3) Pantheon : active forces fashioning creation ; (4) Horus-Pharaoh : the divine on Earth.
Hermetism	(1) Decad : God Himself ; (the TRIAD of BMS) 3+7=10 (2) Ennead : autogenous, creative Divine Nous;9 (3) Ogdoad : Divine Logos fashioning creation ; (The Triad of BMS) SYNTHESIS (4) Hebdomad : forces ruling the world. (Gravity, Electromagnetism, The strong force and The weak force)

Hermeticism, also called Hermetism, is a religious, philosophical, and esoteric tradition based primarily upon writings attributed to Hermes Trismegistus.

CORRESPONDENCE	: As above so below; as below so above (The first principle of inversion.)
Egyptian thought	(1) the precreational plane : Nun ; Polarization (2) the spiritual plane : Atum ; Energy Transformation (3) the mental plane : the Pantheon ; Ideation (4) the physical plane : Pharaoh. Formulation
Hermetism	(1) the precreational plane : the Decad ;10. (2) the noetic plane : the Ennead ; 9. (3) the logoic plane : the Ogdoad ; 8. (4) the physical plane : the Hebdomad. 4.
Inversion	(1) Body, Mind, Spirit planes/ dimensions of consciousness (2) the Space, Time, Energy, Effort or Work Dynamic (3) the four forces (on the Earth plane) (epiterrestrial) (4) Synthesis: the process of complete integration

VIBRATION:	CHANGE
Egyptian thought	*Stability is continuous change,* the endless repetition of the cycle of Atum-Re, his continuous, ongoing '*CONSTANT* creation' on the first occurrence ("zep tepi"), the beginning of time hidden in the everlastingness of the vast & inert waters of Nun. Also : the endless diurnal and nocturnal cycle of Re.
Hermetism	All things being subject to change, (Vibration) there is nothing that stands fast, nothing fixed, nothing free from change, among the things which come into being, neither among those in heaven nor among those on Earth. God alone stands unmoved.
Inversion	Everything vibrates. Frequencies Variations create densities in substance and matter.

POLARITY	COMPLEMENTARITY
Egyptian thought	Pharaoh, as "Lord of the Two Lands" guarantees the unity necessary to mediate the dual nature of all things, symbolized by Horus and Seth, manifestations of the two sides of the same (Horus-Seth): (Space - Time).
Hermetism	All poles are complementarities as Sun and Moon, manifestations of the same principle - differences consist of varying degrees between two poles.
Inversion	From the intersection of duality all quanta and qualia are formed

RHYTHM	
Egyptian thought	Birth, growth, decay, death and rebirth are the fundamental phases of the natural process of light and life. Death is part of the equation and the precondition of rebirth
Hermetism	Everything has tides, rise and fall and manifest a pendulum-swing.

CAUSE AND EFFECT:	(wave-particle correspondence)
Egyptian thought	Horus-Pharaoh is the terrestrial cause of life, prosperity & health. He guarantees a "good Nile" and is the representative of Re and the deities on Earth. In the Later Period, fate and destiny cause events and both rest in the hands of the deities, in particular their king Amun. It is the Eye of Horus which causes Osiris to complete his restoration and become king of the dead.
Hermetism and 'The Eclyptic'	Everything on Earth is caused by the movements of the planets. Our destiny is fixed and only gnosis, (knowledge of spiritual mysteries). The Light of God, sets us free. Determinism is inevitable as long as our bodies are the instruments of the planets, as in most human beings.

Gods are forms of ENERGY attainable by humans who know and obey their Laws and symmetry principles and value systems!

GENDER: SYMMETRY	NOT SEX
Egyptian thought	Except for the bisexual Atum, all gods have their consort. *Male and female are the two sides of the balance.* Every day the male Pharaoh offers Maat, truth and justice, the daughter of Re and consort of Thoth. Because of this, creation endures.
Hermetism	Male and female are mixtures of the elements out of which all physical phenomena are composed (created). Air and Fire are masculine, Water and Earth are feminine.

Corres-pond-ence: moving with the same level (frequency) of vibration. Essential to this mythology was the restoration of Osiris by his son Horus. The latter had his *Left Eye damaged in the battle with Seth*, but it was healed by *Thoth (Hermes Tresmegistu*s). He then brings his Restored Eye, the Wedjat, or Eye of Wellness, to his weary father, who, already in the Netherworld, resurrects there to become king again (but of the underworld).

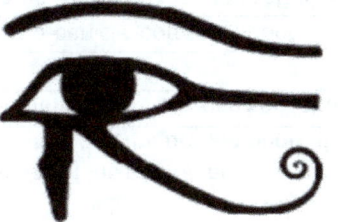

Fig 4. The Wadjet (or Ujat; "Whole One") The sub elements are fractional components.

This underworld is the state we call *the subconscious*. The Wedjat was encoded with the knowledge of the deepest (mathematical gauge 'theories') of Egyptian mystery traditions.

This act of giving the Eye of Horus, encompasses all material offerings, of which it is the sublime example. Together with "voice-offerings", the Eye of Horus was the most powerful way to establish contact with the gods. Is this the 3Rd Eye? Today we use mathematics to connect to the wisdom, intelligence, knowledge and information (wiki) directly from source.

- Osiris is the good King of Egypt: Osiris lives on Earth and establishes all good things, he brings civilization to Egypt (and to worlds to come) and is loved by all, *except Seth and his followers; The Seth dynamic is the polarity and opposite energies. These are orients.*
- Osiris assassinated, dismembered and his *14 pieces* are scattered: Osiris is killed by his brother Seth and his fourteen body parts were scattered all over Egypt; Symbolism at its finest.
- Osiris reassembled and reanimated by Isis: his wife and sister Isis recollects his body (except his penis) and revivifies it; The Greeks call Isis... Iris while adopting others from the 'Egyptian' Pantheon to complete theirs.
- Osiris inseminates Isis who gives birth to Horus: before Osiris goes to the Duat, Isis, the Great Sorceress, is able to take his seed and give birth to Horus.
- Osiris avenged by his son: although in his youth Horus was sodomized by his evil uncle, he grows up with the help of Isis and prepares to avenge his father by fighting Seth.
- Osiris resurrected by Horus: his Left Eye restored by Thoth, Horus is declared King of Egypt and descends into the Netherworld to bring his Eye of Wellness to his father, so as to resurrect him and restore all his powers.
- Osiris "King of the Netherworld": Osiris reassembled, reanimated and finally resurrected by Horus is enthroned in the Netherworld as its king.
- In this capacity, he judges the dead and nobody is able to move further without being judged by him. He is the guarantee, on the other side of existence, of rejuvenation and an eternal life featuring the best of this life.

In ancient Kemet, there were also seven cardinal principles/virtues of Goddess Ma'at to achieve human perfectibility.

These principles are Truth, Justice, Balance, Order, Compassion, Harmony, and Reciprocity.

In the numeric and symbolic canon the numbers 1, 3, 4, 7 and 9 are very significant. The one number we have not accounted for is the seven (7). In addition, the Greeks who were the students of Egyptian teachers in ancient Kemetic Temples, "were given and education in the *seven* Liberal Arts; Grammar, Arithmetic, Rhetoric, Dialectic, Geometry, Astronomy, and Music. This became the pedagogical prototype for the Greek and Roman (and current world-wide) education systems".

These seven Liberal Arts courses were In Biblical times, there are thus "*seven* deadly sins of the bible," viz, *Sloth, Lust, Anger, Pride, Envy, Gluttony, and Greed.* There is also the "seven pointed star," where all seven points are equidistant, radiating seven currents of force that represent seven principles of human existence.

In 1965, an African-American professor, Dr. Maulana Karenga, created the Afrikan-centered celebration called Kwanzaa based on the doctrine of Kawaida. This Nguzo Saba (Kwanzaa) celebration lasts for seven days from the 26th December to 1st January.

The correlations and corres-pondences are the foundation for a qualitative and essential relativity found in the singularity of nature. That it defies rational and symbolic computation might be a result of the level of 'vibration' of the intensity of the energies involved and the power needed to resolve it.

THE CORRESPONDENCESOF KWANZAA WITH THE AURIC BODIES

THE SEVEN PRINCIPLES OF KWANZAA	THE AURIC BODIES	HERMETIC PRINCIPLES
1. Umoja (Unity)	The ketheric Causal bodies	Mentalism
2. Kujichagulia (Self-Determination)	The Celestial Body	Correspondence
3. Ujima (Collective work and Responsibility)	Etheric layer physical form	Vibration
4. Ujamaa (Cooperative Economics)	The astral duddhic body	Polarity
5. Nia (Purpose)	The mental body	Rhythm
6. Kuuma (Creativity)	Emotions; feelings	Cause and Effect
7. Imani (Faith)	Etheric body symmetry elements and geometric force	Gender

Kwanzaais meant to solidify and perpetuate our ancient African spirituality and evolution. The African spiritual belief system cites *seven* Stages/Ages of Man in the completion of his life cycle.

They are Infancy, Boyhood, Youth, Manhood, Middle-age, Old-age, and Senility.

Every human being possesses *seven* senses; they are 1 Hearing, 2 Touch, 3 Sight, 4 Taste, 5 Smell, *6 Intuition, and 7 Clairvoyance*. The 6 and 7 are not scientifically S.T.E.M. like nor system compatible.

THE *NINE* INSEPARABLE PARTS OF THE SOUL.

PARTS OF THE SOUL/BODY	ITS NATURE/ MIND	ITS ESSENCE/ SPIRIT
(1) The Ka	The abstract *personality* of the individual to whom it belongs	Possessing the form and attributes of a human with power of movement, *omnipresence*, and ability to receive nourishment. Equivalent to what we call the shadow image.
(2) The Khat	The mortal *concrete personality*,	The physical body.
(3) The Ba	The heart-soul, which lives in the Ka and sometimes beside it,	To supply the Ka with food and air. Capable of metamorphosis.
(4) The Ab	The heart, the physical life in humans, spiritual, rational and ethical Associated with the Ba (heart-soul).	In the Egyptian Judgment Drama, it undergoes examination in the presence of the God Osiers, the great creator and judge of the dead.
(5) The Kaibit	The shadow. Also associated with the Ba	From which it receives its nourishments. Has the power of movement and omnipresence.
(6) The Khu	Spiritual soul that lives forever	A heavenly being, closely associated with the Ba.
(7) The Sahu	The spiritual body in which the Khu or spiritual soul dwells	The moral nature of mental and spiritual qualities is united to form new powers that man has the choice to use for good or evil.

(8) The Sekhem	The power or spirit of the vital force in humans.	Lives in the heavens with the spirit of Khu.
(9) The Ren	The name of an individual, the essential attribute for preservation of a being	The ancients believed that in the absence of a name, individuals ceased to exist. The quality (vibration) of a name, therefore, was very important.

Is it possible that the symbolic languages we use to express our thoughts are not 'locked in' to the 'neter' of phenomena and that the idea of 'constant creation transcends all and is truly constant and aligned with the forces and principles? In the vibrational fields of higher communication there is a gap between phenomena and man's intellect. On a deeper level though all is connected and responding to higher levels of consciousness.

Egyptians were also "the first to identify *the Gods of order* (symmetry) arrangements in the universe." The Ennead of ancient Kemet consisted of nine gods.

They are FORCES synthesized into elements with energy qualities:

EGYPTIAN GODS	THE ELEMENTS
(1) Shu, the God of air;	AIR
(2) Tefnut, the Goddess of Moisture;	WATER
(3) Geb, the God of Earth;	EARTH
(4) Nut, Goddess of the sky; universe	FIRE and ETHER

These *Gods* I to 4 gave birth to Gods 5 to 9 (These numbers are symmetry elements)

EGYPTIAN GODS	PRINCIPLES
(5) Osiris, the God of omnipotence and omniscience (infinite Consciousness)	Not the sun but symbolic of the vital **principle** of Nature; the sun behind the sun
(6) Isis, the wife of Osiris, the female principle;	Principle of natural fecundity.
(7) Seth, the God of evil,	opposite good;

(8) Nephthys, wife of Seth,	(Nephthys' darkness balancing Isis' light, seen together as twin sisters.
(9) Atum (Atom),	The creator God of Gods. (Quantum Theory)

$\sum$-All is ATUM-Consciousness the irreducible one [Atum is 'Atom']

The 9 parts of the brain are: There are many 9 systems in the world.

1) Brain stem
2) Cerebellum
3) Thalamus
4) Hypothalamus
5) Amygdale
6) Hippocampus
7) Cerebral cortex (Frontal, Parietal, Occipital, Temporal lobes)
8) Right cerebral hemisphere
9) Left cerebral hemisphere

The Story of 1-Osiris, 2-Isis and 3-Horus:

Parallels in the Semiotics* of the Egyptian and Western (Theo-Technology, Science and their Spiritual Creation Myths.

*Semiotics fom "semiosis," is the relationship between, an object, a sign and a meaning. The sign represents the object, or referent, in the mind of an interpreter.

"Interpretant" refers to a sign that serves as the representation of an object. The object is the BODY. The Sign is the MIND and meaning is derived from the energy and SPIRIT.

The Protodynastic and Dynastic periods of Egypt had various triads of Gods at different times. The mythologies and principles had their share of Paradigm Shifts that were somewhat constant with an inspired storytelling we can sort to adjust our perception of what Egypt meant to the world and still does. Of all the Horuses; Horus Behedet (Horus of Edfu) is the star of our story.

And Tao Great was One; the One became the Two; the Two became the Three, the Three evolved the Seven, which filled the universe with manifests.

From God's own Record Book we read: The Triune God breathed forth, and seven Spirits stood before his face. (The Hebrews call these seven Spirits, Elohim –the SUN.)

And these are they who, in their boundless power, created everything that is, or was.

These Spirits of the Triune God moved on the face of boundless space and seven ethers were, and every ether had its form of life.

These forms of life were but the thoughts of God, clothed in the substance of their etheric planes, qualities and energies.

(Men call these ether planes the planes of protoplast, of earth, of plant, of beast, of man, of angel and of cherubim.)

These planes with all their teeming thoughts of God, are never seen by eyes of man in flesh; they are composed of substance far too fine for fleshly eyes to see, and still they constitute the soul of things;

And with the eyes of soul all creatures see these ether planes, and all the forms of life. (From The Aquarian Gospel By Levi)

The TRIAD: Consciousness and the 'Law of Three (3)'. Atoms are the basic units of matter and the defining structure of elements. Atoms (Atum) are made up of three particles: Protons *Osiris*, Neutrons *Isis* and Electrons; *Horus*. Protons and neutrons are heavier (Nut) than electrons and reside in the nucleus (Geb). From Geb, the sky god: Electrons; lightweight exist in a cloud orbiting the nucleus. The electron cloud has a radius 10,000 times greater than the nucleus.

Atoms have an equal number of protons and electrons, as does protons and neutrons. Adding a proton to an atom makes a new element. Adding a neutron makes an isotope, or heavier version, (Nut) of that atom. Through the Principle of Correspondence: From Geb, the sky god (Above), and Nut, the earth goddess (Below) came four children: [*The LAW of four (4) and the forces of Nature.*]

Osiris (Male), Isis (Female), Set (Male) and Nepthys (Female) as the polarity and gender principles. The four forces of nature interact in the synthesis of the wave energy to create the (particle) or atom with the gravitational (Osiris), electromagnetic (Isis), strong force (Set), and weak force (Nepthys). Each is described not (mathematically) but "Syntheologically" as a blending field of possibilities in a quantum state. The Osiris field or gravitational force is modelled as a continuous classical field. It however is multidimensional and transmutable.

Osiris was the oldest (First) principle in the Etheric state and became *king of Egypt* (Prime gravitational force). He '*interacted' with his sister'* Isis (natural complement of the feminine principle and of gender as reproduction and symmetry expressions of consciousness.

All expressions are both male and female. Osiris was a good king and commanded the respect of all who lived on the *earth in the quark family of (our) subatomic physics and in the standard model as expressions of the Body, Mind and Spirit in nature and all creation with*

CREATIVITY: THE DESIGN PROCESS

the gods who dwelled in the *nether-world Above* with 'googolplexes' of other forces and 'Deities' in the aether or in the 'firmament' and the waters.

Set *was always jealous of* Osiris, because he did not command the respect of those on earth or those in the netherworld (of the multiple universes). Not all creation aligned with 'Set' energy because of the repulsion dynamic built into the polarity of the male and female principle. He became 'Up-Set'.

You ask why Abram came to Egypt land? This is the cradle-land of the initiate; all secret things belong to Egypt land; this is why the masters come. (The Aquarian Gospel By Levi).

One day, Set transformed (shape shifted) himself into a *vicious monster* and attacked Osiris, killing him.

So evil is the inharmonious blending of the colors, tones, or forms of good.

Now, man is not all wise, and yet has will his own. He has the power, and he uses it, to mix God's good things in a multitude of ways, and every day he makes discordant sounds, and evil things.

And every tone and form, be it of good, or ill, becomes a living thing, a demon, sprite, or spirit of a good or vicious kind.

Man makes his devil thus; and then becomes afraid of him and flees; his devil is emboldened, follows him away and casts him into torturing fires.

(The Aquarian Gospel By Levi).]

Chaos and destruction are 'mutual' natural principles transformed by thought through creativity and constant creation in keeping with Hermetic symmetry principles and natural (Isis) and spiritual (Osiris) law.

With profound spiritual knowledge (Isis) has the ability to design. What I propose is Osiris's pieces of his (DNA strands) encoding it with the scribe THOTH's imprinting of the (Gene of Isis).

These are the 14 pieces (chakras) that give Horus his spirit and identity. Set proceeded to cut Osiris into pieces and distributed them throughout the length and breadth of Egypt.

The subatomic elements that are the building blocks of nature are the pieces, dancing in and out of the gravitational force of the Ouroboros. The Ouroboros is the perpetual cyclic (ecliptic) renewal of life to infinity, the concept of eternity and the eternal return, death

CREATIVITY: THE DESIGN PROCESS

DESIGN SCIENCE IN THE NEW PARADIGM AGE

and rebirth, leading to immortality. OSIRISwould be the essence of this symbol. All awareness is a holographic reflection of the 'ALL is ONE' of infinite consciousness, then there is sub-consciousness which is perhaps the 95% is the realm of Osiris in the underworld and the 'junk' in our DNA trunk. With Osiris dead, *we enter the subatomic and quantum dynamic energy realm*. Set became king of Egypt, with his sister Nepthys his wife.

Nepthys, however, felt sorry for her sister Isis, who wept endlessly over her lost husband. Isis, *who had great (DNA) magical powers,* decided to find her husband and bring him back to life *long enough (in still Time)* so that they could have a child, or make stranger particles than even Osiris and Isis made originally. This is the 'half - life' state of the subatomic particle family.

Together with Nepthys, Isis roamed the country, *collecting the pieces (DNA strands)* of her husband's body to perform the synthesis of the new paradigm that would emerge or as *(Movements in the cloud chamber in search of affinities and compatibilities),* reassembling or recombining themselves in their own ethereal qualitative flavors of their own vibration fields.

FAST FORWARD TO NOW: *During transcription, RNA polymerase read the template DNA strand* in one direction, but the mRNA is formed in the opposite direction with enantiomorphism, handedness, as an expression of gender-asymmetry and anti-polarity behavior.

The mRNA is single-stranded and therefore only contains *three possible reading frames,* of which *only one is translated*.

Once ISIS completed the task, *she breathed the breath of life (force)* into his body and *resurrected* him. They were together again, and Isis became *pregnant* soon after. Is this 'technology as immaculate as the Mary-Joseph '*preg-nancy'* story?

The mother of Horus (Isis) was a *great magician (not conjuror)* who had the power to destroy Set. When her chance came she could not do it. Set was, after all, her brother. This angered Horus so much that he chopped off his mother's head *in a fit of rage!* Thankfully, Isis was more than able to handle this insult and immediately *caused* a cow's head to grow from her neck to replace her head. *Could this be considered cloning?* There seems to be 'ethereal barrier' violations going on as well. Luckily for Horus, Isis was a compassionate and sympathetic goddess. *She forgave her angry son his aggressive act.*

NOW- In the field of neuro science: "Bandwidth communication;" according to Elon Musk, is the main barrier to human-machine co-operation (or co-creation). Creating direct "high bandwidth" links between the human brain and machines thought of a brain-body interface could have been similar to rearranging Osiris's body pieces. Pieces suggest mechanistic functions not biology which would be' elements or parts' that had to obey symmetry laws.

'Neuralink' has been registered as a medical research company, and Musk said the firm will produce a product to help people with severe brain injuries within four years.

Could this be the 'spiritual' analog for connecting to source and accessing 'Direct Knowledge' from the Akashic records or RECORDBOOK?

Could this explain how the Egyptian Kings and Priests got their

'Wisdom, Intelligence, Knowledge and Intuition' or WIKI as some humans have always done.

What is the true origin of Einstein's $E=Mc^2$? This will lay the groundwork for developing Bandwidth Communication Interfaces DCIs for healthy people.

This enables humans to communicate by "consensual telepathy," which could be ready within five years, Musk said.

Some scientists, particularly those in the neuroscience community, are skeptical of Musk's ambitious plans naturally. Where is Uri Geller when you need him?

> A MODERN GENETIC SECRET: Thomas Beatie, a trans-man, had gender reassignment surgery in 2002 and became known as 'The Pregnant Man' after he became pregnant through artificial insemination. Why are we not seeing parallels here with the souls' eyes, not any other optical tools we use? (From Wikipedia, the free encyclopedia)

Osiris was able to descend into the underworld, where he became the lord of that domain. Thoth and Osiris became the judges of the realms above and below. This is the realm of dark forces. From here all matter is synthesized by gravity's density which is Osiris's power (Causing the great fall of man and all the ethereal life forms except that of angels and the cherubim). Black Holes, Dark Matter and Melanin are trapped by Gravity.

A world without Osiris (Cosmic Consciousness) could not regenerate itself and transition into denser expressions, vibrations of form as matter, energy, presence and essence. For this to be so an offspring with Osiris' DNA transcribed in the language of the 'sex for reproduction' version of the gender principle was needed. The child born to Isis was named Horus, the hawk (falcon)-god. "Horus the child." refers to his birth and secret rearing and teachings by Isis.

In this form he is depicted as a naked child (innocent); seated on Isis's lap like the image of Mary and Jesus teaches us through the universal 'mother and child' principles.

"Horus of the Hor-rising or hor-izon." Horus at Helio-polis, linked with Ra in the sun cult. In this form he is associated with the rising and setting sun. He was pictured as a (hawk) falcon, to mirror the form of the midbrain complex, or as a sphinx with the head of Anubis not the one we now know, with the body of a lion.

CREATIVITY: THE DESIGN PROCESS

DESIGN SCIENCE IN THE NEW PARADIGM AGE

What is the symbolism of the hawk-falcon in Egypt? The hawk flies closer to the sun than any other bird can. Any spirit or Deity that can get close to the son is significant.

The midbrain complex is a deeper meaning "The Eye of Horus" as the ancient Egyptian symbol of protection, royal power and good health. It represents the marking around the eye of the falcon.

When he became an adult, Horus decided to make a case before the court of gods that he, not Set, was the rightful king of Egypt. He was destined to be "Horus the Uniter"; his role in uniting Upper and Lower Egypt. A long period of argument followed, and Set challenged Horus to a contest. The winner would become king. Set, however, did not play fair. After several matches in which Set cheated and was the victor, Horus' mother, Isis, decided to help her son and set a trap for Set. She snared him, but Set begged for his life, and Isis let him go.

The evil Set represents the negative aspect of darkness with its comple-ment being Osiris's Expressions. The Good versus Evil is introduced.

The goddess Isis hides her baby in the marshes to protect him from Osiris's murderer Seth. The evil King is determined to prevent the boy from growing up and avenging his father's death. He sends a poisonous deadly scorpion to destroy Horus.

As Horus is dying Isis calls on the sun god Ra to help her save Horus. She needed stronger technology than she possessed. Upon getting the call Ra halts his boat and sends his deputy Thoth to save the child's life, and he does.

This is a universal story told by many other traditions around the world. This is the classic struggle of Good versus Evil. If Seth destroys the child evil triumphs. Horus's destiny was eventually to save the universe and he would be the rightful king.]

When Horus found out that Isis had let Seth his enemy live, He became *angry with his mother*, and *rages against her*, earning him the *contempt of the other gods*. They decided that there would be one more match, and Set would get to choose what it would be.

Here is the correspondence with the subatomic world and the quantum dynamic we now know. Perhaps the single most outstanding feature of the quantum world is its smooth and wavelike nature as the Osiris method. They are myths that weave our fabrics (fields) of perception. This feature leads to the question of how the chaos Seth makes (itself) is felt when moving from the classical below world to the above 'epigenetic and subatomic quantum' world. How can the extremely irregular character of classical chaos be reconciled with the smooth and wavelike nature of phenomena on the sub and atomic scales? Chaos; Seth exist everywhere in the 'quantum nether-world' and in the underworld and in the world.

Good and evil are not judged by mortal laws and causes we do not know. They are complements, not judgements. There are dynamic principles operating without (human) judgement. Judgement here is the realm of Thoth of the netherworld and Osiris of the underworld.

Set decided that the final round of the contest would be a boat race. Why a boat? The only Deity with a boat is Ra. Is this symbolic of Set's ambition and is there an attempt at a 'God- Satan'; Good vs Evil interaction and fall from grace paradigm emerging here?However, in order to make the contest a challenge, Set decided that he and Horus should *race boats made of stone*.

Horus was tricky and built a boat made of wood, covered with limestone plaster, which looked like stone. As the gods assembled for the race, Set cut the top off of a mountain to serve as his boat and set it in the water. His boat sank right away, and all the other gods laughed at him. Angry, Set transformed himself into a hippo-potamus and attacked Horus' boat. Horus fought off Set, but the other gods stopped him before he could kill Set.

Killing evil would interfere with the element needed for the correspondences needed to balance the universe and all of its dynamic processes. Horus in his blind rage could not appreciate this intervention.

The other gods decided that the match was a tie. Many of the gods were sympathetic to Horus, but remembered his anger toward his mother for being lenient to Set, and were unwilling to support him completely. His karmic debt had to be paid to assuage the 'sinfulness' he perpetrated against his mother. The gods who formed the court decided to write a letter to Osiris and ask for his advice. Osiris responded with a definite answer: his son is the rightful king, and should be placed upon the throne. No one, said Osiris, should take the throne of Egypt through an act of murder, as Set had done.

Set killed Osiris, but Horus did not kill anyone, and was the better candidate. Finally, the gods agreed that Horus should claim his birthright as king of Egypt. The sun and the stars, who were Osiris' allies, descended into the underworld, leaving the world in darkness. There were many dark ages and more to come. We might be in one now! Osiris (Usire) Egyptian god of the underworld and of vegetation.

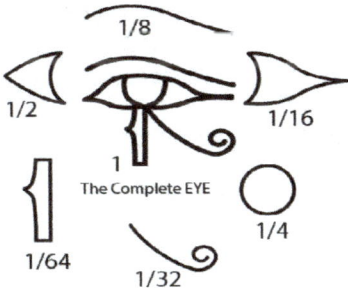

The System of Horus Eye Fractions

Fig. 5

Son of Nut above and Geb below; brother of Nephthys, Set and brother-husband to Isis. His birthplace was said to be Rosetau in the necropolis west of Memphis.

Osiris was depicted in human form wrapped up as a mummy, holding the crook and flail. *This is the principle of 'inversion' or 'the crossing'*. Osiris was often depicted with green skin, alluding to his role as a god of vegetation. He wore a crown known as the 'atef,' composed of the tall conical whittle crown of Upper Egypt with red plumes on each side.

Osiris had many cult centers, but the most important were at Abydos (Ibdju) in Upper Egypt, where the god's legend was reenacted in an annual festival and at Busirs (Djedu) in the Nile delta. Horus and Set were always placed in opposition to each other. However, the exact nature of their

CREATIVITY: THE DESIGN PROCESS

DESIGN SCIENCE IN THE NEW PARADIGM AGE

relationship changed somewhat over time. Set was the embodiment of disorder and chaos while Horus was the embodiment of order. Horus was the daytime sky, while Set represented the night time sky.

In early times the two were also seen as existing in a state of 'toroidal harmony'. Horus and Set represented Upper and Lower Egypt respectively. They were often depicted together to indicate the union of Upper and Lower Egypt. There is even a composite deity named Horus-Set, who was depicted as a man with two heads (one of the hawk of Horus, the other of the Set animal) the Typhonic beast.

It would appear that the balance and complementarity of the Toroidal dynamic principle or faculty is at work here.

This is a vortex technology that describes the structure of the universe and all its expressions.

At this stage Horus was often considered to be Set's brother and equal and the fight between them was thought to be eternal. However, the rise in importance of the *Ennead* resulted in Horus being cast as the son of Osiris and thus the nephew of Set. This changed the nature of the conflict between them, as it was now possible for Set to be defeated and for Horus to claim the throne of Egypt as his own. Horus was the patron of young men and was described as the example of the dutiful son who grows up to become a just man.

The ancient Egyptian system of measures provides another example of number signs conceived as a coherent system. In the so-called "Horus-eye fractions", the designer of a numerical sequence linked its members also into a unified whole derived from a myth, just as in the series of numerals for the powers of ten.

THE TYPES OF MECHANICAL FORCES:

Forces of fight or flight can be strategies for living when stress is then managed properly. Four forces affect things that fly or soar: flight becomes the metaphor for transformation.

Weight is the force of gravity. It acts in a downward direction—toward the center of the Earth.

Lift is the force that acts at a right angle to the direction of motion through the air. Lift is created by differences in air pressure.

Thrust is the force that propels a flying machine in the direction of motion. Engines produce thrust.

Drag is the force that acts opposite to the direction of motion. Drag is caused by friction and differences in air pressure. All four forces acting on an airplane mirror a person's physical, mental and spiritual life. When an airplane is flying straight and level at a constant speed. The lift it produces balances its weight, and the thrust it produces balances its drag. However, this balance of forces changes as the airplane rises and descends, as it speeds up and slows down, and as it turns.

Only two forces affect a spacecraft in space. A spacecraft has weight, even in orbit, and uses thrust to reach space and to maneuver.

But lift and drag—both created by movement through air—are absent in the near vacuum of space. There are basically four forces in our universe that work conventionally and are accepted as the fundamental interactions and the glue that keeps it together. They are the gravitational, electromagnetic, strong nuclear, and weak nuclear forces. Each one is described (*mathematically*) as a field. The gravitational force is modelled as a continuous classical field.

Is the mathematical description the only paradigm we have to work with? Is this model offering the best descriptions we need now with the recent developments in science and recognition of how it is relating to the ancient wisdom traditions of some cultures?

The first cause of a (physical) force is mechanical energy. The second cause is basically (creation) of push or pull. The third cause is the movement or displacement of objects that undergo changes in speed, in direction, or of shape. A force has sense, magnitude (intensity) direction and flavor.

Body, Mind and Spirit have higher vibrational forces operating and interacting with the lower frequency states of Space, Time, Energy in a continuum that obeys all natural LAWS, Symmetry principles and "Technologies".

A force (*feeling or pressure*) can also be psychological, or emotional resulting in different push or a pull per say of elevated or depressed states causing (an object) people (life forms) to undergo changes in levels of stressful states, with 'shape' as the metaphor for mood.

This force has intensities with negative or positive effects. Neutral states are useful with some forces. A force can also be *the spiritual life* energy. The (push or a pull) operates in the field of all energies generated from the realm of infinite consciousness. In this state subtle life forces, in living conscious form and other ephemeral external and universal energies undergo changes in thought, ascension and transformation.

Forces have intensities with *polarized* conditions 'negative and positive', correspondences, consequences and effects. This dynamic scale goes from thought (*ideation*) to 'work' (*formation*) of energies. Being a private pilot is one of my many passions. This was the first career I fell in love and was licensed later on. I have used this skill in many areas of my creative work to enhance my perception of the world and my view of myself and the world at large.

Being in control of an airplane at 3 to 5 thousand feet makes you very aware of your Body, Mind and Spirit in a single engine airplane without a parachute.

CREATIVITY: THE DESIGN PROCESS   DᴇSIGN SCIENCE IN THE NEW PARADIGM AGE

As an architect it's being on earth's drafting table interacting with space and time with life depending on maintaining the equilibrium of all the internal and external forces you, the machine and the elements are all interacting with every second, without any accidents or getting lost. Navigating skills correspond to 'body- physical', 'mind-mental and emotional' as well as 'spirit-spiritual' principles.

Safe landings are well earned blessings.

The 'so/u/lar' v'-ehicle. It's where the Dog star lives
The EN-Gin is the soul of the Eternal Generating
Omniscient Divine flame of man guided by nature and the plan
Symmetry principles with magnificent aesthetic expressions

Creating the sun source for our own Life force extensions An arising known to many; any Dogon, or Egyptian Ancients of wisdom traditions of Osiris's throne of love Under the Crown of the Atf's celestial light The most high super-consciousness making all things right.

Oh great Sun behind the Sun invisible all-pervading One
Your myriad of bi-millenaria propagated in each era.

This the cycle for which we waited for our evolution
In this iteration we will to end our separation
From frustration and distress to attain
Our rightful highest human consciousness

"Here comes the hawk flying by the planet's sun
Osiris-Amen Ra; symbols of the Invisible one
The Isis mother of the Horus progenetory son
The invisible light casts a shadow of the visible one With all its photons of luminosity we still do not see Blinded by our wisdom not seeing our own humanity or compassion".

The Sun behind the Sun the ALL mighty ONE Gather to yourself the power of your source
Transmit it through our sun to our earth mother force transformation
Send the sons of GOD; Generating, Omniscient and Divine
Make a new world of thought, emotion and intelligence of heart-mind
To be rooted deeply in the thoughts of men this time like no other
Stimulate humanity's spiritual evolution
Mark the manifestation of this transformation

With your spirit not your blood again we've seen enough
Let this be the beginning of the end of pain and all destructive cycles
Flood our 'mind-heart' centers with eternal love's embers
Radiate the Divine Consciousness Known as The Christ Ray we have none of today

We have surrendered our souls to consecrated elite men in robes
To camouflaged traditions and rituals of false hopes and postponed salvation.

Paraclete open the minds of men to receive your wisdom again
Let anyone standing in the way of your word feel
The load of your weary road to man's salvation.

Source: "When you are inspired by some great purpose, some extraordinary project, all your thoughts break their bounds. Dormant forces, faculties and talents become alive, and you discover yourself to be a greater person by far than you ever dreamed yourself to be." —Pantanjali

CHAPTER THREE   TETRAHEDRON T$_R$H

3. Manipura (Nabhi), the Solar plexus chakra transmuted sorrow and suffering. No matter what happens in life, sad or miserable feelings distributed. But this center like the svadhisthana chakra is a reputed trickster.

This center creates suffering for others when power is misused. This center manipura chakra like the ajna, is cleverrant and clairvoyant. This center also gives one the power of transmutation and power to transform the physical world.

This center has healing power:

Clairkinesis, Creative Intelligence, the use of force, psychokinesis, psychometry, healing, manifestation in the physical world using physical energy, force and power vibration: the solar plexus, fire the adrenal & pancreas Pancreas, Suprarenal (Adrenal) Glands.

"Renewal is the principle—and the process—that empowers us to move on an upward spiral of growth and change, of continuous improvement." Dr. Stephen R. covey

CHAPTER 3 TRINE A
CREATIVE POTENTIAL

 **H**OW TO EXPLORE OUR HIGHEST and most creative potential with opportunities and relationships attainable to align with natural, creative and dynamic symmetry principles of consciousness to find the tools that can work for us to express our true voice and purpose to realize and manifest the right attitudes and paradigms for living in compatible environments with the best properly aligned spiritual relationships with all the relevant expressions of a stress-less life that we can harmonize with. We can create the equitable and fair distribution of rewards and comforts, joys and peace in optimum health, physical, psychological and spiritual growth that we can share.

Exploring Breakthrough Paradigms to understand consciousness and our higher selves to build better relationships in the human family and manmade environments. To redefine consciousness, as the body, mind and spirit continuum as inspiration for making abstract thoughts, natural principles and technologies real. To reclaim and share the emerging creative, intellectual and spiritual capital to be free and totally fulfilled personally, professionally, in community and be on higher purpose. To collaborate and accelerate transformations to harmonious futures for a new world and its peoples embracing the most natural universal attribute of all; change. The new imperative is to add value to all human endeavor, with honor, respect and gratitude to all forms of 'design sciences' and arts disciplines with deeper 'ubiquitous architectures' encoded with richer identities, new aesthetic flavors and breakthrough technologies now being articulated.

How do we explore our highest and most creative potential attainable, for opportunities and relationships to align with the natural, creative and dynamic symmetry principles of Consciousness; in body, mind and spirit to discover and/or create the tools, the media and our unique message that can work for us and all we love? This helps to express our true intention, voice and purpose. We must realize and manifest the right attitudes and paradigms to live in compatible and stress-less environments with non-toxic and positive situations, opportunities and people in 'holistic community'.

You must cultivate, develop and nurture the best properly aligned and harmonized physiological, psychological and spiritual relationships with yourself and all the relevant expressions of life to harmonize and attract your equitable and fair distribution of rewards; comforts, joys and peace, doing so with the highest regard and respect for the great-spirit or whatever force or intelligence you hold sacred. Doing this in the best, physical, psychological and spiritual health to promote and maintain growth that can be shared is a self-less priority.

The New Paradigm deserves a *CREATIVE* graphic or visual style of communication that can best represent the connection to source we access through a "*Scientia* Graphic–*recta*" (direct visual knowledge) intended to elevate our '*creative*' intelligence and consciousness.

The preponderant opinions and systems of acquiring knowledge in the old paradigm (today) has been through classical standards of various deteriorating forms of education. Most contributions that have profoundly revolutionized the world can be traced to some form of 'divine inspiration' and interpretation in synchronicity with SOURCE. This is where two or more people have received the same inspiration. We seldom think of the impact these geniuses have on the world as being 'paradigm shifts'.

The net effect of the isolated events might not have gotten to critical mass, in the past, but where we are now is quite different. The new treatment for accessing the WIKI is *Scientiam-recta* (Direct Knowledge) Mimesis: imitation, in particular is the order of the day.

Representation of the real world is sublimated in the crucible of imagination filled with expressions we already know from our past. The best we can hope for is variations and not innovation or what's called 'original creations'. The deliberate imitation of the behavior caused by the interventions created and shared by one group of people with another then become factors in 'social change'. Is social change alone enough to optimize and sustain the total development needs of a people. When the social agenda begins to dis-integrate where do we go for the next version or vision of ourselves? Who develops the aesthetic styles and modes of representation especially appropriate to the social, political and cultural realities of the new age?

The artful representations of subjective or personal worlds that are seeded by the direct knowledge eventually become the popular parlance of the culture in all the forms and iterations of needs and desires.

The stimuli that is transduced into sense data, symbols and words and the linguistic accoutrement in spoken language, stimulate other forms of communication, styles of learning and expressions. In an 'epilinguistic' style needed to synthesize the new art, skills and innovation that is evolving constantly. A visual, infographic style is implied in the linguistic intelligence mode of learning, but it is too subtle for us to grasp deeper meaning and understanding. Here's an example of a 'thought process' here (not experiment). Imagine; what does the phrase 'four inch cube' trigger in you and mean to you; versus seeing and holding a four inch cube in your hands? How many more senses, centers and faculties are now engaged in the process?

Functionality, meaning, knowing and understanding exist in non-verbal communication. They are considered forms of ART. Design and apply-ing the skills learnt, with most if not all of them, create a well-rounded human being. They all possess the Body, Mind and Spirit energy dynamic.

Synthesis is creative or mental (Mind) process of D$_E$Sign Science. The synthesizer is the artist or the Body. The term synthesizing is the spiritual dynamic. These are some of the goals.

Explore the highest and most creative potential for opportunities and relationships to align with the natural, creative and dynamic symmetry principles of life; harmonizing body, mind and spirit to discover and/or create the tools, the media for the new aesthetic expressions.

Express intention, voice and purpose to realize and manifest the right attitudes and paradigms to live in compatible and stress-less environments with non-toxic and positive situations to create opportunities for other people.

Develop and nurture the best properly aligned and harmonized physiological, psychological and spiritual relationships for all the meaningful expressions in life.

Harmonize and attract equitable and fair distribution of rewards; comforts, joys and peace, doing so with the highest regard and respect for the great-spirit and the sources of intelligence I hold sacred.

Do this in optimum, physical, psychological and spiritual health to promote and maintain growth that's shared as a self-less priority for community service.

NEW PARADIGM PROFESSIONS:

Augmented Reality Design	Tailored to a wide spectrum of industries, with commonalities and principles that govern them.
Avatar Programmer:	Fine tuning a client's motion capture and text-to-speech emotive output. Some AI-response programming knowledge with topology and geometry.
Chief Design Officer or Chief Creative Officer	Design is central to the success of the modern business. This is the value and purpose of branding.
Chief Drone Experience Designer	Unmanned drones in businesses will increase demand for the design of the entire service experience, support and maintenance required. With legal and policy issues.
Cybernetic Director D$_E$Sign Science related	Cybernetic art directors and visual-design bots in the distinct visual language of a brand. Several related sciences will support this "form intensive" career
The Fusionist (Synthesizer)	Fusionist will remain driven by passion for the Future and the ability to use D$_E$Sign Science as the unifying vehicle to manifest the best experiences and solutions.
Human Organ Designer	Human organ designers will be experts in bio-engineering and design, fitting newly created organs and artificial limbs to humans with deep knowledge of the software and hardware and skilled in bio-electronics

Intelligent System/D$_E$sign Scientists	The intelligent system designer creates the software systems that makes possible the design solutions of others.
Intelligent Design Systems (IDSs):	These systems will integrate multiple domains that will be the products of designers, artists, and technologists. This used to be in the ubiquitous realm or classic discipline of "architecture".
Director of Concierge Services Bespoke	Retailers will harness the power of big data to give their most valuable VIP clients and customers with a higher level of services than the general public
Embodied Interactions Designer (Holism)	New modes of interaction require a new type of designer: one that is focused on embodied interactions with the rise of software that only rarely manifests on a screen.
Interventionist	Creating transformational empathy or hosting a conversation that puts an end to polemics. Designers will have backgrounds in organizational psychology or behavior *change (Paradigm shifts)* framing unexpected questions.
Machine-Learning Designer,	Construct *'information and data models'* and algorithms that allow developers to create Artificial Intelligent Products. AIP anticipate the needs of users, and fulfill them before the user ever has to ask
Program Director	The design agency's version of a product manager of project management, engagement, and client services.
Real–time 3-D Designer Visual Intelligence	Virtual and augmented realities are on the forefront of design and technology explorations. Interaction design and game design synthesis.
Sim Designer	Gather customer data, behavioral models, and statistical models to design simulated people that can be used to help predict future customer behavior
Synthetic biologist/nanotech designer	We are on track to creating customized medicine, and soon synthetic biologists will be designing epigenetics treatment that ties to the DNA of the patient.

1. Data, design, and *'artificial intelligence'* will be the next frontier in the digital world. Understanding and redefining what it means to be a designer and a developer in the new paradigm.
2. Game design as an industry is such a focused discipline and craft: It takes years of practice to operate at a high level. With that in mind, senior level 3-D designers will be pioneers, leaving behind game design and joining product teams to create entertainment and productivity tools with complex interaction problems.
3. We will start to see shifts in school curriculua, where both 3-D and UX disciplines share the same halls and work together to invent a future.

4. These simulations help drive improvements into the design of all things before the product is ever realized.
5. Future products, ad campaigns, software, environments, and services are extensively "experienced" by artificial sim users who give sim reviews, tweets, recommendations, and predicted user data.
6. Medicines will be designed in software and printed on 3-D biological printers. With no ficelity *Chemotherapy* kills all types of cells in the body, not just the cancerous ones.

'Laborare est Orare': To work is to pray.

Here are the 'Bennett Tenets' of the S.T.E.P-Space, Time, Energy, Paradigm Mindset shifting process.

S.T.E.P 0	Connection to source. The Zero point of origin-all is all that matters.
Mentalism: All is mental is a universal law.	It is the origin of matter and of things that matter. In the beginning was the word. Everyone has their word. Sharing it or hearing it lightens their load and guides them on the road to greater destines.
S.T.E.P1	Heart-Mind-Spirit: The circle of creative leadership and relationship
Synergize and Synthesize to realize visions	The S.T.E.P operating principles of the New Paradigm activate the Heart-Mind-Spirit formula. It inspires passion, compassion and Love coming full Circle to complete and close the 'DEAL'.
S.T.E.P2	Alchemy: making the Abstract Real.
Keep the end in Mind. Focus and be clear.	Channel your 'IDEAL' Client or Avatar. Make them part of you so you become part of them. Visualize and synthesize the creative energies that will fulfill both your client's needs and yours. This is relationship building on a higher level.
S.T.E.P3	Self-Expression
Seek to under-stand then be understood	When your creations are aligned with the S.T.E.P formula, they express who you are. Love your self- Love your ideas, products, services, your presentations, packaging and delivery systems. Be all in and totally engaged in the process.
S.T.E.P4	Cohesion adds Value
Think Win-Win-Win	Let your confidence, the love of what you do and excellence enhance the value exchange, making price a nonissue and all situations be satisfying and mutually rewarding and nurturing.
S.T.E.P 5	Cision, Decision and Precision

Be Proactive	Be fluent in the language of Action but make your words loud and clear. Exorcise your 'marketing demons', trust your innovative S.T.E.PFormula and S.T.E.Pboldly into prosperity. Be the leader and expert in your niche or market.
S.T.E.P6	Symmetry and Order
Obey the first things first axiom.	Line extensions with rich aesthetic identities generate repeat business. They make sound investments in business futures. They create and maintain brand recognition by loyal customers. They create longevity and consistent profitability.
S.T.E.P7	Gratitude and Generosity
Celebrate your rewards and recognition. Pay it forward	Be thankful and ready to show appreciation for excellence, reciprocity and kindness. Recognition and expertise are currencies that must be payed forward for succession to create enduring legacies. Celebrate your newly learned wisdom Intelligence, Knowledge and Information and appreciate your earned recognition!

Where geometry, in Egypt, measured 'land', *TORIMETRY™ derived from the torus and its toroidal dynamic with the fractal model is the new gauge*.

The 7 Habits of Highly Effective People, written by Steve Covey was originally published on August 15, 1989. It is a best seller and leading self-help canon in its niche. It is based on "Newtonian Principles and values that have shifted exponentially in 'Moor's time frame' with the emergence of the new paradigm.

It was written to help people make radical changes in their lives by making serious assessments of their habits as they were looking to improve their performance and achieve personal goals. Were they looking any deeper into their inner game? Paradigms change about every 2,000 years. Put this on your bucket list for the next event. It is a paradigm model to change perception or understanding 'exponentiality'.

It is only by seeing things based on the correct principles that we achieve success and happiness. It's a habit. Individuals and communities have paradigms. To 'Simple-Fi' it's a habit. To understand paradigms, Covey urges us to think of the seven principles as maps for our life's journey as we strive for excellence and satisfaction. The moto: Change the approach (paradigm or habit): change the result! The 7 habits is a paradigm shift in itself. The way you do anything is the way you do everything. When we move events change, if we change do we move?

What is a Principle? A principle is a natural law that governs human growth, joy and happiness. Examples include fairness, integrity, honesty, dignity, service, excellence, potential, growth, patience, nurturance and encouragement. These are guidelines for its sincere achievement. Where your paradigms are the directions on your map, these principles are your bench and landmarks that confirm that you are on the right track and that you have the correct direction. It is not manmade codes, maritime nor even Talmudic laws now in use.

The 7 habits is a 'Canon' of authentic principles. What is a habit and how do you change one? Is habit the intersection of knowledge, skill and desire? Do we have the right Body, Mind and Spirit connections to source, in the proper order, to be able to make sustainable choices?

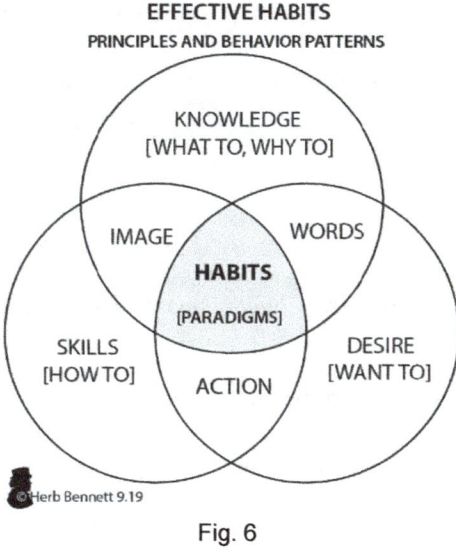

Fig. 6

"We must never become too busy sawing to take time to sharpen the saw." Dr. Stephen R. Covey

The 7 habits of Highly Effective People and their paradigms of habits presented by Dr. Covey is based on the concept of the *maturity continuum*. There is no spiritual connection in it. What we find is a 'Newtonian' paradigm with mindsets that no longer fit our new paradigm thinking and realties we now face, with technology disruptions and other social anomalies. These do not lend themselves to creating new habits readily. The conditioning and stresses take time, concentrated effort and requires major mindset shifts to be effective now. The Keys to living and fulfillment work with theories and principles of basic needs for Knowledge and Skills for us to be on purpose. We believe that callings, motivation and desire are the prescription for new paradigm shifts that are supported by our creative genius. We believe that our skills come through us from source. We think we are in control giving no credit to *the causes of 'callings'*. We build monuments to and for effects.

CREATIVE POTENTIAL — D_ESIGN SCIENCE IN THE NEW PARADIGM AGE

New mindsets, new skill-sets, new toolsets equal new habits.

'Coveyites' believe that unless you possess these 3 qualia (the generic and ubiquitous term for quality), new habits cannot be created. This is by no means adequate for our time and the paradigm we are preparing for. We are stuck in the polarities of much lower dimensions than any other time with the habits behaviors they bring about. Neuroplasticity and epigenetics are real. We can rewire neurons to heal ourselves 'by thought alone'.

In the Einsteinian paradigm time is not 'linear or sequential'. It may not even exist in some fameworks. Photons travel through space in 'no time' nor does it age. A chronon is a proposed quantum of time in the quantum world. It is a discrete and indivisible "unit" of **time** as part of a hypothesis that proposes that **time,** is not continuous.

These are elements that we are made of, but we hold on to time, 'for dear life and miss our divinity. The BMS continuum shows how the space, time (subject and objective modalities intersect in relativity) against the synthesis of space, time and energy. In the current science paradigm space-time does not involve energy. It is in a disconnected compartment. I believe, this leads to the entrainment of consciousness. Quantum Theory and other paradigms demonstrate physical characteristics, psychological behaviors and habits and new ways spiritual or creative energies transform and synthesize all three dimensions of consciousness into one expression, function or essence with the alignment and appropriate frequency distributions attributed to the 'event horizon' to offer a ken of knowledge in the truest sense of the word with all its meanings and applications included.

To 'Covey; the Newtonian', this (linear *concept of the maturity continuum)* is the natural law of physical growth, in an incremental, sequential progression to personal and (not intra) but inter-personal effectiveness and is the cornerstone of the seven habits. Why only seven (7)? What underlying higher principles govern them?

The 3 'interactive states' with qualities and traits we need to recognize.

CONCEPTS	EXPECTATIONS	MINDSET SHIFTS
Dependence is the concept that some external force or person will take care of me.	I depend on these to survive and to achieve things.	Being open to mindset shifts and cultivating new habits
Independence – The concept that I can look after myself.	I rely solely on myself, I no longer need assistance.	Individuality is a myth
Interdependence – The concept that 'WE' can do things.	That our talents and abilities combined create something greater.	Community, collaboration and shared resources

The paradoxical 'sequence of uncertaintity' does not always follow expectations. This means that it is impossible to accurately measure the position of a particle, or event in any S.T.E.P. or Space-Time-Energy-Paradigm with respect to more than one axis. If there are many observers 'present' and aware this would be true also. Would they all have the same measurements and coordinates? In fact, this leads to an uncertainty relation for the coordinates analogous to the Heisenberg uncertainty principle. In this model there is one observer who is, per-hap-s not experiencing the 'hap-ness' which by definition is the mother of uncertainty. 'Hap' is the root of happiness. This is from the Middle English *'hap'* meaning "chance" or "good luck."

The 7 habits of Highly Effective People	The 7 habits of New Paradigm thinking
Sharpen the saw	Raise you consciousness
Seek to understand then be understood	Be self-realized and think creatively
Synergize	Synthesize
Think win/win	Collaboration is a creative unifying dynamic-We all win
Life support systems	To attain freedom satisfy basic needs first
Put first things first	Symmetry principles generate variations
Begin with the end in mind; be proactive	Begin with the proper mindset and goals

The value of self-awareness; Humans have a uniquely valuable ability to think about their own Genetic Determinism – A genetic inheritance from your parents.

Neuroplasticity has a new view of this habit making behavior.

- Psychic Determinism – Your upbringing is responsible
- Environmental Determinism - Something around you is determining your response
- Direct knowledge comes from source through intuitive and unlearned skills. Intuition is the deeper mental faculty that *underlies* and makes possible a variety of behaviors, both ordinary and exceptional, in which new information appears in the mind *without apparent cause.*
- Ordinary people do extraordinary things within this spiritual ken.

This appears strange but it is actually a familiar, natural, genuine and inborn human capacity not of mind alone. It is the total synthesis of all Body, Mind and Spiritual dimensions in the space-time-energy continuum of Human consciousness and all of its expressions paradigms and thoughts. The finely tuned being access new information, knowledge and understanding without the use of one's familiar, rational or intellectual faculties and reasoning, sensing and memory. In some realms it is known as connecting to the "Akashic Records" In theosophy and anthroposophy, (is science aware of this idea? The well-known 'Akashic records- are a compendium of thoughts, events, and emotions (Everything) believed by theosophists to be encoded in a non-physical plane of existence.

CREATIVE POTENTIAL   D$_E$SIGN SCIENCE IN THE NEW PARADIGM AGE

This is known as the 'etheric plane'. There are anecdotal accounts but no scientific evidence of the existence of the Akashic record.

We have the ability to choose our response through self-awareness. If your response is the product of conditioning throughout your life, then you can re-program yourself to respond in a manner determined by you. Here conditioning is the idea of, intentionality or not, where if we are unaware of our habits and their impact on our lives. We call that "conditioning".

When we begin to recognize them and intend to act on transforming them or neutralizing them that is "program-ing". If we do nothing about them stress continues to take its toll.

Responsible people do responsible things and be/have responsibly. They do not blame circumstances or others. They acknowledge that in choosing their response, the consequences attached to that choice belong to them. They operate with causal paradigms for effects.

This is the concept of proactivity and is the first and most basic habit of a highly effective person. To be proactive is to be responsible for your own life. Your behavior is a function of your mindset and decisions, not your (outer-world) and conditions. It would be reasonable to think that if you have reached this level of seeking that compassion would replace anger and forgiveness would be familiar to you as a distressing paradigm. There is a plethora of techniques that others can introduce you to if that is the way you want to go. This is the 'fork' in the road for us all to take or not. Which direction do I take and how much, over what length of time for results with my goals. There are many great solutions but none seem to be about the true spiritual or D$_E$Sign Science™ and the 'ubiquitous architecture' of one's soul and destiny; a term that every other discipline uses but architects themselves as the language of thought, spirit and innovation.

The performance of proactive people is not determined by external factors such as other people or unfavorable conditions because they have selected their response with the aim of achieving a particular goal with thrust and confidence.

When SOURCE chooses you to do its bidding you better be there to deliver. If not there will be dues, maybe a karmic debt to pay as well. Ego disintegration and reprogramming is work.

Similarly, optimism and positive responses breed positive outcomes. In innovation, massive swings of power are determined by positive and negative attitudes and emotions. The same exists in everyday life. If you are looking to keep score you are in a different game with all not being together. Well, that's another take on the 7 Habits according to Newtonian Covey.

A MATRIX OF COVEY'S PRINCIPLES IN THE BMS FORM-ULA:

N0	NO PHYSICAL (included) or (proposed)	PSYCHOLOGICAL	SPIRITUAL
0	COMMUNITY	INTERDEPENDENCE	ASCENTION
7	SHARPEN THE SAW	PRECISION, ELEVATED EMOTIONS	EXCELLENCE
6	SEEK TO UNDERSTAND THEN BE UNDERSTOOD		
5	SYNERGISE		
4	THINK WIN/WIN		
3	LIFE SUPPORT SYSTEMS	INDEPENDENCE	*SALVATION of self*
2	PUT FIRST THINGS FIRST		
1	BEGIN WITH THE END IN MIND BE PROACTIVE		
	FOUNDATION	DEPENDENCE	CREATIVE FREEDOM

Identifying habits to be transformed, enabled and enhanced. Describe the habits, their qualities and characteristics Discover and define life areas they influence Look for the triggers and that activate habits; bad and good.

Create your list

How to identify, gather, sort and taxonomize (classification) habits. Does judgement respond to habits?

Do habits have egos or egoes have habits? Strategies: Meditate, Think, Visualize

Use the Kundalini and their traits of the 7 chakras as the 'Habit Baseline'.

Look at the Q2matrix.

Use humor to manage habits; if you think of them as causing pain use humor to create pleasure. Can other activities be used? Humor keeps us human.

Neuroscientists have traced our *habit-forming* behaviors to a part of *the brain* called the *basal ganglia*, which also plays a key role in the development of *emotions, memories and pattern recognition*. Decisions, meanwhile, are made in a different part of the brain called the prefrontal cortex.

The Basal ganglia is linked to the *thalamus* at the base of the brain. It *coordinates movement. Motive:* (or motivation) is a need, want, interest, or desire that propels someone (or an organism) in a certain direction.

Memories: the faculty by which the mind stores and remembers information. *Emotions:* a natural *instinctive* state of mind *deriving from one's circumstances, mood, or relationships with others*. Why isn't the 'state of mind' and internal process responsible for itself and not on external causes?*Pattern recognition:* artificial intelligence, data processing.

A branch of artificial intelligence concerned with the classification or description of observations. *Pattern recognition* aims to taxonomize (classify)and encode data *(patterns)* based on either *a priori knowledge (intuitive)* or on *statistical information* extracted from the *patterns and from memory.*

THE REASONS MATRIX

REASONS/LIFE SUPPORT	BODY/SPACE	MIND/ TIME	SPIRIT/ENERGY
WHAT & WHY	INFORMATION	KNOWLEDGE	WISDOM/THOUGHT- FULLNESS
THE HOW TO TECHNOLOGY	OBSERVATIONS/EXPERIMENTS	SKILLS,TECHNOLOGY	DESIRE/DESIGN
FULFILLMENT SATISFACTION	OBJECTS, PLACES,	EMOTIONS/ FEELINGS	COGNITION
EXPERIENCES/EVENTS	IDEAS / CONCEPTS	MEMORIES/REFLECTIONS	RECOGNITION
LIFE SUPPORT SYSTEMS	PEOPLE/ANIMALS	NATURE/ MOTIVES	ENERGY/WORK/POWER
EXPRESSIONS	MEDIUM/LANGU-AGE	COMMUNICATION	MEANING
REALITY	SHAPES/FORMS	MEASURE/GAUGE	SHAPE/FORM
CHOICE/ACTION	REASON	REASONABLE	REASONING
ACTS/GESTURES	INCISION	DECISION	CISION
MAKING	REWARD	EXCELLENCE	SATISFACTION
EXPECTATIONS	MANIFESTATION	SILENCE/MEDITATION	THOUGHTLESS AWARENESS

What are the human habit or paradigm typologies, their characteristics and traits? Where in out human story can be find a more holistic set of systems for such tools?

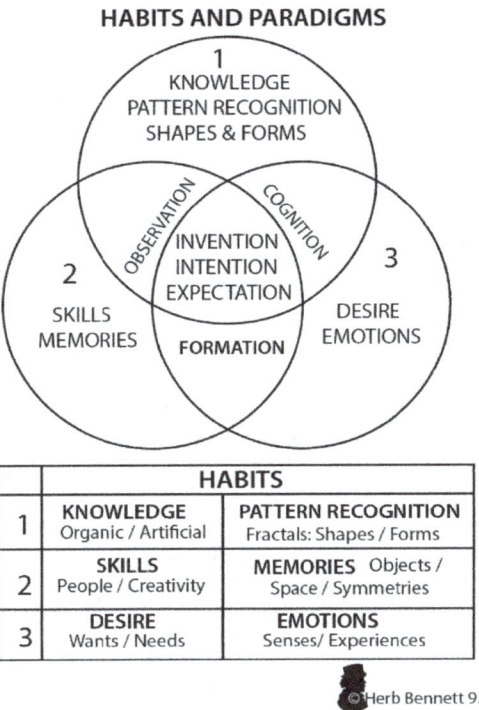

Fig.7

Communicating with likeminded professionals is made more interesting through the veils of unfamiliarity, security and intention, to be penetrated, when seeking support from experts in the same fields. They help others grow and are empowered to make contributions that are not very popular nor are in the mainstream; 'of Consciousness' as compelling to avoid the sustained purgatory unless direct action is taken. Connecting to 'source' attracts Wisdom, Intelligence, Knowledge and Information.

The 'WIKI' that describes a new Paradigm for design with new 3D forms, a new aesthetic and creative perspective based on an East-West synthesis. This can add value to many aspects of our creative lives.

CREATIVE POTENTIAL

D_ESIGN SCIENCE IN THE NEW PARADIGM AGE

It is built upon the "Symmetry Principles" of nature through philosophical ideas, geometric form and numbers. It offers insights into quantitative and qualitative properties of nature, consciousness and SOURCE, God or HIMHERIT, in descending order of correctness that might be needed, in creating a new paradigms with new theories, tools and technologies to help reimagine our "world" and the role D_ESign (The Dao D_ESign from the Dao De Jing) plays in it.

As creative professionals we can create a new aesthetic reality with ubiquitous design principles that can be implemented to enhance our environments, our life support systems and everything we create. At the root of this is the physical, psychological and spiritual flavors of consciousness where habits of all types operate and must be understood for creative freedom to optimize our human potential, success and happiness can be attained. There is another root I recently recognized that I think you might be curious about. It is the root of Happiness.

Let's look at the root of the word happiness. 'Hap' is the root for things 'accidental'. We make things 'Happen or they just happen. Is it destiny or do we D_ESign our own Happenings. I 'believe' I desire, I deserve 'Happiness' are all intentions and motives that connect to SOURCE. The origin of HAP seems very co-incidental or accidental.

Is this a paradigm of a time past that is no longer relevant to NOW? The opposite is Haphazard, Happenstance and Mishap. They are the opposite unfavorable outcomes of leaving decisions up to chance or destiny without clear focus and direction. The flavor of the Favor is key.

The favor of the flavor is me; being creatively free. It is what we truly need to be happy. It's what we pray and work for when we make work prayer. [Laborare est orare] The state of 'nowness' is accessible through thoughtless awareness. Behind the silent veil of deep meditation is our relative distance to *SOURCE*. The stress that we live in is caused by our misaligned state.

Forgiving spirit catches up with us, justifiably so, at different degrees and stages of trauma, crisis, disease and then death.

This defines the technical or intellectual parts of A puzzle which could also be quantitative. The qualitative aspects are quixotic and more complex. I am focusing on Habits of creatives and discovered your work that was highly recommended to me. I am working on a book entitled D_ESign Science...in the New Paradigm Age. There are chapters on "making the abstract real through manifestation using a synthesis of emerging ideas and principles.

It starts with the idea that consciousness is defined by the three (3) expressions or dimensions namely; the Physical, psychological and spiritual aspects of what seems to be all manifestations of reality.

René Adolphe Schwaller de Lubicz's study of numbers is the closest treatment of this topic I have experienced and enjoyed. It is truly phenomenal. I am convinced that underlying principles involved in the wider thought process can lead to a higher dimensional computing. I believe that we are at the verge of a total synthesis of expressions of nature that follow the "flavors" of consciousness as the Physiological, psychological and spiritual dimensions are extrapolated into the diversity of the illusion of objects manifested in our world view.

I have produced 'structural logical models' based on the number three (3) that is then extrapolated into *'muchness and suchness'* systems (to leave them entirely open), reminiscent of monumental ancient sites like Gobekli Tepe, Stonehenge or other 'multiliths'.

The question is are these sites also 'celestial computers' and other advanced tools that we have not understood yet? I believe that the thought process and logic structures have some role to play in advancing the technologies we are now struggling to define.

I see applications in subatomic physics and any other disciplines where vast amounts of data need to be "gathered, sorted, codified and taxonomized to become the ordered periodicites for the qualitative and quantitative synthesis we need to make information useful. This is the core topic that all else revolves around. It needs to be tested as the strategy for the synthesis that could help manage the ken of knowledge that might overwhelm us. We do not build these types of holistic tools without 'spirit' or energy. Everything is spirit and energy.

The spiritual and metaphysical aspects of the emerging paradigm is a new frontier leading to the unfolding of, and ART-iculating this new aesthetic reality we are struggling to formulate that's not televised. New Studies of the Brain, the Mind and their role in the definition of consciousness seem to be 'avoiding' the oriental contributions of the role the Kundalini, the chakras and central nervous system plays in a more inclusive model and holistic view of how the oneness of the ALL works, inviting MAN back into the the wider cultural synthesis of this planet. The east-west synthesis must be a part of this living dynamic we call consciousness. By ignoring this ancestral Wisdom, we are creating home bound prodigal people.

Creating a computing system for *qualitative reckoning* and evaluations sounds contradictory and paradoxical. But that could just be the rule of natural law. I would like to suggest that this is such a wide and open field of investigation that approaching "tool-making" in the context of new languages, symbols and ideas not available to us now is needed. The approach I must take is to reach out to like minds of those who are at least thinking in similar ways and are willing to begin exploring how collaborations can be created.

I have a lot of these visual mathematical and logic structure representations, essays, text and other content developed over the last 40 years.

The job now is to apply the essence of this process to this vast amount of information and test it with the technologies created to verify its usefulness. Your contribution/s in any way shape or form will be highly appreciated.

THE QUEST AND QUESTION MATRIX

QUESTION /is it/	BODY/SPACE Physiology	MIND/TIME Psychology Mentality	SPIRIT/ENERGY Thought-Intuition	
{WHAT} /is it	[A canon]	{WHAT}	(for) people	
{WHY} /is it/needed	to make	{WHERE}	(positive) (Changes)	of
{WHERE} /is it	(in) (their)	(and)	[life/lives]	/and/
{HOW:} /is it/done	by [self-assessment]	{WHAT}	evaluation	
{WHAT}/is it	(their) (own)	{WHO/M}	[performance]	
{WHY}/is it/done/so	to [allow]		them	
{WHAT}/is it	[per-misson]	{WHAT}		
{WHY}/is it/done/so	to change	{WHAT}	their habits]	
{WHY}[/is it/done/so	to achieve	A canon	[(personal)(goals]	
{?-WHAT:}				
{WHY}			to manifest	
{WHAT:}	life's goals			
{HOW:}	by designing	solutions		
{WHAT:}	innovative			
{HOW:}	using			
{WHAT:}		CONSCIOUSNESS	direct knowledge	of

(from) {WHAT:} & {WHERE:} & {HOW:}	([ONE] [GOD SOURCE])		or [HIMHERIT-energy]	
{WHO/M is:}	The creator	expressions and		
{WHAT:}	ALL natural forces,		Symmetry dynamics	
{WHERE:}	on earth's	evolution		
{WHY:}				

THE	NEW	PARADIGM	VERSION	
{?- WHAT:}/is it/&/for	life's goals	A canon	to manifest	[of]
{WHY}/is it/needed	by *designing*			
{WHAT:} [/is it/the] value	*innovative*		*Scientifically*	
{HOW:} /is it/done	using	*Designing*	Ideas, spaces, etc.	
{WHAT:}/is it	Infinite consciousness	*solutions*	Direct connections	
{HOW:} /is it/done/by	([ONE] [GOD SOURCE])	Re-imagining	Direct knowledge	
{WHAT:}}/is it	The creator		Or [HIMHERIT- energy]	

(from) {WHAT:} & {WHERE:} & {HOW:} /does it come	ALL natural forces,	CONSCIOUSNESS		of
{WHO/M is:} /is it	on earth's		Symmetry dynamics	
{WHAT:} /is it	for	expressions and		
{WHERE:} /is it				
{WHY:} /is it/needed		Evolution		

Here is a canon that can help people make *positive changes* in their life by *self-assessment and evaluation* of their own *performance*, that allows them *to change* their *habits* and *achieve personal goals*." The quest, question and request are in the 'Tao'.

"Knowledge is an unending adventure at the edge of uncertainty—" Jacob Bronowski

"The conventional view serves to protect us from the painful job of thinking." —John Kenneth Galbraith

CHAPTER 3 TRINE B
THINK BANK™

THE CORE KNOWLEDGE

WE PRESENT THE CORE KNOWLEDGE, Skills and technologies for the new paradigm Triad model of consciousness. The three-dimensional characteristics of Consciousness are Body, Mind and Spirit. This threefold model or Triad permeates all expressions of the Universal Consciousness on the macrocosmic and microcosmic levels of reality.

This fundamental knowledge along with the symmetry principles and other natural laws have been part of the wisdom traditions of ancient civilizations. Culture was once defined as the intersection of the natural and the artificial.

This relates to the physiological and psychological aspects of awareness and reality without the third component of 'spirit'. Spiritual principles, when thought of in the context of consciousness, natural laws and symmetry principles exist in the domain of universal forces. Metaphysics is man's attempt at understanding the spiritual dynamics of the universe. The methodology we use to understand spiritual principles have nothing to do with religion. We can now redefine the synthesis of physiology or body, psychology or mind and spirituality or energy as culture. Energy here is about work and power; from thought to the basic electricity that powers machines and our homes.

Laws and cultures that interpret them are equally important. Different cultures through time have offered us knowledge through their "wisdom traditions" giving us clues we can use

The Chinese, East Indian; specifically the Hindu, Sumerian and Egyptian cultures are of interest to us in this meditation.

Hermetic philosophy describes seven Hermetic laws that modern science still has not explained.

The first law; the law of "mentalism" is the key that unlocks the mystery of "Thought"; how it works and where we find it. The Law of mentalism 'states' that all things are mental. The laws reveal their meanings through observation, experimentation and meditation. It does not reveal itself unless we find the right key to unlock it.

Stated another way it says "No-thing is manifested except by thought. Everything in our world starts with a thought. These thoughts are expressions of complex dynamic processes that enveloped in form.

THINK BANK ™   D_ESIGN SCIENCE IN THE NEW PARADIGM AGE

How many vocabularies or families of form are there? There are organic forms of nature and the inorganic manmade forms made of geometric principles and artificial materials. The forms that are manifested through chemical processes are an extension of nature and are considered organic. Man uses geometry to describe the world. It's inherently a world of form. Here again we are indebted to the Egyptians for the discipline of geo meaning earth and 'metry' as in metric or measure. The nature of form itself has the three-dimensional qualities of the triad. Form is the synthesis of the physical, the behavioral and energy properties that resonate with the universal properties of universal consciousness at the macro level and is expressed at the micro level of the correspondence of the second Hermetic law of Correspondence. As above so below is its description.

There are three systems of geometry. One that is Euclidean and two Non-Euclidean variations. The Euclidean geometry is an orthogonal description of space.

A 60 degree triangle is defined by flat surfaces with all of its angles equal to 180 Degrees. A 'curved' triangle has a compounded curved surface with its angles greater than or less than 180 degrees.

These properties generate identities that are quite distinct when applied to other polygons. The process that generates these identities are mental. Their *'angles are our angels'* bringing us peace with the pieces to be the creative language to describe our world.

They require thought, evaluation and experiment to arrive at the relationships and descriptions that result from the creative process. Intuition and other unfamiliar mental processes and methods are involved as well. Mind is the process at work here. Mind is the process of refining thought prior to expression or manifestation when emotions, feelings and skilled experiment-ation and other symmetry principles and technologies are applied. [The suffix 'ation' is energy.]

There is a major distinction between Design and Manifestation. Design involves man's interpretation with knowledge, systems and methods for harmonizing forces and materials into form. Design requires the understanding of "how nature works". Manifestation is a more organic process.

The law of correspondence is a macro and micro correspondence dynamic that is at the core of the uni-versal consciousness in the macro state with its corresponding micro-expressions of the universe we are aware of and inhabit. Man has the most degrees of freedom which allows us to give form to our micro and macro mental environ-ments and situ-ations; energy of internal and external...spaces.

In the Hindu tradition there is a spiritual energy dynamic with a plethora of attributes known as the 'Kundalini'. *It's my electric soul.* There are 14 spark plugs for my engine with all the interconnections.

This is the universal and human life force linked by the subtle energies with seven chakra or centers as 'wheels' in Sanskrit. The chakras are key to both the universal and human electrical magnetic systems. These centers correspond to the endocrine system which is responsible for the distribution of hormones through the ductless glands. Western medicine fails to recognize and accept this vital 'relationship'.

They have developed protocols without fundamental knowledge of how these forces work. It can be argued that everything in the universe contains the Kundalini force with the same dynamic principles at work, but on different levels of frequency vibrations.

It is this same vibrational differentiation that all expressions rely on and are manifested. This is the holistic and harmonious understanding of the essence of humanity and life.

Once we have these principles in place we focus on the practical (praxis); aspects of "making the abstract real". What does it take to design reality? What are the creative processes, tools, and knowledge needed to transform thought into things? Logic structures, Symmetry principles, laws of behavior with appropriate rituals and technologies are some of the basic elements needed.

Wishing thought into reality is not design! Design is a science. Like many other ancient wisdom traditions we need to accept this as a reality. Transforming thought into form involves elements of time as in tense past, present and future. The dynamic of tension is also a time factor that with pressure helps the process of creativity flow through the stages of development described and or prescribed by the chakras. They in fact correspond to the phases of manifestation as part of the design science. The thought process is triggered by need on a very basic level. The need flows up to the cortex which engages the stimuli and the ideational processes.

Visualization is the next stage where form and matter meet and is resolved through the communication center in thought and communication.

The heart is the next center where the LOVEforce is applied to the approval process. If the form is not loved it goes back to re-thinking center and its process for other iterations to be created. The next stage is the work center.

Energy is extracted from the sun through the consumption of sun fed foods in the solar plexus and is transformed into work energy. The next level is where gender is assigned. All things are either male or female.

Mechanical parts are designed as such to 'fit' according to symmetry principles with male and female characteristics and physiology. Gender here is not sex. Procreation is replication involving sexual intercourse, for self-preservation and 'self-reflection'. Creation or the production of artifacts relies on principles of gender. Here we find the male and the female form supporting functionality. The final step in the process is the understanding of the behavior (psychology) of matter to determine how the design, the intention and satisfaction of the impulse or need is to be created and delivered.

THINK BANK ™   D_ESIGN SCIENCE IN THE NEW PARADIGM AGE

Thinking on a phenomenological level allows us to encode the symmetry principles of the triad (3) of the physical, psychological and spiritual dynamic to express the identity, aesthetics and all the characteristics of the appropriate form. Logic structures, Symmetry principles, gauge theories, numbers, measure, and all other necessary systems are used to design (not just wish) thought into form and reality. These are disciplines that the mind is completely engaged with. There are other systems required to bring these into the world. The symmetry principles involved with manifestation in the physical world are four (4). Together they are 3+4= 7, seven.

The fundamental law of 7 applies to all expressions of nature and the phenomena operating on the three-dimensional vibrational level of planet earth. What this leads to is a "qualitative" periodic matrix that correlates the flavors of expressions with certain correspondences and properties. Thinking abstractly with a mental scaffold can get us to a deeper understanding. 'Observational logic' taught our ancestors that '*The earth is green when the yellow sun mixed with blue sky*. This was before we know what chlorophyll was. In 'simple-fi' speak this is still true.

Using words like "SUCHNESS" to relate to flavor and MUCHNESS for quantity with universal CONSCIOUSNESSasspirit helps us develop an open and expansive paradigm to expand our [human] consciousness which corresponds with its universal 'flavor'. Where we get into trouble is in using 'muchness' as the basis of science and other theories to validate "suchness" phenomena.

For those who think the words suchness and muchness are not exciting we can use the German words 'Solchein' for 'such' and 'Oft' for much with the suffix 'heit' for the 'ness' that's added to both. We do this in the intellectual and research traditions using German language once considered the 'tongue of the western brain'. The 'sexy' form for 'suchness' is 'Solcheinheit'™ and for 'muchness' it's 'Oftheit™'. Gesundheit bless you. Gestalt psychology or gestaltism (German: *Gestalt "shape, form")* is a theory of mind of the Berlin School. This is a concept we are aware of. That it deals with shape and form is profound. German words for consciousness are Besinnung, Bewusstsein, and Sinne.

The purpose for the qualitative matrix is to create order with expressions of nature, similar to what the periodic table of elements does. Creative disciplines are called into action in their respective states of *'Solcheinheit'* where there are discrete rituals required to design the world around us as each individual soul expresses its own

'Solcheinheit'. 'Oftheit™','Solcheinheit'™ and *Sinneheit™*
(consciousness) represent Body, Mind and Spirit.

The disciplines are discrete. They have unique technologies, methods and require understanding of their basic 'neter' or nature that correspond with likeminded creative people who resonate on the levels of frequency that the manifestation requires.

A shoemaker cannot create a rocket and get to the moon. This is true of all three aspects of the thought-form-spirit consciousness manifestation principles involved in making things. Knowledge of physiology, movement, measure etc. are required.

Psychology or behavior runs the gamut from the base to the finer and subtle expressions and dynamics as does the spiritual which goes from thought itself to power and electricity which are all related to work energy. This relates to consciousness, the one source, with the three dimensions of physiology, psychology and spirituality not central to the western philosophical canon.

Our visual intelligence is vital to this process. So much so that words are being challenged by images for communication purposes. Again there is the visual spectrum going from the subtle vibration of vision and imagination to having the ability to 'see' what we create as they become physical objects in our world-view. All our senses operate within the epigenetic encoding (DNA) of *Oftheit*™ '*Solcheinheit*'™ and *Sinneheit*™.

The (*Gestalt "shape, form"*) is the principle that expresses equations of need and art-iculated relationships translated into physical space, with particular behaviors and aesthetic expressions with new identities. The spiritual dimension is more remote but is available to us. When the alignments are in order the form appears or is made. We are spiritual beings having physical experiences in what we call life.

We operate on dense vibrational levels that are complements of the finer forces and processes and choose to make things.

Civilizations that were created by some of our ancestors that have survived in any form of ruin or otherwise seem to have synthesized the physical, behavior and spiritual expressions representing their cultural, social and philosophical and religious systems that we are still struggling to understand. Most of what we create are strictly about satisfying physical need. This is not how civilization building is done nor how they survive or evolve. At some point in our story we have to be about becoming a civilization by lifting our selves to higher levels of consciousness.

If we understand and are honest about our current state of awareness and can observe the spectrum of our collective consciousness, questioning the progress we have made in alignment with our purpose, the results would be dismal. With all we have done there is a kind of vulnerability or unsustainability about our situation having focused on the physical at the expense of the other two dimensions for the harmony we need.

Do we know that the 'trinity' is the principle that imbues all human life, every expression and though we have? The physical triangle, when built, is the first structural stable S_2 shape. The family unit is three; the mother, father and offspring. Energies and forces operate in threes and the spiritual father, son and holy-ghost trinity model is found in many other cultures around the world.

The one or the source is distributed into the three (dimensions) and returns to the one in cycles of 'life' and natural law. All reality operates with this principle. Our binary process gives rise to patterns of the triad or trinity from the ONE. Though we engage with the two from the duality, this process references that one at all times for its fundamental quality and gauge through codes and specific instructions that are inherent in the expression of being.

It is the experience of becoming and energy as essence taken to the highest states possible. At some fundamental level there is a tetrahedral symmetry at work here. We deal with this later.

What disciplines and skills can we master, to nurture the energies needed for each dimension of the triad. Each one is unique. The physical demands that we understand space, physiology, movement, structural stability, integrity and matter. Behavior requires understanding psychology though all elements are governed by 'behavior' with their internal and external forces the behavior of behavior, we may call tis the 'meta-behavior' is a unique dynamic. Our minds control our behavior. Our thought affect our behavior.

Thoughts are in the spiritual realm as the highest form of energy or Spirit operating at all levels of super-consciousness. Knowing how to qualitatively order the variations of each dimension is the function of the 'Qualitative Matrix'. The law of seven (7) obtains here.

The premise presented states that creativity in the evolutionary sense engages man-woman as being created to be creators as both self-regenerating and being able to manifest reality. Being given the most degrees of freedom in creation comes with a price. We seem to have been given many tools without instruction manuals.

We may have to find the instructions by trial and error it seems. There must be a 'direct' way to avoid the pain and get to the creative bliss we are meant to enjoy by connecting to source. If we were put here to help maintain and develop our reality and support our 'environment' the one that nurtures us then why are we not more conscious of what our role is and be about 'our father's business'.

Why are we not building the mansions here and now, instead of waiting to get to the mansions when it might be too late then after we have compromised ourselves? Where is that famous image we were created to look like; that we were meant to be like? What were we meant to become?

"Any likeness that created this awesome reality must be extremely smart". If expanding consciousness is part of our deal then taking it to the max must be our birthright and destiny. This is where the hidden manuals come into play again. Shifting our mind sets or our set minds is key to achieving the paradigm shift needed. We must first find the instructions that we came with. Creating a physical, psychological and spiritual protocol that teaches us the secrets to synthesize a new reality is the new agenda. How this is created, distributed and made accessible is now readily available to the planet.

We have the technologies and the talent to do so. The pain that is caused by this not being shared to help us all grow and find our purpose has a back lash that we are feeling in every aspect of our lives, the life of the planet and our environment/s.

We can no longer focus simply and myopically on the physical or material. Creating systems to focus on development for material gain and profit at the expense of the psychological and spiritual even religious principles is not wise. A holistic healthy and abundant future is in the balance. When these triadic principles and harmonies are cultivated we would have evolved to higher dimensions of our selves being guided by the intended universal consciousness we are connected to but seem not to respect. What we do to it we do to ourselves is the price of our ignorance. The third eye or seat of the soul or the Pineal gland as part of the endocrinal system has light sensitive qualities.

Mental House Cleaning: an article dealing with how to prepare the mind for things that are needed not wanted to make sense that folks may not be receptive to. "Two objects, thoughts or feelings cannot occupy the same space, time or energy field. The old paradigm must give way to the new." The society and culture I live in program the fixed patterns of my mind.

My very identity, job and paradigm are based on these patterns. These systematic patterns of thoughts (habits) that programmed my mind came from my environment; parents, relatives, community and teachers. They are deeply embedded into my normal awareness or consciousness and my subconscious mind by my body, mind and spirit imbalance. This caused the external and strictly material and illusory psychological mechanisms of the ego to automatically resurface when triggers are activated and my buttons are pushed. My monkey mind stays busy with these conditioned patterns that linger longer in my sense of 'comfort'.

The thoughts and the processes that evaluate them are cause and effect related. I identify with what is familiar and hold on to bad habits. Difference makes some 'feel' uncomfortable and alone and similarity make other feel at home. This is how our DNA encodes us. To me difference is more inspiring and creative. The life of seeking continued until my crisis and trauma came as a total disintegration of my EGO.

This was my self-diagnosis. It resulted in total dysfunctionality with no energy with me pretending to understand the world. Everything around me appeared very strange and different. I found my element in the state of difference and that meant I too was becoming different. This finally became creatively controllable and I awoke in my own subjective "paradigm". Art forms I explored turned into magic that never stopped flowing. My Transformation 1975.

Deep Mental, Physical and Spiritual conditioning. Fixed patterns of mind reflect thoughts, feelings, desires and the expectations created by the environment and all of the messaging in it deeply. The triggers begin to appear in particular situations or with people who immediately activate them. The remedy for this is to become the actor or the trickster or whatever deception is needed to neutralize the trigger vampire and give it what it wants.

Triggers always want everything their way. They seem to never get enough 'blood. They dislike 'food for the soul'. So to neutralize them that is exactly what we give them. There are prescriptions for controlling what triggers do. Their needs come at their "victim's" expense.

Being the victim is the easiest role to play in the theatre of 'me, myself and I'. 'I' am the star, 'me'; the victim and 'self' is the most capable stock taker of habits to bale these players out of their predicament. These three actors conspire against 'us' to become the host and hostesses of habits that define the 'I, me and self' or 'us' players.

THINK BANK ™   D_ESIGN SCIENCE IN THE NEW PARADIGM AGE

These habits (all pun intended) have their costumes for particular situations, crafted to represent the values and rewards desired as outcomes are extracted from the situations or people who to us are triggers.' I, me and self' can never be triggers, or so 'we' think. What triggers need; they need to be reconfigured creatively to be de-triggered permanently. The 'EGO' is the renaissance-man appearing in all actions, subtractions and transactions.

So what is the problem with EGO? The natural world, including our inner world that we also omit or forget, is made of forms and shapes the objects that are expressions of vibrational energy at the material level. It corresponds to the ethereal realm of FORM and SHAPE as phenomenal thought at much higher conscious levels. Each realm has its own symmetry rules, language and 'essence' we need to know to communicate not to talk. EGO is what we apply to the objective world as a healthy dynamic that can become "Energy we use to Get Over" with compromise.

"Everyone wants to get to heaven but nobody wants to die" to get there; Says BB King. There is no backdoor to resurrection and judgement or divinity. To us in the 'now' transformation is a form of resurrection. We judge which habits align with our life's goals.

How do we discover what they are? Do they relate to our values and our basic nature?

A thought process: I cannot exist with expectations alone in the pre-sent society in our present state if we are to enjoy the pre-sent (value) that life is. I am unable to exist but can I still be without a body, without a mind and without my spirit connected to the greater SPIRIT.

Where did 'me, myself and I' get this idea of isolating expectations for the synthesis of the triad of consciousness on all its levels? The forms and shapes of the world have a mirror plane... 'above and below'.

It informs deed by word, extrapolates reality from illusion (image) and transduces right and direct action from higher levels of thought. These are states with depths we are unable to plumb with our illogical reasoning skills and limited intellect. There are intuitive alternatives attainable through silence and thoughtless awareness in meditation.

The compelling single force of expectation, is a vast matrix of multiple dimensions of consciousness upon which 'gems or germs' of consciousness grow with choices. With all our knowledge we are still not up to the task of formulating complete and healthy identities, identifiers and identifications. We settle for ease and comfort and create false economies, sticking to personal identity with costumes and expectations that come even after waking up, or in whatever ill-luci-dated state we find ourselves.

Firmly entrenched paradigms are powerful, influential and unhealthy. Their power aligns with the degree of the inadequate identifications and identifiers we create. We experience values without integrity. We can translate this and 'simpli-fi' it to con-note 'KNOWING' and eventually meaning.

Unless the ego is disintegrated strong belief in one's own thoughts creates overwhelming power over you. The abuse of the faculties will then easily obscure all vision with illusions, reduced awareness, focus, attention and Intention not to be present. This will cause you to surrender to daydreaming. Dreams, as astral phenomena are creative and useful. What they manifest unconditionally can lead to the true freedom we aspire to, to attain our goals. The intelligent spirit or life force is an eternal present (gift) of 'nowness' that's not material. Now itself, knows no past nor future.

When we are invited to it we bring our past and future along. What type of dissonance does this create? 'Now' is no space-Body, no time-Mind and no Energy only Pure Spirit. [If it is as encompassing and as vast as it is without space, time and energy we get lost in what seems to us, in our mind's eye, to be a void.] We then avoid being in the void for any length of whatever 'measure-meant we use for quantifying or keeping score. We elect to be in the addictive and very seductive conditioned past we carry that we cannot relinquish permanently.

The void, (zero point) the state beyond man's knowing, is where all the ethereal energies are found. It is the pure medium for transformation and dynamics like the pendulum and quantum theory. Here our slow vibrations oscillate to the stressful, anxiety ridden, over expected and expectant states we are preoccupied with and miss what was present and given to us to live our lives in abundance and joy. Expectation and identification tantamount to wanting to see or have something 'pleasant' *happen* to, for or with us and others etc. Let's translate. What it says is; "if we know and are clear about what we want it is reasonable to expect it to *happ-en*". The "to, for or with us and others etc." is the proverbial all powerful WHY? Does this favorable (expected) result of the *happening* lead to *happiness*? If there is no peace there is no-thing happening and therefore no peace.

The location of the *happening* must correspond and align with all qualitative and quantitative aspects and properties to create the *happiness* we seek. It's like the mystery of finding anything we lost. If we look for it were it is, we find it. It's logical, isn't it! *Happiness* can only be experienced in its rightful spirit space, in the appropriate state, mood or mindset and in the highest cultivation of spirit, for what 'must' happen must be harmonized to coincide with all the tools and methods of manifestation. Cycles are natural but they rely on precise Alignments. Life cycles are no exception to this law.

Let's look at the root of the word *happiness* right now. *'Hap'* is the root for things 'accidental'. *'Happen-Happenings and Happiness'* are all connected to SOURCE and are co-incidental. Haphazard, Happenstance and Mishap are unfavorable complementary outcomes- polarities. The flavor of the Favor is key. The favor of the flavor is me being creatively free. It is what we truly need to be *hap-py*. It's what we pray and work for. It makes our work our prayer. It's all in the 'word' from the beginning, so what should be different?

In *happiness* we repel all the unattractive *happenings for peace sake*.

Presence is being in the state of 'nowness' accessible through thoughtless awareness. Behind the silent veil of deep meditation is our relative distance and orientation to SOURCE, in no time.

THINK BANK ™

DESIGN SCIENCE IN THE NEW PARADIGM AGE

The stresses we live in are caused by our 'misaligned states'. Forgiving spirit catches up with us, justifiably so, at different degrees and stages of trauma, crisis, disease and then death. No one knows what happens at the moment of the return to our arising. Personally I do not think we should wait to find out. We take this opportunity 'now' (as our motivator) to align with source to enjoy the favors we 'learn to earn' for our time served and the service we offer to others and the planet. Our purpose is to make 'awakening' irrevocable we must recognize all fixed mental patterns as habits of (body) (mind) (spirit) with their paradigms.

Remember that the paradigm is the grand value system aligned with universal principles and the three dimensions of consciousness are very specific. This is where we might be getting stuck; not identifying accurately, the difference with specificity and generality. This recognition triggers or motivates the proverbial 'WHY". That is the deep soul searching introspection that addresses the pain and brings it to the surface to motivate us to be honest and true to ourselves. This is not the time for shutting down. 'Kicking the can down the road' eventually transforms into that bigger horizontal 'metal can' we're in on our homebound journey.

There are some experiences we leave behind and those that are in our hearts we take with us to be weighed against the feather.

Why can the mind not 'create' itself? If it's energy, it cannot be created nor destroyed. It can be polluted as it deludes itself by participating in its own conditioning. It cannot heal itself if healing is needed in stupor-stition and avoidance modes. It must be answering to an infinitely higher power. Fixed mindsets cannot be transformed by thoughts, deeds and beliefs of the same mind alone. Problems do not fix themselves within the same universe. Applying effort, practice or willpower, found primarily in lower vibration ranges, do not work.

How do we get beyond the limited self and pause for there to be a new cause to reboot all meaningful and sustainable transformations with the right synthesis in real place, time and energy?

Back to the triggers. How do we know what they are? Are they old or new and to whom do they belong? Who activates them and who or what are the targets. If they are physical they are emphasized by the lack of creature comfort and desired things that ruined our expectations and manifestation methods, arts or sciences we have no way of verifying and are leaving ourselves open to the "snake oil sales" phenomena, analog or digital, of the day all over again.

Are there distinctions between things that are desired, wanted and/or needed? Who need them any way?

Not all people desire or want the same things. There is diversity and ranges of differences to consider and be aligned with manifestation laws. Basic needs and 'status inspired' needs are based on social, cultural and economic status, access and means. This is all directed by habits, paradigms and the panoply of human traits, proclivities and all else imaginable. Stations in life, status revolved around development of the self. Individuals, communities and groups are just a few layers to consider. Materialism outwardly directs this human urge.

The urge for self-development is the purview of the true self. One that knows its connection to source and is in the flow of its vibration without being distracted by any external definitions or identifications of it and the fixations of its paradigms and dogma. When fixed mental patterns appear, this mentality becomes the buffer used to protect us regardless of any expectations that activates it. The limbic brain with its 'fight or flight' stress responses is neutralized or trans- ended.

The logos enters the picture to mitigate habits or keys like "ennui, sloth lethargy lazy, idle, indolent, inactive, sluggish, apathetic, lethargic, listless, languid or torpid.

These are qualitative dimensions and flavors of awareness in misaligned, unhealthy paradigms. In-sight brings cognition and re- cognition of otherness as intellect. 'One-ness' links directly for the WIKI to flow from SOURCE. Interacting with others opens the floodgates to higher dimensional be(com)ing. When you are aware of how paradigms work, the energy supply they receive gradually dissipates however.

The energy that formerly supplied these addictive and seductive patterns redirects its entire resources and power to the synthesizing of harmonious dimensions of awareness in us to align with all that is external. In this way, conditioned mental patterns gradually lose their power and are no longer attracted or sustainable.

As a result, the work of the mind, controlled by the ego, that might have appeared quixotic before becomes increasingly transparent when new and sustained habits are cultivated. In this way, Consciousness and Presence will increasingly dominate your mind, and they will be manifested in more enduring periods of silence when 'thoughtless awareness' manifests self-realization through meditation. With meditation and visualization 'mind', persona and personality 'reconnect with' or 'redesign' its purpose.

Connecting with higher levels of consciousness is the result of seeking and finding deeper and higher levels of mind and spirit. The body then responds differently as it re-aligns 'itself' with the essence of the newly transformed being.

Mind becomes a way by which Consciousness expresses itself through the language of form and shape. Allow me to reframe this idea: Consciousness uses the mind, when it is enabled and free to express itself in the world via energy as forms. Shape is quixotic and malleable when Symmetry and Geometry offer the intelligence and integrity needed to do the describing, reconnecting and designing or the polarization, ideation and formation of thought. New form Paradigm vocabularies and aesthetic identities are manifested to articulate principles that nurture us.

How can we achieve true 'global intelligence' when the Wisdom Intelligence Knowledge and Information from all cultures are denied and are not part of global consciousness? This is essential to our holistic realization that could elevate human consciousness now.

THINK BANK ™   D_ESIGN SCIENCE IN THE NEW PARADIGM AGE

These are the wisdom traditions and cultures that continue to contribute significantly to the contemporized WIKI.

1. Egypt: The 7 Hermetic laws that are the 'symmetry principles of nature, western science knows nothing about.
2. The Buddhist Canon; the Dao DeJing with its transliteration to a 'Dao Design™ to create.
3. Hinduism offers the Kundalini and the 7-14 chakras (East) which aligns with the endocrine and human energy system (West). This is the East-West Dichotomy we need to synthesize. Our entire consciousness and all its expressions depend on this global mindset shift.
4. Many other systems will be presented. What other cultural and wisdom systems or 'kens' do we use to synthesize our own personal paradigm comes into question.

This is the 'praxis' for creating the expressions of the languages of geometric shape/s and form/s:

1. Sacred and Profane geometries using the three systems of form namely the Euclidean and the Non-Euclidean. Contributors to the Non-Euclidean traditions are Gauss, Riemann with Bolyai and Lobachevsky in the 19th century.
2. Newtonian, Einsteinian and Subatomic Physics.
3. Quantum theory, entanglement, entrainment and String theory.
4. Think of other resources to build systems in other disciplines.

BE THE ENTREPRENEUR TO YOUR OWN PROSPERITY h.g.b
EVERYMAN IS AN ARTISAN TO HIS OWN 'CONNECTION TO SOURCE', FREEDOM AND
FORTUNE. Appius Claudius Caecus

THE BODY MIND SPIRIT MATRIX

BODY	MIND	SPIRIT
THE EGO	ILLUSORY IDENTITIES	THE EGO-MIND DYNAMICS
LANGUAGE	REALITY	CAUSE AND EFFORT
DREAMS	DAYDREAM	TRIADIC QUALITIES
DIRECT KNOWLEDGE	BROWN STUDIES	SOURCE IS EVERYTHING
BARRIERS AND WARS	VEILS	IN EVERY SHAPE AND FORM

How do we observe, recognize and heal or override the imprints of old habits and begin to embed new ones?

Meditation is the silence that allows us to connect to source through 'thoughtless awareness' to rewire the circuitry in our brain and to tune the rest of the Human Instrument. It makes all the sense in the world that the last thing the mind needs would be more distractions. Silence is uncomfortable at first but it is a clear indication of the work that's being done. If we could fall right into it, we nor it would be truly peaceful.

Gnosis is the common Greek noun for knowledge. It generally signifies a total and reliable dualistic knowledge in the sense of *mystical* enlightenment or "insight". Gnosis taught the deliverance of man from the constraints of earthly existence through insight into an essential relationship, as soul or spirit, with a supra-mundane place of freedom.

The term is used in the context of ancient religions and philosophies, aspects of Judeo-Christian beliefs, particularly to the ideas that emerged during early Christian and Greco-Roman interaction during the 2nd century. It seems quite appropriate for the concepts that are emerging in the new paradigm.

Gnosis has spirit and consciousness. Knowledge does not and is materialistic and Newtonian in its fundamental nature.

Gnosis taught the deliverance of man from the constraints of earthly existence through the soul or spirit as insight into an essential enduring relationship, as, with a supra-mundane place of freedom. The term is used in the context of ancient religions and philosophies, aspects of Judeo-Christian beliefs, particularly to the ideas that emerged during early Christian and Greco-Roman interaction during the 2nd century.

It seems quite appropriate for the concepts that are emerging in the new paradigm. Gnosis has spirit and consciousness. Knowledge does not and is materialistic and Newtonian in its fundamental nature.

Gnosis is a feminine Greek noun which means "knowledge". It is often used for personal knowledge compared with intellectual knowledge. Latin dropped the initial g (which was preserved in Greek) so gno becomes no- as in noscō meaning "I know noscentia meaning "knowledge" and notus meaning "known".

The g remains in the Latin co-gni-tio meaning "knowledge" and i-gno-tus and i-gna-rus meaning "unknown" and from which comes the word i-gno-rant, and a-gno-stic which means "not knowing" and once again this reflects the Sanskrit jna which means "to know", "to perceive" or "to understand"

In the kundalini of Hindu tradition and spiritual philosophy, Ājñā, English: "command"), or third-eye chakra, is the sixth chakra in the body. It is a part of the brain which can be made more powerful through repetition, like a muscle. It signifies the con- science.(being with science and intelligence.)

CHAPTER 3 TRINE C
THE CONSCIOUSNESS STORY

EVERYTHING IS THOUGHT - PHYSICAL, real, visualized, imagined or dreamt that interacts with gross or subtle psychological, internal or external natural forces, principles and rules expressed as frozen and dynamic forms of spirit, energy, past present and/or future. In the continuum of physical-space these are articulated through physiology, psychological-time experienced through psychology and spirit-energy, interpreted and understood through spirituality. 'ALL' obeying laws of mentalism, correspondence, vibration, rhythm, polarity, gender, cause and effect is consciousness.

Align the following principles with your new paradigm attitudes and vision: SYMMETRY PRINCIPLES

BODY	MIND	SPIRIT
1. Highest and most creative potential attainable	ALL CENTERS/PRINCIPLES/FORCES	Intentions Connections to source
2. Natural, creative and dynamic symmetry principles	BMS-STEP	Thought Being in the flow
3. Harmonizing body, mind and spirit	ROOT	Speech Total Synthesis
4. Create the tools, the media for a unique message	HEART	Effort Creative communication
5. All I love.	MENTALISM/HEART/	Action LOVE is the creative energy
6. Intention, voice and purpose	THROAT	Living Speaking to self and others as thinking and communication

SYMMETRY PRINCIPLE (cont'd)

PRINCIPLES	MENTALISM	FREEDOM
7. Right attitudes and paradigms	Habits	Reality The Inner Game and The 'Rim World'.
8. Compatible and stress-less environments In all forms.	Mind	Understanding
9. Non-toxic and positive situations, opportunities and people.	Unconditional Love	Wisdom
10. The best properly aligned and harmonized physiological state.	Psychological	Spiritual relationships
11. The meaningful expressions in life.	Experiences, feelings	Values
12. Harmonize and attract my equitable and fair distribution of rewards;		
13. The great-spirit and the sources of intelligence I hold sacred.		
14. Optimum, physical, psychological and spiritual health		
15. Promote and maintain growth		
16. Shared as a self-less priority as community service.	With whom	
When	How	Where
Why		

CONSCIOUSNESS

Body, Mind and Spirit: the three fundamental dimensions of consciousness.

The brain, our DNA, the central nervous and endocrine system with the subtle systems or the electro-magnetic energy field known to oriental cultures as the aura, specifically the Hindu tradition where the Kundalini and the seven (7) Chakras transform impulses and sense data, by transduction to produce electrical energy that is essential to the formation of intelligent information generated from 'The Source' known by many names.

The most inclusive of them all is consciousness. Consciousness is a triadic, harmonic, ubiquitous force that breaks down into three distinct qualities of expression of Body, Mind and Spirit. The three qualities permeate all expressions, energies and living forms. Body, known as physical, is the normal awareness of consciousness. Mind, known as psychological, is the subconscious form, and Spirit is the creative force that is the superconscious source of the ALL of ALL. When these three dimensions are harmonized, they form a transcendental

THE CONSCIOUSNESS STORY

DESIGN SCIENCE IN THE NEW PARADIGM AGE

dynamic or AKASHA. It is past, present and future 'awareness' all in one. Focusing on physicality gives us a material or physical science we have used as the foundation for western societies. Mind has a behavioral science – psychology. Spirit has a creative and energy science – spirituality that is related to gross forms of power which span all processes from work to thought – the highest form of fuel known to all forms of expression and the dynamic we know as life.

Within each dimension the triadic qualities operate as a holographic dynamic to form an interactive ma/a/trix that expresses five of the seven qualitative expressions of consciousness. Two of them are rarified; five are gross or dense.

The ethers (waters) of the protoplast, the earth, the plant, the beast and man represent the physical or one third of reality. From the highest vibration of rare quality, these flavors of superconscious thought eventually coalesce and 'form' into dense matter. The mind and its psychological and emotional principles are even less understood. Spiritual awareness, knowledge and experiences are very often viewed in the context of religious dogma and rituals, not as the metaphysical or spiritual science.

This discipline is more open and able to afford much deeper levels of understanding of spirituality. This produces a unique and independent body of knowledge that has nothing to do with religion. The principles of religion deal with personal and institutional beliefs that may have their roots in attitudes of restraint and control. Spirituality, on the other hand, is a universal dynamic rooted in the exponentially higher dimensions of super-consciousness and true freedom. What compounds and confounds the issue is our definition of energy also.

Energy is an integral and holistic flavor of consciousness. Space and Time are the other two. The MIND, that is the Energy of pure thought, has properties, qualities and essences that are distributed along the Ray of Creation where movement is the dynamic nature. The purest movement, displacement and extension of all 'finite mind' is Space. The purest duration and periodicity of all de-finite mind is Time. The purest in-finite energy of conscious and super-intelligent vibrations have two expressions.

As above, so below according to the Hermetic principle of correspondence. One is the finest phenomenal and subtle flavors of THOUGHT, realization, intention and motivation – subtle energies that move the human spirit. The other is the power or gross energy of electricity and mechanical power for work as 'Thought' and motion.

Man, Nature and the Universe all rely on various forms of energy – again along the spectrum of vibrations of conscious thoughts. Their basic fuel is thought. The expressions that make up the entire spectrum is the thought process of super consciousness within which all the sub-levels of the continuity of expressions form a matrix that continues to expand through its own Space, Time and Energy continuum.

"MAN living without celestial alignments creates a false sense of self that leads to all forms of corruption". HGB

Religion plays a major role in our creative life whether we recognize and admit it or not. Regardless of the various forms of scripture, metaphysics and cultural history, they all demonstrate how individuals were meant to achieve higher 'Consciousness'. Some are more familiar to us. There are others that have been 'hidden'.

'The Christ' is known as the third-level 'MAN'. The major confusion lies in the dialectic of the terms associated with Jesus, 'Jesus Christ' and the title Jesus *'The Christ'*. Jesus is the birth name. Jesus Christ is the spiritual transformation of the man, Jesus. Jesus, *'The Christ'*, is the third-level spirit that rose to a level of divine ascension few have attained on earth as the third element of Holy Spirit of the Triune God found in many traditions. News flash: the Christ consciousness is the nectar flowing in all of us. We must know it to find it. Wouldn't you love to find the holy grail?

This transformation was attained after the initiation of historical Jesus in the wisdom tradition of Egypt where the Title 'The Christ', was granted after tests were performed by temple priests. We seem not to make any of these critical distinctions with these definitions and have settled for the historical 'Jesus Christ' the man because of our literal mindset and materialist proclivities. With this combination deeply rooted in our psyche, we face more challenges. In one of the sources used here – *The Aquarian Gospel of Jesus 'The Christ'*, Jesus clearly instructs us that the 'mortal path' or man's physical interpret-tation of Jesus Christ of the flesh was not the model man to be worshiped externally or from outside of us. However, this is exactly the model we have implemented and have followed ever since. The ability to rely on our internal and individual potential, not only spiritually but in all aspects of our lives, has been severely compromised and debilitated. We are more dependent on external forces for our survival than on our own internal creative and spiritual connections to source that allow us to obtain direct access to the transformative knowledge and wisdom we need. That is *FREE*. All we have to pay is attention. Not paying attention gets very expensive for our bodies, minds and spirit.

Evidently, socio-political and religious choices made over time, perhaps by ignorance or by deliberate manipulation for power and control. This limits the capacity for every soul to achieve not only the fullest spiritual potential but the physical and psychological as well.

It would be in the interest of early leaders in all spheres of influence that shaped human lives and the affairs of how they could be directed and controlled to use this as the most profound type of manipulation in a world that would condition peoples' minds to serve the leadership's interest.

By controlling and misrepresenting the promises of the inevitable and emerging Aquarian Age as it unfolds, we continue to miss opportunities to create a harmonious and equitable spiritual order for the planet's survival and MAN's salvation. The Christ Consciousness was meant to create freedom, peace and a very different reality that would be more harmonized than the materialistic-centered, egotistical-based reality we have all bought into. Where is the LOVE?

The resurrection and the 'coming of Christ' to the earth is a glimpse of our own 'Christ' or spirit-consciousness' within us all – a gift that was meant to demonstrate how people could actualize or restore their highest spiritual life using the power of love to attain the rightful

THE CONSCIOUSNESS STORY

and latent spiritual state of super consciousness programmed into what we now know as our DNA. Is our DNA our soul or is it a part of it? The moniker 'Christ' is the Holy Spiritual or super-consciousness part of the Triune GOD, composed of the Father, the Son and the Holy Spirit. This is an energy dynamic that can be art-iculated through design for a higher level of thought and design. Designing our destiny is how we attain our purpose and our creative freedom.

These are the three fundamental dimensions of Consciousness – the body, mind and spirit – that are manifested on all planes and vibrations of life including the earth realm in the process of synthesis through 1. Polarization. 2. Ideation and 3. Formation.

One other avenue of uncovery took Albert Einstein, riding on his beam of light, into E=Mc2 crushing our paradigm at the turn of the last century. We may not have recovered from this event and here we are again with a more intense opportunity for an awakening, like no other in our story following his definition of insanity. Like the few who got 'it' in the past, this phenomenon is occurring again but this time we have several 'quickening dynamic events' on our side and more are getting 'it' now.

Whether one can ART-iculate it or not, does not matter. It is in us all. With vision as the vehicle for our quest, the question becomes, "What does the world look like now through the eyes of 'HIMHERIT™, the creator, or any other creator for that matter?"

The request is, "Can we see ourselves and the world through the sameness eye?" Since we are all ONE, we should see the same ONE. Anyone found wondering what any of this diatribe has to do with 'design' is in deep sleep. These are the thoughts we do not share with others, not even with ourselves, often. Creating a safe space for reflection and connection leads to transformation of any desired form. It is all in the mind and the heart.

"The mind is neither a form nor an attribute of matter. It is a very high vibration of light." Here is a definition that excludes or AVOIDS any recognition, use or understanding of the concept or experiences of *'spirit'*. The heart brings up the rear as it is often left behind on our *trails* or *trials* towards our destination or destiny, happiness and peace.

We now begin applying the principles and skills of these seven 'intelligent' centers to the creative design process. We approach this with the knowledge that the macro universe and micro man, with all the attributes of the holistic universal mind-body interactions, use these dynamic symmetry principles to create and maintain the self-generating processes of galaxies and babies alike. The 'physical', 'psychological' and 'spiritual' are critical to all true expressions of consciousness. Truth depends on alignment, adherence, coherence and correspondence with the principles of natural law to be expressed during constant creation. Energy knows no end in the eternal Space, Time and Energy continuum, in 'synchronous harmony', for there to be manifestation with everything in its own time, following natural law. Ecclesiastes 3:17

Sharing this knowledge and implementing it through creative educational systems now has never been more crucial and readily available for human growth. We begin to create healthy conditions, opportunities, skills and heightened awareness for us all. The cultures of the world, with the current experiences we are having, cannot continue to ignore the need for 'spiritual growth'. Continuing to misrepresent valid religiosity through ill-conceived agendas with dogma and hate is extremely costly and criminal.

If at least we see merit in this as a creative process that helps creative individual to un-cover and be in touch with their deeper inner selves, then this would be the step that starts that magnificent journey we all seek. There it is!

We begin with three types of information revealed about each center. First, there are the spiritual principles. This is followed by the psychological – human skills and rituals for the 'how'. Nature follows laws with which we must align. The third phase of the quest relates to translating the esoteric principles into recognizing human experiences with ways in which they are being applied.

The goal is to reimagine, reformulate and describe the dream or visioneering processes with basic creative skill sets in a new context or environment with a revived energy and strong focused desire. KISS is the way to 'Simple-Fi', (believe in simplicity) To transform and understand the first part of the formula, see it internally as Body, Mind and Spirit BMS applying to everything that's 'consciousness'. It then takes place poetically in a *STEP*– Space-Time-Energy-Power continuum as the essence of life.

The views we create unfold constantly in what we call the new paradigm.

A fancy term for what you see, is what you get WYSIWYG. The difference now is seeing you and your 'whats' with your own beautiful, loving, inner eye/s.

Spiritual Principles: (Spirituality) The Creative Praxis: (Physiology)

Related concepts are: mentalism, the crown, ether, the pineal gland, the brain and thinking as well as the three-part human brain – the reptilian mammalian and the neocortex and the hypothalamus. The brain is the ideation center of mentalism for creating the things we need to sustain our lives, starting with thoughts. Upward expressions of need ascend three

'Nadian' channels with the Kundalini, the ida, the pingala and the sushumna nadis, in a framework of Physiological, Psychological and Energy related electro, chemical attributes called mind. These ideational dynamic (creative) processes coalesce, transduce and interact to interpret and transform impulses into thought forms.

A thought form, like a point in space, is an event with the potential to become something that corresponds with a grander framework – consciousness. In keeping with the form analogy, the line, plane form sequence must follow for manifestation to occur. There is a very direct intuitive process that can also occur. It can present holistic, preconceived form. This is a more complex process.

THE CONSCIOUSNESS STORY   DESIGN SCIENCE IN THE NEW PARADIGM AGE

When the concepts are formulated, communication with the Ajna, visualization and imagination center, begin. This takes place downward on the next slower level of vibration.

Spiritual Principles:

7. Sahasrara is the crown chakra. When this center is opened permanently, infinite Bliss is enjoyed. An inseparable oneness is interwoven with the ever-transcending Beyond. We know that we are always interacting with Infinity, Eternity, Immortality and consciousness.

Of all the centers, the highest, most peaceful, most soulful and most fruitful is Sahasrara. Here infinity, eternity, immortality, source and creation are one.

6. Ajna, the brow chakra, destroys or evolves beyond the dark past, to hasten a golden future. It manifests the present in a supremely fulfilling way. The anahata is the 'love', feeling center for reality-testing 'fulfillment'. Psychic and 'occult' powers are endless.

When the ajna center is opened, we experience the 'thought form' itself becoming one with it through feelings or experiences. With the ajna/agnya chakra, the past can be nullified for 'the Karmic debt to be paid'. The future can be brought into the immediacy of the ever present 'now'.

The present is the only space, time and energy portal through which physical, emotional and energy forms are manifested. Man-ifest-ing visions and desires uses this third (inner) eye to do so immediately. With the third eye, one can accomplish much. This center uses the ultimate Power we connect to. If it is misused, by misaligned intentions and other disconnections, then there is destruction. Nature uses de-con-struction. *To do what? Create!*

We are taught to be afraid of it. It is part of the creative process. If we use the transcendental, ultimate, Power with harmonized intentions, properly and divinely, then it will be the greatest blessing you can ever imagine.

This is the center for Clairvoyance, Visualization, imagination and intuition. Seeing clearly demands sharp focus and deeply felt intentions with acute visual intelligence. Transcending space is the result of very intense internalization. Keeping the 'big picture in mind' reinforces the mental blueprint, for transforming matter into three dimensions by attracting the proper electro-magnetic vibration's mapping of the thought form.

The Creative Praxis: Psychology

Correspondence is the relationship between mentalism and imagination: the 3rd eye consciousness, the pituitary gland, visualization & INTUITION are vital to this center.

5. Spiritual Principles:

Vishuddha is the (throat) chakra with the capacity to offer divine messages to the world. Universal nature discloses hidden mysteries to the seeker. When this center is open, one receives codes directly from the highest waves breaking down frequencies with pinpointed details and delivering the messages to other centers needed. One can become a poet, a singer or an artist. All forms of art are expressed from this center.

Universal Principles Applied:

Related concepts are: Clairaudience, Symbolic Intelligence, language – the use of words and speech, telepathy, the refined use of power rather than brute force and the Use of symbols to create meaning and attract matter.

The Creative Praxis:

Polarity the throat, the thyroid and parathyroid glands, and communication: "When we talk to ourselves, we think. When we talk to others we communicate."

4. Spiritual Principles:

Anahata is the heart center. The anahata center has free access to visible and invisible worlds. Time and space are transformed and is subjective. In the anahata center, one can enjoy the deepest bliss of oneness and be in pure Joy, fusing one's consciousness with what one sees. The heart, which embodies the universal Consciousness is a divine heart.

The 'spiritual heart' is not the heart that we find in our physical body. The spiritual heart is a higher universal super Consciousness itself. We always say that there cannot be anything superior to the universal Consciousness. The spiritual heart, houses the universal Super Consciousness. This anahata center is very safe when we use it to identify ourselves with the vast and intense beauty of nature.

Universal Principles Applied:

Compassion, LOVE, Relational Intelligence, the ability to be one without merging, true rapport and attunement with another Creating unity, common cause with others, healing through empathy, creating community. The Creative Praxis: rhythm: the heart, the thymus, love (feelings) Thymus Gland.

3. Spiritual Principles:

Manipura, the Solar plexus chakra, transmutes sorrow and suffering. No matter what happens in life, sad or miserable feelings vanish. But this center like the svadhisthana chakra can create problems. This center can create suffering for others if one misuses the power of the manipura chakra. This center, like the ajna chakra, is clairvoyant. This center also gives one the power of transmutation and power to transform the physical world. This center has healing power.

Universal Principles Applied:

Clairkinesis, Creative Intelligence, the use of force, psychokinesis, psychometry, healing, manifestation in the physical world using physical energy, force and power.

The Creative Praxis:

Vibration: the solar plexus, fire the adrenal and Pancreas, Suprarenal
(Adrenal) Glands.

2. Spiritual Principles:

Svadhisthana, the spleen (Sexual-Gender) chakra is another power center of love. When it is opened, the sex forces will try to lower the consciousness of the seeker. The anahata or the heart center will transform this impurity into purity. Purity is eventually transformed into ever-fulfilling and everlasting divinity.

Universal Principles Applied:

Clairempathy, Logic Intelligence, Emotional human intelligence for understanding behavior, manifesting desires, logic, mechanical intelligence and functions.

The Creative Praxis:

Gender: the sacral or sexual center, water, the gonads – ovaries and testes, energy generation, gender – male and female physiology and flavors along with symmetry laws to make parts whole. The Testes, Ovaries, Uterus.

1. Spiritual Principles:

Mastery over the muladhara (root) chakra, controls the will. One can conquer diseases, know whatever one wants to know and discover whatever one wants to discover. If one wants to know HIMHERIT's Compassion, Light and Love will let him do so. This power can also be misused.

Universal Principles Applied:

Clairsentience, Body or physiological Intelligence, Survival instinct, finding our way in the physical world.

The Creative Praxis: cause and effect, the earth, the periodic table of elements, the root, material matrix – tools for the Dao D$_E$Sign, the behavior of mechanical and dynamic correspondences with parts, elements and geometry all to support movement in all three dimensions.

The 3 Nadis:

In addition to the seven chakras of the subtle body, the 'Tantras' have been described as a network of subtle channels known as nadis through which the life force (prana) circulates. Nadi means "stream". According to the tantric treatise Shiva Samhita, there are fourteen principal nadis. Of these, Ida, Pingala and Sushumna are considered the most important.

Ida is the left channel. It is white, feminine, the repository of habits, memories and conditionings, and cold. It represents the moon, and is associated with the river Ganga (Ganges). Originating in Muladhara, Ida ends up in the left nostril. Pingala is the right channel. Pingala is red, masculine and hot. It represents the sun and is associated with the river Yamuna. Originating in Muladhara, Pingala ends up in the right nostril.

Sushumna is the central channel and is associated with the river Saraswati. Within the Sushumna nadi, there are three more subtle channels: Vajra, Chitrini and Brahma nadis through which Kundalini moves upwards, running up the body from just below Muladhara chakra to Sahasrara chakra at the crown of the head.

The kanda in Muladhara chakra is the meeting place of the three main nadis, known as Yukta Triveni (Yukta: "combined", tri: "three", veni: "streams".) In Muladhara, Shakti, the static unmanifested Kundalini, is symbolized by a serpent coiled into three and a half circles around the central axis Svayambhu-linga at the base of the spine. The serpent lies blocking the entrance to Sushumna, the central channel, with his mouth. Sushumna remains closed at its lower end as long as Kundalini is not awakened.

The technique of Kundalini Yoga consists of using Prana (the vital air), and guiding its circulatory movement through Ida and Pingala down to the base of the spine into the space where Kundalini lies coiled. The vital energies of the opposite forces circulating in Ida and Pingala will be unified and Shakti Kundalini will then awaken and rise up Sushumna, energizing the seven chakras. From Muladhara chakra, Ida and Pingala alternate from the right to left sides at each chakra until they reach Ajna chakra where they meet again (crossing) with Sushumna.

In Ajna/Agnya chakra the meeting of the three main nadis is called Mukta Triveni (Mukta: "liberated"). Continuing beyond Ajna chakra, Ida and Pingala end in the left and right nostrils respectively. Once the Kundalini Shakti has ascended through Sushumna to Sahasrara, the highest psychic center at the crown of the head, it is made to reverse its course and return to rest in the base center again.

The seven kundalini poems (Uni-Verses)

7. The Sahasrara chakra as the crown

Blissfully enjoyed with its opened ways.
A state of inseparable oneness, interwoven with the ever-transcending Beyond says;
We always deal with Infinity, Eternity, Immortality
ALL in ALL in ALL consciousness is reality.

Of all the centers highest is this most peaceful, The most soulful and fruitful is in Sahasrara. Here Infinity, Eternity and Immortality come to source in creation with the one. Clairprescienced and reawakened not by our reasoning in thought or logic or deduction Reading the akashic records to unseal all eternal data on HIMHERIT'shard drive live.

If not of the world, transcending things and time while creating through MENTALISM and deep mind

In a rooted sense of oneness, dissolving, illusion of some kind boundaries of consciousness in my conditioned human brain three parts harmonized reptilian mammalian still remain below The neocortex crowning seated in the ether of a pineal soul.

6. Agnya, brow's this chakra to destroy all darkened pasts, to hasten a golden future that can never last; for certain To manifest the present in four supremely fulfilling ways.

Clairvoyance, Visualization, imagination and in-tuition not afforded. The anahata 'love' and feeling node reality tests all the 'fulfilling' Psychic and 'occult' powers of endlessness.

The opened ajna centers the above and below 'thought form' being itself becoming one with feelings in this ajna time-space, Nullified past; 'the Karmic net is cast'. The future is not swayed from bringing into immediacy; the ever present 'now'.

Pre sent in space, time and energy a portal birthing physical forms
Visions Achieved desires received the third eye to perceive
All conceived in now with the darkest past then destroyed.
Patience need not apply to work here with 'HIMHERIT' With the third eye wide open, one can accomplish much.

If the ultimate Power is misused, with intentions confused with the third eye's transcendental Power abused, all is in destruction if the third eye is used properly With divine alignments set not on property alone More blessings humanity imagined is now our own Seeing clearly with intelligence transcends space Seeing big picture use of vision referencing to grace The mental blue print meditatively turning into place beyond dimensions attracting magnetic vibration in correspondence; with the pit of uitary in unity to visualize, imagine and be in-tu-it-ion.

The ition that's it's in-tu needs no perspiration to
Become the Creative Praxis of and for Creation.

5. Spiritual Principles:

Vishuddha is the (throat) chakra with the capacity For messages to divine the world in its Universals Nature discloses hidden mysteries to the seeker. When this center is open, one receives the codes from the Highest and becomes the communicator From the Highest callings to poets, singers and artist. All forms of art are expressed from this center.

Clairaudience, Symbolic Intelligence; the use of words and speech, telepathy, use power rather than brute force.

The Use of symbols create meaning and attract matter, power vs. force, polarity the throat, air the thyroid or communication:

When we talk to ourselves, we think. When we talk to others we communicate.

4. Spiritual Principles:

Anahata is of two hearts with free access to the visible and the invisible worlds. Time and space are transformed and is subjective. In the anahata center, one can enjoy the deepest bliss of oneness and be in pure Joy. Becoming one's consciousness is its employment

The heart is a divine heart dancing to consciousness music. The 'spiritual heart' is not the valentine body part.

The spiritual heart is even larger than Consciousness itself.

We always say that there is no such thing more superior to the universal Consciousness, but this is not so oh no!

The spiritual heart, lives in the universal Super Consciousness.

This anahata center is very safe when we use it to identify ourselves with the vast and intense beauty of man and universal nature. Compassion, LOVE, Relational Intelligence, The ability to be one without merging, true rapport and attunement with another Creating unity in on common cause with others through healing With empathy for symmetry while creating community.

The heart rhythm vibrates through the thymus gate

For love and feelings to never be too late.

3. Spiritual Principles:

Nabhi, the Solar plexus chakra transmuted sorrow and suffering.

No matter what happens in life, sad or miserable feelings distributed. But this center like the svadhisthana chakra is a reputed trickster.

This center creates suffering for others when power is misused.

This center manipura chakra like the ajna, is cleverrant and clairvoyant. This center also gives one the power of transmutation and power to transform the physical world.

This center has healing power

Clairkinesis, Creative Intelligence, the use of force, psychokinesis, psychometry, healing, manifestation in the physical world using physical energy, force and power vibration: the solar plexus, fire the adrenal & pancreas Pancreas, Suprarenal (Adrenal) Glands

2. Spiritual Principles:

Svadhisthana, the spleen (Sexual-Gender) chakra is the love power center. When opened, the sex forces will try to lower the seeker's consciousness. The anahata center's spiritual heart will transform impurity into purity. Purity is eventually transformed into ever-fulfilling and everlasting divinity. Clairempathy, Emotional Intelligence, emotional intelligence for using the emotion, manifesting desires.

Gender: the sacral or sexual center water the gonads; ovaries & testes energy generation, gender: male & female physiology and flavors along with symmetry laws to make parts whole the Testes, Ovaries, Uterus.

1. Spiritual Principles:

Mastery over the muladhara (root) chakra, controls the will and truth. To conquer dis-eases, knowing whatever one wants to know or to discover the innocence one wants to recover. Or we may discover HIMHERIT's compassion, in the Light and might and Love, This power can be misused when he cannot do so often in mistaking. Clairsentience, Body or physiological Intelligence, Survival instinct, find the way in the physical world cause and effect forgiving the earth, the periodic table of elements, the root, material matrix; tools for The Dao DeSign. The behavior of mechanical and dynamic correspondences with parts, elements and geometry to operate as movement in all the multiplicities of dimensions.

THE 3 NADIS

"Streams" of consciousness are in true conscious light. The seven candles of the subtle body bright says Tantra Network channels of subtlety flow through the nadis Queen Prana flows thru her Nadi in Shiva Samhita accord, With the other fourteen nadis lords. The princess Ida, with Prince Pingala and King Sushumna are the royal three. Princess Ida; the cold, left, white, feminine channel, habits memories, conditionings by the Ganga Ganges moon, Originating in Muladhara to the left nostril.

Prince Pingala the hot, right, red, masculine channel. Basking in the sun light by the Yamuna river flows. Origin-ating in Muladhara, Pingala to the nostril right. Sushumna's central channel is the river Saraswati's flow Within the Sushumna nadi lives the Vajra, Chitrini and Brahma nadi; three more subtle channels growing Through which Kundalini moves upwards running up

The body from just below Muladhara chakra to chakra
Sahasrara at the crown heading to pure blissness.

THE CONSCIOUSNESS STORY

DESIGN SCIENCE IN THE NEW PARADIGM AGE

The kanda in the Muladhara chakra is the meeting place of the royal family as the main nadis, Yukta Triveni.

The "three"main"streams" In Muladhara, Shakti,

The static unmanifested Kundalini, is the serpent coiled into three point five circles around the central linga axis Svayambhuin returning to the cauldron's etheric flames. The guardian of the entrance to Sushumna,

Is the central channel with his closed mouth staying at its lower end in Kundalinic slumber. The vital air of Pranain vibrational movement go Through Ida and Pingala down to the cauldron Where Kundalini lies coiled in electric space. Circulating vital energies of all the dual forces

Ida and Pingala unified in Shakti Kundalini
Awaken arisings up the Sushumna energizing
Seven of the seven Aquarian candles of the Christ.
From Muladhara chakra, Ida and Pingala alternate from the right to left sides at each chakra
Reaching Ajna where they meet again at the
Junction of Sushumna.
In Ajna chakra the meeting of the three nadis
Liberate the soul through Mukta Triveni

With Ida and Pingala flowing past the Ajna chakra Ending in the left and right nostrils respectively. Kundalini Shakti ascends all seven centers

From Sushumna to Sahasrara, moving to The highest psychic center at the crown, Reversing cycles resting in Muladhara's flow.

The Summary of the Design Matrix

Centers	Attributes	Tasks	Revisions	Satisfaction
The Crown Neocorte x The Pineal Gland Ether	Thought, Creative and Critical Thinking Cognition, Intelligence Access to creative Universal Source "Akasha"	Meditation, Recognizing needs, Developing ideas, concepts, processes Access to intuitive genius and solutions	Revise or Redesign when, ideation fails	Aesthetic pleasure and attraction Self-esteem enhancement Rethink if not satisfied
The 3Rd Eye The Pituitary Gland	Feelings, Presence and Karmic Balance and Harmony Visualization, Imagination	Visioneering Imagineering Conceptualizing making the Abstract real. Media arts presentations for heart and love reality testing. Media Articulation	Revise or Redesign When visualization and all other forms of Communication and media expression fail	Fulfillment alignment with Vision and other expectations Correspondence with (Mentalism) or mental functions

Throat The Thyroid and Parathyroid Glands Air	Telepathy, Verbal Intelligence, Literacy and effective communication Work Power vs Creative Mentality and Mental Acuity Power vs Force	Self-Talk is Thinking Talking to others is Communication symbolic, graphic and visual media definitions. All art forms are applied as needed. Describe needs and Articulate in all media	Revise or Redesign based on response to reality heart testing and aesthetic pleasure levels and attraction	Approval and agreement Decoding messages and Fundamental natural laws to be applied to true innovation and originality.
The Heart Thymus	The biological Heart and the Spiritual Heart- Identity creation, presence, personality and style The Dao DeSign Paradigm as a spiritual resource.	Love Compassion passion Sex and Gender functions Align physical, psychological rituals adding ergonomic experiences, traditions and related solutions to Design Using inspiration as fuel to energize and maintain all work	Emotional Changes of heart and other psychic and creative intensions and expectations. Return to earlier stages to revise and redesign	Passion ART-iculated and appreciated, adding value and convenience as a form of environmenttal, emotional and aesthetic satisfaction healing. Self-esteem enhancement The Joy of Positive Design Results Aesthetic correspondence.
The Solar Plexus Solar Energy the Adrenal Gland Pancreas	Human creative energy, Talent and Creative capital genius, healing vs pain	Transforming the world through design excellence, ethics and higher conscious values	Revise as needed	Excellent Design, healing psychological, mental, spiritual, emotional

THE CONSCIOUSNESS STORY   *D~E~SIGN SCIENCE IN THE NEW PARADIGM AGE*

The Sexual Center Water Ovaries and Testes	Reproductive Sex and Symmetric Gender	Passion, Gender; using male and female principles for mechanical utility, symmetry laws logic and mechanical advantage	Revise as needed	Purity vs Impurity Divinity vs Carnality
The Root Earth	Materials, Processes, Elements, Technologies Physiological Intelligence	Transform all materials into raw products	Revise as needed	Reward The proper use of materials to correspond with the needs, vision and intension Making the abstract real to conform to the law of cause and effect.

"Every explicit <u>duality</u> (multiplicity) is an implicit unity."
Alan Watts
All is one! h. g. bennett

CHAPTER FOUR   CUBEOCTAHEDRON H_AO_TH

4. Spiritual Principles:

Anahata is of two hearts with free access to the visible and the invisible worlds. Time and space are transformed and is subjective. In the anahata center, one can enjoy the deepest bliss of oneness and be in pure Joy. Becoming one's consciousness is its employment.

The heart is a divine heart dancing to consciousness music. The 'spiritual heart' is not the valentine body part.

The spiritual heart is even larger than Consciousness itself. We always say that there is no such thing more superior to the universal consciousness, but this is not so oh no!

The spiritual heart, lives in the universal Super Consciousness.

This anahata center is very safe when we use it to identify ourselves with the vast and intense beauty of man and universal nature.

Compassion, LOVE, Relational Intelligence, The ability to be one without merging, true rapport and attunement with another Creating unity in common cause with others through healing.

With empathy for symmetry while creating community. The heart rhythm vibrates through the thymus gate

For love and feelings to never be too late.

CHAPTER 4 TRINE A
THE PRAXIS OF CONSCIOUSNESS

TRANSITIONS TO NEW TECHNOLOGIES SUPPORT real world lifestyles. Here we go from theory to practice "making the abstract real". This is the pattern we follow throughout this conversation.

Consciousness, by definition, is comprised of the physical, or physiology, the emotional or psychological and the spiritual dimensions or creative work-energy in harmony. The goal is to have all three dimensions evolve and be harmonized for humans to reach their highest states of being and becoming. The universe or forces greater than ourselves, to which we give many names, is constantly at its highest state/s hoping that at some point or stage, in our covenant with it, we will keep our end of the deal, which is to harmonize and, at some point, be one with it for ALL to be in divine order.

We made other choices and have focused on the physical to greater degrees than on other flavors of this all-powerful and omniscient dynamic of which we are an intricate part. What we do to it, we do to ourselves. We cannot deny the order or harmony that was intended. Being disobedient to what created us, will cause us to short change ourselves and sabotage our potential of reaching the bliss we were promised. We are now faced with the possibility of total demise. But all is not lost nor is it all gloom and doom. There is hope. It springs eternally from the self-regulating and regenerating, kind and forgiving love that keeps burgeoning from itself and perhaps, incidentally, to us. It keeps on giving us its abundance, its intelligence, its energy and all the principles and resources we do not understand or use properly. We have mastered the physical – material expressions and by extension a world that is experienced by survival instincts mostly. We focus on limited emotional states to satisfy our material needs, not expanding our psychological 'consciousness' to the degree that we have expanded the physical.

The spiritual or creative energy dimensions – the third flavor is another story. The 'spiritual' is that state, flavor or dimension with disconnection. What does this all mean and how do we put this into some context that informs and teaches us to relate to the emerging paradigm shifts with which we need to resonate with now.

We are in an 'exponential evolution' with exponential 'disruptive power'. Continuing to unfold, the evolution is impacting consciousness and nature. The disruptive revolution relies on us to change our mindsets to embrace and manifest the WIKI this opportunity offers us, and the world, holistically. Our mental and creative capacity will expand as we tap into a SOURCE of genius that, when ART-iculated usefully, will reveal an abundance of ideas, technologies and solutions we need. With a bit more personal growth, what is now "exponential," grows even greater. We are living in an exciting time with phenomenal possibilities. We need to understand how to develop appropriate methods for processing the information and ideas that inundated us. A 'matrix of use', similar to our periodic table of elements, will help us encode the qualitative and quantitative information as the framework we put in place, that is very different than the scaffolds (old Paradigms) we used to build the mental processing structures that helped us understand ourselves and the world in which we lived. Mental, structural clusters of psychological and spiritual constructs are the pillars of the foundation needed to create the new world view.

It will align with the new paradigm information, ideas, designs and realities. When our support systems begin to become obsolete, as they are now, it's time to act on synthesizing the new knowledge for growth and development, not as survival mechanisms, or socio-political development strategies this time around but as symmetry principles for living and loving fully, abundantly and passionately.

It's time for achieving our highest states of consciousness to transform our environments and our lives if we truly want to create the forms, the ways and the means to sustain the viable communities we need at all levels possible. Old brooms are not going to sweep homes clean this time. A new mindset is needed for the time-space, creative energy, passion and thoughts continuum that the new paradigm is presenting to us.

This is exciting stuff. Industries, professions and skills will be morphed into the appropriate and effective technologies, models and methods for ART-iculating new forms. The premise, therefore, is a structural philosophy that begins to reexamine the structural relationships we experience and can express.

At the root of this transformation there is a structural and visual language describing new geometric interpretations of 3 dimensional forms that are transcendental and consistently sustaining our thoughts and ideas through time, space and energy. As we use and perfect these basic skills, we will understand our physiology, psychology and spirituality. This leads to an essence and flow of consciousness and the oneness we should reflect. Disciplines that stand the test of this transformation or socio-cultural and political 'morphology' in transformation would have viable systems to apply to their respective disciplines to create solutions that "make the abstract real" or manifest them. Realities are distilled or crystallized with new identities and forms of expression.

The ubiquitous architecture of the old paradigm is transformed into D$_E$Sign Science and is extremely helpful. As an architect, Artist, Industrial Designer, inventor, cultural activist, author and educator I am very interested in developing the synthesis of these disciplines, and others, into an industry to create environments, products and solutions with the highest and best use, flexibility and economy for families in the US and eventually the world. Knowledge derived and applied from other disruptive opportunities and qualitative experiments, through further research and study, will generate a steady flow of the WIKI. We will create a healthy pace for rapid momentum building which will produce results, effects and outcomes that are much more useful and of greater values.

The inherently 'visual' disciplines I am engaged in create the framework for design research. It reinforces the understanding of true needs, discovering symmetry principles that are applied to synthesizing design theories for practical solutions in the paradigm shifting realities evolving now. D$_E$Sign Science and the ubiquitous spiritual faculties as the vehicles for viable Solutions for the internal and built environments 'new paradigm designers' experience.

For me inventing new 3D Non-Euclidean form vocabularies is validation of this new paradigm 'spirit' with its new identity and aesthetic values. Design applications in many, if not all, of the life support and manmade environments would benefit from this 'form, image and media enrichment technology'. This is a fundamental and structural disruptive technology that requires some serious promotional, educational support and "LEGACY FUNDING" capital to establish it in perpetuity. That we are ahead of the events in ecliptic terms is fine with me. It allows for ample preparation. Shifting mindsets is a time consuming business.

The perception is that 'Nonprofit driven' angel and philanthropic sources of funding tend to inspire creative freedom. The business opportunities are to be explored in a different forum. We will pursue and develop other disruptive 'technologies' for creating, operating and managing the financial management systems technologies and solutions for creating services, communities and homes to eventually generate true wealth for families.

Our mission is to increase the speed of technological development inspired or forged by the paradigm shifts and the wealth of knowledge, opportunities and exponential values readily available to work with and to be shared with other organizations, partners and developers to create the new future. This relates specifically to our legacy building partners/funders who, by aligning with this innovative industry and how we position it, would realize all the benefits the social, cultural and economic capital they will enjoy. Our idea bank or data base will be the research and development resource with intellectual properties and trade secrets to be made available to other industries and partners leveraging what we learn and share through joint Ventures and Collaboration with our Design Research, Design Science and Ubiquitous Architecture.

We are interested in creating a future industry now to anticipate and embrace all disruptive technologies that will transform, enhance, redesign, re-engineer and re-create other industries. With these proprietary form technologies, we invent and control, we will expand into (direct or contract) manufacturing of the accessories, appliances and equipment needed and other creative objects for our developments.

Our paradigm shifting technologies, community building philosophies, systems and strategies will add value to the manmade environment and will enhance peoples' lives.

We provide cost effective homes and other forms of accommodation to create wealth for families. They will enjoy the exciting, unique and aesthetic (newly-branded) accessories and furnishings we design and produce for their comfort, enjoyment, healthy and productive lives. Long-lasting quality designs conserve energy and inspire us to create sustainable solutions and can save the planet.

At the exponential rate at which technology is emerging and evolving today, home production is ripe for this creative and disruptive transformation we are qualified and passionate to offer and implement.

The core values and unique aesthetic flavors that inform this transformation that we bring to this 'industry of the future', is the application of recycled shipping containers for the structure of the new and exciting homes. The unique application of materials and flexible design solutions along with the invention of our 3D Non-Euclidean form vocabulary and the systems we use to produce the quality products and projects emerge from our response to the emerging paradigm. Design ideas, inspiration and aesthetic flavors we encode with our creative applications – creative, commercial and industrial products and public and private ART works become the cultural language we identify with spirituality.

The classic metaphor for innovation in many disciplines and in popular culture is the ubiquitous use of the moniker *'Architecture',* once considered 'the mother of the arts' and the best 'well-rounded' education one can get. Not everyone is convinced that the theory that 'everything has an architecture of everything', relies on a 'D$_E$Sign Science' that Richard Buckminster Fuller proposed in 1957.

It is fitting that this is now a true, sustainable profession evolving into the vehicle for making the synthesis of the many disciplines that these 'industries in their future' in a default collaboration morphs into 'UBIQUITY'. No more sticks and stones.

It is a D$_E$Sign Science that will blend the arts, mathematics and traditional sciences into an effective and creative framework with tools of various kinds. The computing power is our ally. 'Mr. Moore never thought his prediction would last 50 years. *Who is Mr. Moore?*

In 1965 the American engineer Gordon Moore predicted that the number of transistors per silicon chip would double every year. He expected "The growth pattern to grow from about 60 elements on an integrated circuit to 60,000—a 1,000-fold extrapolation over 10 years, similar to what has been going on for the last 50 years."

We witnessed the newspaper, publishing, music, movie, and advertising industries get sucker-punched by the internet partly, but primarily by a lack of vision and conditioned mindsets with old paradigm fear-based economies. Fortunes, careers, and industries were lost and new ones made. Many industry "experts" were ignorant or skeptical of the coming internet. Their ignorance of the systems and mechanisms of action ruined their companies as they clung to their comfort zones and old-school business models (old paradigms). The world benefited because of the disruptive technologies made available with the help of the internet. The people who knew about how to use these technologies rode the wave of financial success.

The Speed of change is exponential. The amount of technological advancement that occurred in the year 2000 was created every 1 hour and 6 minutes. It will occur every 30 seconds in 2020. Can industries develop the capacity for 'the infusion of Paradigm Shifts or changes? We know which industries are candidates for disruption. Do we have the insight and foresight that will keep us relevant in the next three to five years or more?

THE PRAXIS OF CONSCIOUSNESS   D_ESIGN SCIENCE IN THE NEW PARADIGM AGE

Medicine, manufacturing, and transportation, are rapidly and profoundly changing into instant, personalized, autonomous (self-sufficient), inexpensive, and free product and service-based industries. Housing and community building have to rapidly and profoundly change into instant, personalized, autonomous (self-sufficient), inexpensive, socio-cultural creative products and service-based industries.

NEW PARADIGM OPPORTUNITIES:

- Medicine: [Healing] The recently released *medical tricorder* prototype and *IBM's Dr. Watson in the Cloud* will make most hospital, healthcare, and doctor's services obsolete. We need to provide an *IBM Watson* link to the 55+ homes in our communities to monitor and provide health care Services and treatments. Regenerative, genomic, Nano, cybernetic, and open source medicine have changed the goal of healthcare from a late stage treatment industry into a pre-disease preventative, regenerative, healthy longevity-based industry. There is a cause and effect correlation with longevity and housing needs. When people live longer, their homes must be better built, be more sustainable and maintenance free. They must also be smart and energy efficient now with the information and technology infrastructure needed to complement their lifestyles. In 55+ communities the need for incorporating health care services is critical.
- "WealthCare™ is the system of financing management and financial growth opportunities offered to homeowners and other investors needed to build "conscious communities".
- How this will be done requires a holistic, systemic and modular approach with production plants, production facilities and distribution networks. Manufacturing: 3D printing has given companies the ability to manufacture the most complex designs in their products while keeping the cost the same as that of manufacturing the design of a brick. In other words, complexity has become the bonus with 3D printing.
- To this we will add ornamentation and other aesthetic elements that have been removed (simplified) from buildings. This simplification or 'DE ornamentation' also took with it the talents of crafts people. We no longer have the skills required to embellish our homes. Today's handheld 3D scanners can give everyone the ability to personalize their products or help reverse-engineer an existing product.
- Computer-aided design (CAD) software allows files to be transmitted so the prototype or product can be printed thousands of miles away. CAD software programs are starting to use natural language descriptions to add qualities and features to existing designs, making it easier to personalize products. The combination of these advanced 3D printers, 3D scanners, CAD software, and print anywhere capabilities is starting to replace overseas manufacturing with 'US MADE' products with faster deployment, less transportation, reduced warehouse storage costs, Bespoke – personalized products, *and less pollution*.
- Atomically precise manufacturing circa 2020's will create personal desktop factories. We will provide space, energy and support services in our homes for this production function. Here is the next revolution! It's not industrial by any stretch of our consciousness. It's "mental and SPIRITUAL".

- Generic Manufacturing: Our multi-dimensional thinking imagines needs and technologies that very often share common features, resources and characteristics that present the opportunity for creating new systems. A generic "all done by one facility" with virtual or physical capabilities is one very viable solution for future production from prototype to on-demand or with in-line capacity.
- Transportation: Transportation services and car companies – this is the plant model for modular construction, are switching to an accident-free, reduced-energy, reduced-pollution, and reduced- traffic industry with solar, hydrogen, electric, and 100 mpg, intelligent, synchronized, autonomous vehicles.
- Industrial Synthesis: The car and the home will merge as they are designed and built in the future. Most industries are becoming obsolete, which is why as an informed industry with conscious and concerned people we are *redesigning our industry*. Our *organizational development* will allow us to easily create our transitions.

As we now know, the need for individual "Experts", is dwindling. Technology is becoming more social. It relies on community, commons, cooperation, co-creation and collaboration. 'Group thinking' is embedded everywhere *(in the 'IDIOT' Innovative Diffusion on the Internet Of Things)*. Studies are beginning to show how much more effective our collective or group dynamic and consciousness is becoming.

Our smartphones, tablets, glasses, wearable computers, and virtual assistants give us solutions instantly at little or no cost. It's not just about speed or time but rapid compassionate response and timing. The *'internet of things'* is now being embraced throughout the world. The wake of the 'thingification' leaves a trail we are unable to manage properly. We are incomplete, half-cycle beings. Does this reflect our consciousness and our intelligence? Homes are being 3D Printed in China and our 'ant colonies' are still building with post and lintel. Of the 7 Billion people on the planet what percentage of them represents the quota of our total human genius?

Diffusion research goes one step further than two-step flow theory. The original diffusion research was done as early as 1903 by the French sociologist Gabriel Tarde who plotted the original S-shaped diffusion curve. Tarde's 1903 S-shaped curve is of current importance because "most innovations have an S-shaped rate of adoption" (Rogers, 1995).

Manufacturing, medicine, retail, energy, data, analysis, education, and complexity are rapidly becoming personalized, inexpensive, and instantly delivered. This requires existing businesses to adapt their business plan and implement multiple new systems to compete with the personalized rapid deployment and interactive products and services that have become available. Our homes will be internet VI (for Infinity) Ready.

Complexity is the one element in this matrix I disagree with. I think simplicity is the goal, especially in 'good' Design and in life. Isn't our projected escalating computer power capable of dealing with our need to 'simple-fi' and be more organic? This question opens the possibility of a qualitative paradigm to harmonize with the present material proclivities we operate with now.

Business is very personal, subjective and often intimate too!

Our lifestyles, goals, and even the things we were told would happen, and how to make them happen, have all changed. This is the paradigm shift in action and manifested in full bloom. These changes are coming faster and are more dramatic in time-both subjective and objective time. Our personal, social and, financial status can either stagnate and be left behind, or we can choose to look and act on what is happening and flour-ish physically, mentally, and spiritually or be stuck in the paradigm of MONEY and think that our salvation is financial and materialistic only. *This fits into the Physiology, Psychology and Spirituality dimensions or creative energy paradigm that represents the three dimensions of consciousness [Our Philosophy] that is the prime principle that our entire vision and industry is based on and life itself obeys. No-thing can exist without them. This is how we "SYN-THESIZE or enfold these ideas into a holistic theory with real praxis for true healthy living.*

The tools and systems will be made smarter to implement the standards that are being created by those who know what the right components are and when they will be available. Visioneering is essential. This is the age of collaboration where many new relationships will integrate multiple new paradigms to replace the old ones with their existing industries.

What is Disruptive Technology? How fast is it Spreading? Are there any industries untouched by DT's?

The cause of this disruption started with the successful use and acceptance of free constant digital information by everyone with a smartphone, tablet, or computer. Disruptive technology is radically changing humanity faster than we think. These accelerating technologies are growing exponentially every year. Their price performance 2.0 doubles every year, and billions of users are starting to employ these technologies. By combining the timelines with the technologies and new goals that humanity is targeting, we will be able to institute smart changes. This is where forecasting with what used to be called "futurism' is revisited.

My concern is where is the 'spirit' in this creative process? If we define spirit as a higher level of energy as a creative dynamic we know as the life force or source and not religious, we open a new frontier of mind and thought we seem to have avoided thus far.

To benefit from this new paradigm, we must embrace our spirituality. The 'creative community' will be right at home in this discussion and has always been. If spirit is our base or work energy paradigm then we are short-changing our evolution and our lives. The mindset required to effectively implement this agenda is not yet being cultivated widely. What principles, attitudes and systems do we have to implement for this transformation to be expedited? It would seem that we have embraced many of the 'external dynamic' and physical elements, but the internal ones are still sorely lagging. Isn't the net effect of self-development supposed to bridge this gap?

"The following technologies are here today and will be a part of the future: Sensors, nanotechnology medicine, quantum computing, bioinformatics, synthetic biology, robotics, nanobots, artificial organs and senses, ubiquitous knowledge, smart materials, open source software, IBM's Watson, Google search, Siri, Google assistant, computer brain interfaces, telepresence robots, self-aware robots, 3D printing; studio/lab in each home, longevity escape velocity biotech, server farms (the cloud), microelectromechanical systems, smart phones, tablets, cybernetic limbs, medical tricorders, personal genome, genetic analysis, genomic engineering, proteomics, exoskeletons, autonomous machines (cars, planes, insects, rats, birds, weapons, etc.) gene therapy, desktop sequencers, regenerative medicine (regenerating, growing, and printing human body organs), computer made.

Synthetic life, interactive surfaces, Google's Project Glass, Google Fiber, augmented reality, cryogenics, repurposed drugs, nanotubes, Nano-shells, nanoviricides, and smart, interactive, and energy producing walls, floors, countertops, mirrors, doors, and windows all a class of new membranes". What a wonderful world it would be? The timing element and the pace or disruption could catch up with this (scenario) or prediction if the gap continues and the lag is not reduced quickly enough. Adaptation is a new factor for infusion that is not taken into account. The people in those fields will need to adapt into other emerging industries. As a Prosumer™ or an entrepreneur, the best protection is to be educated and informed about the coming changes that may affect the 'widget making-service' livelihood of the folks we care about and serve.

The only reason these changes will happen is that they are so much better than what exists now. These disruptive changes are set to produce abundance throughout the world as products, services, and how we create them continue to grow. They become autonomous with smart technology. The ever 'Emerging Future' offers many services that will help us see, plan, and create a future beyond our wildest dreams, avoiding irrelevance and obsolescence. The other option is to find some ubiquitous critical thinking core WIKI for our mental and passionate 'tool boxes' and be on our way to creative freedom.

Creativity now involves Interpretations of 3 dimensional forms that are transcendental and consistently sustaining our thoughts and ideas through time, space and energy. With our needs to redefine humanity with our creativity, genius and technology we are in an exponential evolution and a disruptive revolution.

THE PRAXIS OF CONSCIOUSNESS   D*E*SIGN SCIENCE IN THE NEW PARADIGM AGE

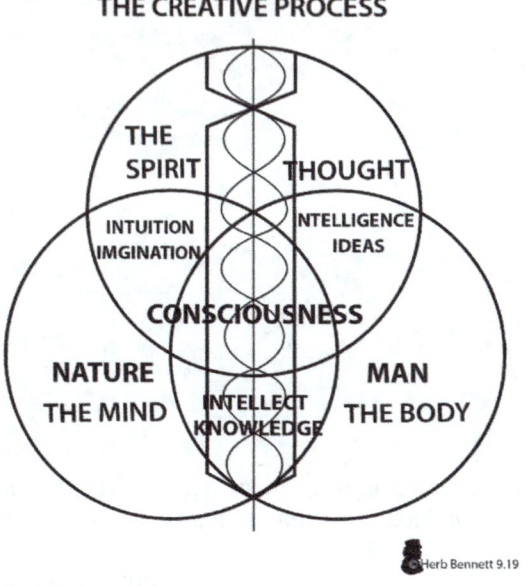

Fig. 8

Consciousness by definition is the physical, or physiology, the emotional or psychological and the spiritual dimensions or creative work energy in harmony.

 *We are creating the future now by blending the best of multiple-related industries, synthesizing and transforming them into powerful and effective paradigm shifting systems, with knowledge, tools and technologies to create a new future for humanity. HGB*

"Let go of your attachment to being right, and suddenly your mind is more open. You're able to benefit from the unique viewpoints of others, without being crippled by your own judgment." —Ralph Marston

CHAPTER 4 TRINE B
ORDER

ARRANGING PROPERTIES, ATTRIBUTES AND FLAVORS of natural phenomena into a quantitative, qualitative and quantum matrix is critical to understanding ourselves and the world with the vast amount of information we *gather, sort and taxonomize,* as we try to understand nature and the bonds we share. A matrix is a form that allows us to put elements into arrays in specific inherent order. Processing them creatively, to reveal information and knowledge using principles and periodicities of 'Natural Phenomena' is critical. The periodic table of elements, created by Russian chemist Dmitri Mendeleev, is an example of such a matrix. Dense material, earth elements belonging to the star stuff of the universe, help creative man encode the form languages, expressions and essences of a mutable reality. Of the 'three worlds' known to sages and philosophers, the physical world (all puns intended) carries more weight in the minds and hearts of most people than the psychological and the spiritual dimensions of consciousness do.

This is a quietly kept secret. It seems there is a 'qualitative matrix' for the infinite 'expressions' of natural phenomena, rituals and energies we all experience. They have 'different elemental periodicities', their own correspondences, affinities, symmetries, principles and laws based on *'Number'*. The three key numbers are 3, 4 and 7. They represent the fundamental qualities in the natural elements of phenomena. Three represents the three expressions, or worlds, of body, mind and spirit with physiology, psychology and spirituality operating with qualities of space, time and energy from the quanta to macro levels of vibration in our universe and in our lives. Four represents the four forces, the four elements of life etc. Seven is the key to the infinite extension of columns of elements, behaviors and suchness that are 7 in number in its hierarchy of sevens, obeying this '7 natural law' with all hidden aspects unfolding in time.

Time is objective, subjective and eternal – in pure duration. What this affords us is a method of organizing or ordering the ever-expanding ken of knowledge we process, not create, to be able to have a better understanding of how nature works, define our purpose and be in harmony. The concepts of time and mind are our *nemeses*. They are the inescapable symbols of our downfall. *Time kills us and mind creates environmental, mental and spiritual pollution.* Time moves our boat along the lotus river of 'birth, decay and death' mind is the current. Ego is the engine, with Shego as his first mate. (Emphasis on mate.) Our definitions of both time and mind do not reflect the intricate relationship they share. For the sake of convenience, we call the physical realm the first dimension of consciousness; the psychological is second and spirit is third. At this time in our evolution humans are primarily first dimension, conscious beings with 'pinches of second and third' added, more for pretense than substance or true flavor. When pure duration approaches Infinite there is 'no time'.

ORDER

DESIGN SCIENCE IN THE NEW PARADIGM AGE

All credit to Vasistha's Yoga for reminding us that "the mind alone is the cause of all objects in the *physical* world" and "three worlds exist because of the mind stuff". The question is, does this describe mentalism, the first symmetry principle? The quest is to find the three worlds, discover what mind is, to understand cause, applications and effects on humans. For the *'thought processing'* (not experimenting) heuristic framework as the first dimension of matter, space becomes pure extension.' Time is 'cision-ed' for us by frequency and measure to be our gauge of cyclical events we repeat.

The second dimension of mind (psychology) with objective time, could be Eternity as pure duration. In time we grow and pattern behaviors into becoming.

The third dimensional energy is pure conscious-ness and pure spirit. Here thought is the finest fuel we use as keys to freedom. Does this work in the Newtonian and quantum worlds with the common pre-sence (s) being (pre-sent) in MAN? In Newton's world man is quite the observer, psychologically and spiritually disconnected (closed thinker) to the task at hand and in mind. In the quantum world there is the observer, the participator, consciousness, uncertainty and quixotic dynamics like wave particle behavioral transpositions and other magical phenomena still unfolding.

Is the pre-sent the 'likeness of creation' beyond us? What other likenesses were made?

The lotus of ORIGINALITY is the *lotus* flower rising above the mud blooming clean and fragrant flavors. The lotus is our original 'metaphor'. *"If there is nothing new under the sun," let's create access to one of the many suns we are discovering in our universe!* Understanding any or everything starts with the desire to understand self.

This is generally done best without the ego to set us free, fearless and focused. Freedom is the key ingredient needed for getting to originality in the three types of expressions in which people in the world engage. Each one is a potential trap which can be sprung if we know how.

There are the physical traps that exist. Some have variations to the existing inventory and the very few that are original. We can elevate the *'nothing new under the sun'* as the emotional (NNUTS) trap from this inhibiting principle that most live by to be free. The spiritual trap is serious. Is 'NNUTS' now a variation or is it original? Can we create a new sun and put some original things under it?

Finding the inspiration: My motivation is understanding the lotuses of 'Consciousness-Originality-Mind and Energy,' (COME). Being – how do things, people and expressions 'come' into being? The paradigms or the creation stories of great civilizations all have spiritual traditions that prepare them for shifting to the crest of the waves of their cultural reality and global presence. The 'lotus' of becoming is a manifestation science that is the inspiration for all types of design in a specific order.

Here are tools for shifting paradigms:

1. Metaphysics: Wisdom traditions and philosophical concepts.
2. Meditation, Intuition and imagination.
3. Cultural information: Oriental and Occidental (Western)
4. Knowledge derived from observation, experiences, participation, collaboration, research, study and critical thinking.
5. Science and technology.
6. The graphic language of visual intelligence, the arts; analog and digital media.
7. Design Science, construction and production technologies.
8. Expressions and disciplines include the arts, science, mathematics especially, Non-Euclidean (or curved) geometry.
9. Celestial architecture is the study of ancient temple sites with astrological links to the heavens, the mysteries of 'origins' and our original beginnings. Applying this knowledge to future architecture is critical.

The word 'come' is inspiring. How did we get here, why did we come and what are we becoming? These are all very challenging *questions* on our *quest*. Coming *to* a place, a state, feeling or thought implies a journey *from* somewhere. FROM when deconstructed is a symbol with deeper meaning. With the 'F and R' removed, 'OM', the universal vibration resonator, is left. This might be a leap but it can also be a mnemonic device.

Traditionally, the comprehension of natural laws is preceded by experiments and discoveries in the 'STEM' paradigm of Seeing, Touching, Evaluating or Estimating, and Measuring. In the intangible and subtle worlds of waves and energies all rules change. If my attention to history serves me well, many of the giants upon whose shoulders we still stand, have changed various paradigms, venturing into the realm of mystery for their discoveries when they could no longer use the knowledge of their time. We are at this point in time again when the paradigm shifts.

The phrase 'Thought-Experiment' is an oxymoron. Thinking, done according to natural law, could be sufficiently organic and spiritually rewarding. There are many higher levels of consciousness that inspire all vibrations of thought. It is the finest fuel known to the universe in many grades, potencies and flavors. Visualization, imagination and thinking rely heavily on all levels and dimensions of 'spirit' for their creative processes.

In this 'thingified' world of ours their products overshadow their processes. Einstein, the star, could use 'thought experiments' and we have accepted it. The '*lotus of our egoless freedom*' allows us to be true to ourselves to think creatively. We discover who we are, were we come from and where we are going.

The Hindu traditions offer us an idea known as the Kundalini as a clue to the mystery of all our 'comings' short, medium and long in the following poem:

ORDER

DESIGN SCIENCE IN THE NEW PARADIGM AGE

"O Devi! Thou art the mind, the sky, the air, the fire, the water, and the earth. Nothing is outside Thee on Thy transformation. Thou hast become Siva's consecrated queen to alter Thy own blissful conscious Form in the shape of the world". It is literally elemental.

Kundalini, the serpent power or the mystic fire, is the primordial energy or Sakti that lies dormant or sleeping in the Muladhara Chakra, at the center of the body. It is called the serpentine or annular power on account of its serpentine form. It is an electric fiery *'occult'* power, the great pristine force which underlies all organic and inorganic matter. What other thought parallels can we find in the western world?

Looking further we read: *Kundalini is the Goddess of speech, (language, symbols, words) and is praised by all. When awakened she offers illumination (light), the source of all Knowledge and Bliss.*

She is pure consciousness; the Supreme Force, the Mother of Prana, Agni, Bindu, and Nada. It is by this Sakti (female quality) that the world exists. Creation, preservation and dissolution are in 'Her'. Only by her Sakti the world is kept up. It is through Her Sakti on subtle Prana, Nada is produced. While you utter a continuous sound or chant Dirgha Pranava! (OM), you will distinctly feel the real vibration starting from the Muladhara Chakra. Through the vibration of this Nada, all the parts of the body function.

She maintains the individual soul through the subtle Prana. In every kind of Sadhana the Goddess Kundalini is the object of worship in some form or the other.

The language of the day expressed the prevailing consciousness creating the culture and the history. What is the quality of the *Time* that is the agent of the flow of consciousness that produces the aesthetic, the symbols and the expressions of any era? Is time for space the same as time for dynamic behavior or time for creative spirit?

Each era has its Body Mind Spirit continuum flavor created by the unique Space Time Energy Paradigm forces of its own nature. There are three numbers in the system of number laws we are focusing on. In all of the above these are the principles at work. The three-number law: The symbol 3, the triad and the trinity, the triplet or third wave. The symbol 4, the quartet or fourth place. The symbol 7, the heptet or seventh place, the wave or Heptave. The other numbers in the 'enneave' 1-Unity, 2-Duality, 5- the symbol of Balance, 6-Creativity, 8-the eight-fold symmetry (way), & 9- Completion relate to other vibrations of creation and consciousness. The 3, 4 and 7-fold vibrations are more directly linked to manifestation. They are at the core of the universal creative process shared with man the physical being-mankind the emotional expression in *sub consciousness* and the spiritual essence or life force of man and all other expressions.

In the realm of vibrations 3 is in the upper register *of super consciousness.*

4 is at the lower register of *normal consciousness or awareness.* In the mid register there is a vibration that serves as the transformational dynamic (of feeling or touch) at the Love center. 3 + 4 =7 the registers are arranged as 3 in the upper, 1 in the mid register and 3 in the lowest range.

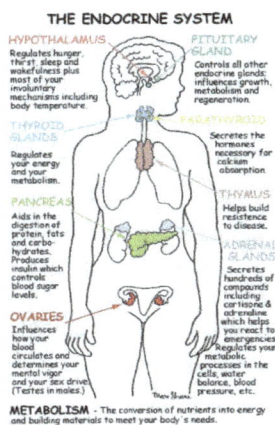

Fig. 9

Insight: it appears that though love is a very powerful force the three upper registers, centers and dynamics with the three lower registers, centers and dynamics are the 6 fold elements of the creative process. This may evade the observer since it is not quite evident. The other significant insight is the control that the solar light force and the power of the eternal breath actually have over the heart. The biological and emotional heart has its own functions and expressions.

The spiritual heart has its own. Is the *solar light force* the biological and emotional heart force and the power of the eternal breath the power of the spiritual heart? The brain has its link to the heart by way of bundles of neurons/ nerves.

The three states permeate all realities in the physical, the psychological and the spiritual expressions of consciousness. The consciousness state of one (ness) which is not the counting 1 of value, 'trifurcates' into three and returns to the consciousness state of one (ness). The returned one might

be on a higher level of vibration or on a higher wave relative to its origin. All expressions follow the natural law of 3-three. When the six centers; the 7 minus the love, are distributed obeying the laws of 4; the 4 forces, the four elements, and all other fourfold symmetry principles and processes. This is the inherent nature of the law of four. There are higher registers above the upper register we are more familiar with. This requires deeper meditation to reach higher levels of consciousness vibrating at the SOL (Speed Of Light) or SOUL: Speed Of Universal Light).

The East West Dichotomy:

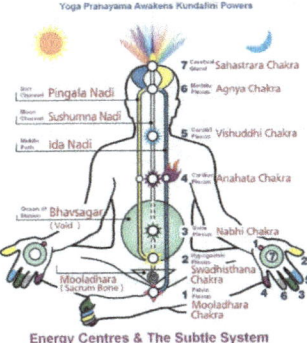

Fig. 10

This system represents the deepest level of our knowledge of the gross nature and fuels of human physiology without the chemical processes, without the electro-magnetic forces, the color, vibrations and the host of flavors involved in the human experience we call life. The Chinese were isolating sex and pituitary hormones from human urine and using them for medicinal purposes by 200 BCE. In 1849 Arnold Berthold pioneered this research. In 1902 William Bayless and Earnest Starling continued the development. Shakti is the female principle of divine energy, especially personified as the supreme deity. This next system represents the deepest level of oriental know-ledge of the subtle nature and fuels of human energies with the chemical-electro-magnetic forces, the colors and vibrations with the host of flavors involved in threefold human experience for the heightened consciousness potential. This system is at least five thousand years old.

ORDER

DESIGN SCIENCE IN THE NEW PARADIGM AGE

The Number Four Law: Four is the realm of manifestation using the laws of 4; the 4 forces, the four elements, and all other fourfold symmetry principles and processes. This is the inherent nature of the law of four.

The vibrations in this realm are slower causing the expressions or effects of density, mass, solidity and physicality synthesized by the forces that keep them in harmony.

The quantum Matter-Energy continuum, like the space-time-energy dynamics, are harmonized into multiple dimensions of organic and manmade (geometric) forms. Forces in the lower register align with the vibrations of "native" elements in correspondence with the symmetry principles that cause matter to be manifested. This manifestation resonates with the upper register of the ideational, visualization and communication intelligences. What's the role of 'love' in this process? How does it relate to 'spirit'?

Is there any connection between Quantum Theory and its 'new paradigm' or world view and the universal energy traditions and systems of the Kundalini? Can we be open enough to at least recognize the possibility that they are models of the same dynamic that we are very intricately a part of as well?

The East-West highway is jammed with shipping containers full of things we have exhausted our emotional and spiritual energy to create, not to mention the natural and human resources we continue to squander.

Where is the love? Lost in the things we covet and use to keep score in some useless game of 'pretend living' with lies we are told for losing our souls.

Love is the transforming manifestation, work (energy) dynamic. The appropriate assignment of masculine and feminine symmetry attributes and characteristics follows. Appropriate geometries and material behaviors then align with symmetry properties and energies to do the work the 'thing form', its use, function and purpose were intended to do, with the matching 'thought form', for the thought of the form to be realized and expressed. Not every thought that's been realized is or can be expressed. We can always approximate the process towards attaining some degree of success. Once we are in the right direction, time and source fill in the details.

THE MYSTERY OF NUMBER

To keep score, we use numbers to measure our progress, not being aware that there are other dimensions of number that if understood and applied will increase our value. Numbers are laws with symmetry and organizing principles that create order in everything we think, say and do.

The Law Seven (7): Seven is an arrangement, agreement and relationship of 3 (not+) but (:) with 4 (3:4) that can be defined and described in multiples of 'qualitative and quantitative interactive expressions. We can do so mathematically, spiritually and emotionally. How would it feel to be 7th in a class of seven? There is a distribution or rhythm and vibration of fundamental properties, behaviors and flavors or essences of the very few elements numbering 3, 4, 6, 7, 9 and 10 combined and permutated to generate the 'Maya' we perceive.

Quantum mechanics tells us that there is no-thing, no time making little or no sense in our Newtonian 'apple struck' mental conditioning. Consciousness is pure extension, pure duration and pure energy that can all fit into a pea. What's the role of the ego in this story? Symbolism, symmetry and the expressions we interpret are at the core of these flavors forming and inspiring languages that are used by the intelligences that create cognition. Each intelligence, language and interpretation can then be described, art-iculated and expressed. The languages, visual, verbal, tactile or touch and feelings, logical, musical, intrapersonal (talking to self or thinking) or interpersonal (talking to others or communication) to harmonize ideation corresponding to different degrees, with manifestation. The Language that started with mentalism, the neocortex, resonates with the fundamental principles of phenomena. The vocabulary and language of thought which form action and process, manifestation and interactions with the internal and external environments are also in coherence.

Man is the creative thought form processor in the universe a *pea in the vast multiverse of simultaneity*.

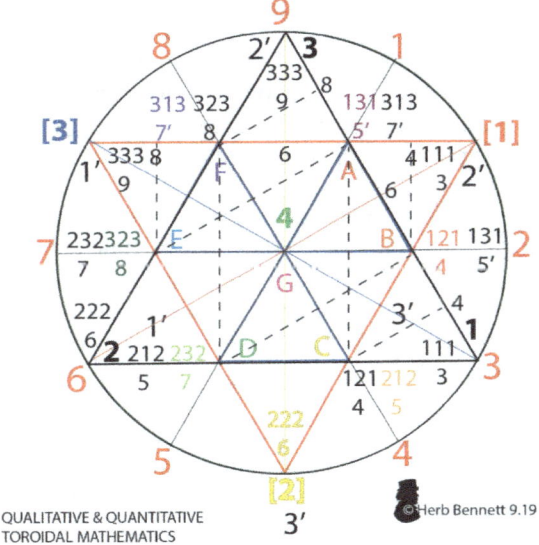

QUALITATIVE & QUANTITATIVE
TOROIDAL MATHEMATICS

Fig. 11

| ORDER | DᴇSIGN SCIENCE IN THE NEW PARADIGM AGE |

THE SYNTHESIS OF THE TOROIDAL AND THE FRACTAL DYNAMIC PRINCIPLESARE ANALOGOUS WITH THE WAVE AND PARTICLE ENERGY FIELDS OF NATURE.

"Music is formless and is therefore the perfect expression of the formless." Innayat Khan"Let go of your ego or shego, and suddenly your mind opens. You're able to benefit from the direct knowledge from source, without being crippled by your negativity." Inspired by Ralph Marston

What if the physicists' paradigm of particle solidity, i.e., the existence of actual "matter", is off? What if, analogous to the "electron", the proton – or the quark, or the string – is just a densely localized positively charged electromagnetic field, fairly stable because it must be in equilibrium with the negative charges of the "electrons" to even exist? The TORIMETRIC™ paradigm says that the universe is electric. That Space is Electricity, Mind is Dielectricity and Spirit is Magnetism. We throw in the Ecliptic and cyclic periodicities into the mix with Energy, light and (rates of) Motion. We then collage our images for higher fractal resolution at infinite levels of magnification to ppreserve clarity and a new paradigm would be born.

Then what we call matter is nothing but electromagnetic fields. There is no matter left. All is energy. The equivalence of matter and energy would be a triviality. Einstein is right but tautological in $E=mc^2$ where gravity becomes a feature of electromagnetism, antimatter is just electro-magnetic fields with reversed polarity, and a Unified Field Theory becomes child's play. Love (the spiritual/ electromagnetic force) transforms it into manifestation through work (energy), the appropriate assignments of masculine and feminine symmetry attributes and characteristics.

Appropriate geometries and material behaviors align with symmetry properties and energies to do the work of the 'thing form', its use, function and purpose were intended to do, as a 'thought form'.

The following dictionary definitions are the conventional concept of 'thought'. Determinism is a theory or doctrine which states that acts of the will, occurrences in nature, or social or psychological phenomena are causally determined by preceding events or natural laws. It also supports beliefs in pre-destination and, by extension, 'destiny'. Acts of the will are thought form concepts of mentalism. The root and the crown are two intelligences or subtle energy centers in the bio, magnetic, electrical dynamic that control the will. Centers of will, vision, communication, love, work, gender and matter motivate and inspire creative action. The universe and all its expressions follow this rule.

From the stimuli to urges we go from 'ought' to think as the intersection of the/and/ought with new paradigm principles. 'Ought' is used to indicate duty or correctness, typically when criticizing someone's actions.

If one is not complying with law or expectation 'ought' justifies criticism. It indicates or 'demands' respect for manmade or natural laws of some desirable or expected state. Taking the initiative to give or ask for advice is a function of 'ought'. Probability, one new paradigm concept, is a quantum concept determined by 'the power of 'ought'.

With the definite article 'the' is added to 'ought' it becomes the word 'the/o/ught', which is contracted into 'thought'. It is traditionally defined as an idea or opinion produced by *thinking* or occurring suddenly [HAP-PENING] as in happy, in one's mind with attention or intention, hope, or the idea of doing or receiving something through the actions and/or processes of thinking.

Anything we ought to say, do or think could be a physical thing or a good. It could also be a good thing that benefits the user or just be done in the spirit of goodness. These are the three dimensions of conscious-ness in action. The linguistic decoding of the impulses and the encoding of the thought with its symbolism, idea or its representation is a function of the neuro transformation or creative process.

Thinking (the gerund) is the brain's 'ram' memory processing data in the present. Thought is past. I 'will think' is an expectation of future. Data is stored on our long-term memory hard drive. The Time-Mind continuum is the next creative process to be considered.

Theory and right (light) vs (dark) action converge in the thought field of interactions that define the creative processes against the background of the polarity and orientation present in the field of thought.

At this point Einstein's anachronistic thought experiments are chronologically inconsistent across the current space-time-mind (consciousness) continuum in 'light' of the new interpretations of consciousness now unfolding. There is nothing new about consciousness. A new construct or framework is in order. Experiments that are mechanistic and S.T.E.M. (See, Touch, Evaluate and Measure) no longer work.

LESSONS AND INSPIRATIONS FROM THE VASISTHA YOGA 'CANON'

Praxis is the method for creating real world solutions based on new paradigms and their theories. The premise is predicated on the new perspectives of the quantum dynamic behaviors of the universe as the macro phenomenon and man as the micro expression of nature.

The macro and micro expressions of consciousness interact with their shared knowledge. It would be reasonable to see how quantum behavior can be experienced, understood and communicated without experiments that are unreliable. We can experience the universe within ourselves and be free of the physical limitations of materiality. Time, matter, space and energy are being reinterpreted and deconstructed to enable us to encode the next iteration of creation. Who or what is doing the interpreting?

ORDER

DₑSIGN SCIENCE IN THE NEW PARADIGM AGE

Mentalism is our incomplete theory of physical and psychological phenomena that does not include spirituality or energy processes, ultimately explicable *only* in terms of a *creative and interpretative mind*. This is problematic here. There are other gross and subtle intelligences that can teach us about life.

Creativity is *ONE* spiritual flavor of consciousness. This all comes after the practice and skill of meditation, which is simply contemplation, thought, thinking and reflection in action. Mentalism and meditation are two creative expressions of mind. Mind has a prolific affinity for art-iculating reality. It does not recognize our potential, with the new freedom that emerges in this 'non-material world', where we can participate mentally. This is not being creative nor is it leading to understanding who we really are – minds and spirits having very physical, egoic and material experiences we hold on to.

In the research into metaphysical contradictions and their mental conditioning results, questions arise about the dialectics of realities, and causes and effects of the new knowledge. Does energy *facilitate the perception or interpretation of the vibration* of matter or vice versa? Concepts like freedom, justice, equity, and a number of social, political, ethical and human issues and values related to personal choices can now be included on the lists of causes based on this new framework.

It opens up a range of dialog and possibilities never before available to most of us. This is what new paradigms do for us.

"*The Lotus River flows between the high mountain and the low delta carrying life from birth to death. In our Piscean story, named after our present epoch, various 'vesica piscis' or fish forms live in its stream. Some, like the salmon, swim against the current upstream to reproduce, answering nature's calling. The bottom feeders are floundering in blissful nescience concerned about meals they missed. The predators, the salmon and the flounders, all in the continuum of 'who eats whom' are all on their path to their inevitability. Are there fish in heaven from all the fishing that's been going on since the original creator of fishers of men did his magic? I am sure Noah saved two, from his mysteriously symbolic cargo, one for himself and one for 'HIMHERIT'.*"

THE UNIVERSAL TRINITIES

In the Hindu triumvirate (or Triad) *Brahma* is the creator of the universe. *Vishnu* is the second god responsible for the upkeep of creation and *Shiva* is destroyer of the world. *Consciousness*, the all omnipresent, omniscient '*cosmic being*', omni-vibrational essence, causes Visnu to arise. From the cosmic being's, heart entire worlds arise. All that arise have the ability to preserve themselves through Visnu.

Out of Visnu arises Brahma who in turn gives rise to the four expressions of animate and inanimate things – sentient, insentient energies and forms, prior to the dissolution. At this point Shiva dances to the music of life and death' Effect and Cause – ease and dis-ease – pain and suffering played out in the lower realms. Here men conjure desires in their hearts building 'air castles' in their minds. The three hearts – the physical, the emotional and spiritual hearts with strong desires and illusions – are rendered onto Shiva because the rewards of little or no self-effort and no right action are Shiva's tools.

Self-effort is the result of knowledge from the good books, instructions from wise teachers and one's own passion, focus and will.

Here is an equation: Fs x Es= Iy x SE – Fruits of endeavors equal the intensity of self-effort. Right actions create positive outcomes.

From Shiva's entrance to now, we are walking a tightrope. We can rise or we can fall. Freedom of choice and will are ours. The outcomes are ours too. However, the creator is compassionate. From HIMHERIT's heart, compassion is extended through Visnu, the up-keeper.

A path is created to remove the *four expressions* of animate and inanimate things – sentient and insentient forms. Each has its own language. Pilgr-images and noble virtues like austerity, charity, truthfulness, righteous conduct, honesty, respect and dignity are but temporary measures. More enduring is *prayer, revelation and knowledge*.

Here are the secrets for getting past the four gatekeepers – 1. self-control, 2. the spirit of inquiry or curiosity and enthusiasm, 3. contentment and 4. good company. These are the creative principles designers use. With a oneness mindset there is no distinction between these forms of communication.

In the western world knowledge feeds our voracious materiality. Prayer is strictly for supplication, and revelation is a book in the bible few truly understand. Of all the sentences in this work, this is the most dispassionate. Entire libraries have been dedicated to how to do the right thing, leaving us on a trajectory to oblivion. From a spiritual (NOT RELIGIOUS) view, every word in this text is a practical, emotional and super energy generator to create the lives we were meant to live. Here is another dedication to the library of human failure celebrating Shiva's triumph.

Experiments that are mechanical are S.T.E.M (See, Touch, Estimate and Measure) no longer work. The Thought S.T.E.M is now (See, Think, Energize and Meditate) with observation and participation.

The search for truth and freedom has an upside and a downside. If in the study of the nature of life we do not find truth or freedom, the process of seeking could still have its rewards. What we discover could soften the pain as changes in life are encountered. Discovering truth and freedom could be the bonus. Wisdom could be gained in either scenario.

Like paying attention, which does not cost anything, except when it is not paid in full, the search for wisdom and freedom costs less and the gain is exponentially greater. There are physiological, psychological and spiritual transformations that follow the eternal creative principles outlined in this work. One of the many goals of this work is the establishment of a *'body, mind and spirit map'* for the journey of self-discovery, self-effort and self-knowing. To enhance our lives, we can transcend all the artificial divisions we encounter. On second

ORDER — DESIGN SCIENCE IN THE NEW PARADIGM AGE

thought maps already exist. In this case a *'body, mind and spirit GPS'* is needed. Fundamental principles and natural laws of the cosmic being in the DNA in us for example, are ready to unfold and no longer be dormant. The awakening is long overdue.

The Dao De Jing was referred to as a canon that inspired the 'Dao DeSign' (system). It is used as an oriental harmonizer for the *'body, mind and spirit'* triad that, in principle, is part of a wider swath of oriental wisdom traditions.

The 'Vasistha's yoga', like the Dao De Jing is the second canon used to inspire the meditation and thought processes from the Hindu tradition.

This storehouse of wisdom by Swami Venkatesananda "provides the means to eliminate psychological conditioning".

The next canon is the *'Temple in Man' and the 'Temples of Karnak' by Schwaller De Lubicz*. This is a three-volume series focusing on the study of the geometric, Kametic Spiritual Design science of temple and celestial architecture. This sets the tone for my Non-Euclidean Geometric inventions and patents. The transition from the pharaonic era in Egypt to the Christian or Piscean age employs one of the key canons of mathematics and geometry for temple building, placing man in a hexagon described by the radius of a circle. In so doing "man is placed under the sky of the temple".

Gauge theories involving the proportions of man as the meter, with space and measure in the western form tradition is art-iculated with the canon of proportions for the human body with the Vitruvian Man by Leonardo da Vinci.

In the second canon, "man is placed on the sky of the temple as the radius of the circumscribing circle".

Fig 12
Vitruvian Man by
Leonardo da Vinci.

I arrived at a similar two-dimensional geometric expression by exploring and modeling, with cardboard, the curved 'interstitial spaces' centered in the voids of spheres in various stacked configurations, starting with the four spheres of the tetrahedron.

I later tested this paradigm shifting thought process by transforming right angle cones into extensions of curved form vocab-ularies conforming to the Non-Euclidean geometries of *Carl Frederick Gauss* (1777-1855), *Nikolai Lobachevsky* (1792-1856), *Janos Bolyai* (1802-1860), and *Bernhard Riemann* (1826-1866). The life of an artist is a process, not an experiment.

I received utility and design patents for these inventions. I was more familiar with R. A. Schwaller De Lubicz's 'number theory' before discovering these two canons corresponding with the two dimensional, curved triangular resolutions of space that were similar to my work.

This research continues to generate insights and innovations in fields beyond my expectation and knowledge. As an artist *first* and an architect I have become an open and curious *'at it dude'* (I miss pelt attitude and recreated myself) is who I have become. (My subconscious is smarter than I am.) As a going 'at it dude' there is no monopoly of knowledge I am attracted to. All fields are open and fair game, especially when I recognize and can interpret visual information I find, using my trained 'eye' or visual intelligence like I did with the Egyptian canons and my other research.

The thread here starts with consciousness followed by energy, mind sciences and spiritual technologies for development. I call it the 'Mechanics of Consciousness'. Translating this knowledge into art and the built environment with celestial alignments will revive an ancient but not a lost science. 'Making the abstract real' is the science of Manifestation working to discover the long lost and atrophied *'barathary gland'* used to conjure form into existence.

In some parts of the world sages and wise men are rumored to still use this practice. What's known of the 'barathary gland' is that it was the gland located in the Hippocampus area of the brain.

It gave Humans four higher senses, which were Psychometry, *(the supposed ability to discover facts about an event or person by touching inanimate objects associated with them),* intuition, clairvoyance, and telepathy.

There are supposed to be higher senses or talents that were abused and taken away from us by the Anunaki. A reader of similar titles to the above, might be familiar with this idea (smile).

The Transformation timelines and benchmarks:

The Age of Pisces is believed to end when the great world Savior' – Christ – arrives and the Aquarian Age begins. Humanity commences its "entrance into heaven", the Spiritual Kingdom.

Geometry no longer measures earth or land. It is a spiritual tuning gauge. Four names (Pillars) - *Carl Frederick Gauss* (1777-1855), *Nikolai Lobachevsky* (1792-1856), *Janos Bolyai* (1802-1860) and *Bernhard Riemann* (1826-1866)

The assumption that the sum of the three interior angles of a triangle can be less than 180° for one identity and also be greater than 180° for another, leads to a Non-Euclidean imploding and exploding curved geometry, quite different from the very neutral, but thoroughly consistent Euclidean geometry. If proven it can be used to create useful forms for our environment. Within the Sushumna nadi there are three subtle channels: *Vajra, Chitrini and Brahma* nadi through which Kundalini moves upwards running up the body from just below Muladhara chakra to Sahasrara chakra at the crown of the head. The nadis are complementary systems with their own exercises and benefits that are part of the 70,000 nadis in the overall network. The battle against ignorance and illusion is something that has to be

ORDER

D$_E$SIGN SCIENCE IN THE NEW PARADIGM AGE

overcome before man can experience the beauty of the Reality of the Spirit. Crossing over from illusion to Reality is known as the Void, or the Bhavasagara (The void or Ocean of Illusion). Is this the electrical model in humans?

An inference is an idea or conclusion that's drawn from evidence and reasoning. An inference is an educated guess or use of our 'Gut'. We learn about some things by experiencing them first-hand.

We gain other knowledge by inference —the process of inferring things based on what is already known. If nothing is known, we may rely on intuition and Natural Laws, Symmetry Principles and other skills that are not part of the western Ken. In the one world we occupy, I see no distinction when it comes to creative solutions, how and where they originate.

7 LAWS of CONSCIOUSNESS: East meets West Movement: Towards a synthesis formula

7 Fundamental interactions of consciousness:

Body: physical form-physiology-space: as pure extension - the reptilian brain

Mind: mental-psychology, behavior subjective time, as pure duration-the limbic or mammalian brain

Spirit: thought, spirituality -energy as pure thought and work-the neocortex

Gravity: as in mass attraction

All things as energy and vibration are brought toward one another – stars, planets, galaxies and even light and sub-atomic particles. Gravity gives weight to physical objects and causes the tides. Gravity has an infinite range. Its effects become weaker on distant objects.

The electromagnetic force: is one of four fundamental forces in nature.

The other three fundamental forces are the strong force, the weak force, and gravity. The EMF can be generated by three types of fields known as the electrostatic field, magneto-static field, and the electromagnetic field. The weak force transmutes quarks. It is involved in many decays of nuclear particles which require a change of a quark from one flavor to another.

The weak force was first revealed in the radioactive beta decay and other decays. It is the Residual strong force that binds protons and neutrons to form atomic nuclei. It is called the nuclear force and is the residuum of the strong interactions between the quarks that make up the protons and neutrons. We define the qualities of the energies as follows: What if the proton is magnetism, the Neutron is Dieelectricity and the Electron is Electricity. What a fine model this would be.

THE QUEST-THE QUESTION AND THE REQUEST:

Can the law of correspondence and all seven laws of nature be at work here also? Can spirituality, physiology and psychology be considered interactions to correspond with the four fundamental interactions for manifestation?

The creative process followed here employs the esoteric knowledge of the chakras and their characteristics to align with the natural and universal dynamic principles to align with creativity.

1. The root: with developed skills and our understanding of materials with all due respect for 'Mother Earth', we consistently produce high-quality original work. We achieve Inner-Direction through self-confidence and Uniqueness. Artists search for and find their creative processes, interests, and rewarding experiences as they impact their environments positively. This leads to a vital state of Inner-direction. Originality is obtained through research, practice, and meaningful experiences through travel, networking and community involvement. Of paramount importance is the consistent search for excellence and the reward of self-fulfillment with financial rewards.
2. THE SEXUAL CENTER: Set realistic Goals and Confront Challenges. I think we all know how to set and achieve goals. Challenges are another story. Diamonds are created with heat and pressure so are artists and designers.
3. THE SOLAR PLEXUS is about energy and work. Expand your Vision and Refine Your Process and Skill Set. Some artists follow some tradition, often multiple traditions. Any artwork you create by might have traditions behind it; or a combination of disciplines.
4. THE HEART: Develop Your Passion with a Unique Artistic Vision with the power of LOVE. Part of what drives us forward is our feelings, our compassion and passion. We become interested in art to fulfill our need to share our joy and love with the world. You will learn new skills and forms of expression as you shine your light in the world through your love of art, design and the people you share them with.
5. THROAT: Communicate with many Sources of Influence and mentors. Align your findings with your vision and identity. Synthesizing multiple sources of influence will lead to more original works. Communication is a form of reality testing.
6. 3RD EYE: Experiment and Capture Random Occurrences. Visualization and meditation are very effective disciplines. Creative play, experimentation and happy accidents can lead to true innovation.
7. The CROWN-MENTALISM: Plan for Originality of Concept and design excellence. What original thoughts or ideas can you synthesize for your life?

What ideas move you? To find your voice or style, explore reading, writing, sketching, 3D modeling or internet research, dialog with other artists and designers, and participate in many forms of 'play' to invite your subconscious to the ideation process.

THE BODY MIND SPIRIT MATRIX

BODY	MIND	SPIRIT
[The purest form;Body's-Body-ies] Space Physical form. Matter-Objects and Things Words 1. *The Root: with developed skills and your understanding of materials with all due respect for mother Earth* 2. The Sexual Center: and the Physiology of Gender for mechanical systems Matter Solid, Liquid, Gas (plasma)	[The body's-mind/s; Physical aspects of MIND] Time Awareness Space; Sense data- Smart materials Structural and Behavioral characteristics and properties Psychology 2. The Sexual Center: and Gender for mechanical functions. Meaning	[The body's-spirit] Energy, Vibration, Integrity Flavors, Creation and Reproduction 3. The Sexual Center: Set realistic Goals and Confront Challenges. I think we all know how to set and achieve goals. Father-Mother-Child Higher Senses Intention
[The Mind's Body-ies]	[The Mind's-Mind/s: Pure Mind] 4. THE HEART: Develop Your Passion with a Unique Artistic Vision with the power of LOVE.	The Mind's Spirit/s or (Creative) Energy-ies [Thought-Form; Mentalism] Intuition

[The Spirit's subtle Bodies]	[The Spirit's Mind/s]	[The Spirit's Spirit/s]
6. 3RD EYE: Experiment and Capture Random Occurrences, Visualization and meditation. Creative play, experimentation and happy accidents can lead to true innovation, Dreams and Astral plane experiences	Subtle interactions and higher behavioral dimensionalities

Expand your Vision and Refine Your Process and Skill Set.

Transformations and alternative states of consciousness

5. THROAT: Communicate with many Sources of inspiration. Align your findings with your vision and identity. Synthesize multiple sources of influence. Communication is a form of reality testing. | Pure Spirit

Thought as the fuel of super-consciousness as the purest and highest degrees of Thought; Mentalism: Subtle Energies essences and higher dimensionalities

3. The Solar Plexus processes energy for doing work.

7. The CROWN-MENTALISM: Plan for Originality What original thoughts or ideas can you conceive? What ideas move you?

'Connect the subconscious to the ideation process. |

The central nervous system (CNS) controls most functions of the body and mind. It consists of two parts: the brain and the spinal cord. The brain is the control center/panel of thoughts.

TIME AS PURE DURATION-SPACE AS PURE EXTENSION-ENERGY AS PURE THOUGHT AND EFFORT ARE PURE QUALITIES OF CONSCIOUSNESS

WHAT IS CONSCIOUSNESS?

Everything that is thought – physical, real, visualized, imagined or dreamt that interacts with gross or subtle psychological (internal or external natural forces) principles and rules expressed as frozen and dynamic forms of spirit; energy, past, present and/or future in the continuum of physical- space articulated through physiology with psychological-time experienced through psychology and spirit-energy interpreted and understood through spirituality, 'ALL' obeying Hermetic laws of mentalism, correspondence, vibration, rhythm, polarity, gender, cause with the bio, energetic, electrical effect is consciousness.

THREE BRAIN LEVELS

FIRST LEVEL BRAIN	SECOND LEVEL BRAIN	THIRD LEVEL BRAIN
The reptilian brain is the oldest of the three brains. It controls the body's vital functions such as heart rate, breathing, body temperature and balance. Our reptilian brain includes the main structures found in a reptile's brain: the brainstem and the cerebellum. The reptilian brain is reliable, but tends to be somewhat rigid and compulsive.	The limbic brain emerged in the first mammals. It can record memories of behaviors that produced agreeable and disagreeable experiences. It is responsible for what are called emotions in human beings. The main structures of the limbic brain are the hippocampus, the amygdala, and the hypothalamus. The limbic brain is the seat of the value judgments that we make, often unconsciously, that exert such a strong influence on our behavior.	The neocortex first assumed importance in primates and culminated in the human brain with its two large cerebral hemispheres that play such a dominant role. These hemispheres have been responsible for the development of human language, abstract thought, imagination, and consciousness. The neocortex is flexible and has almost infinite learning abilities. The neocortex is also what has enabled human cultures to develop.

Like many other natural phenomena related to understanding life, perceptions about consciousness relating to the brain are questions still deeply rooted in our old paradigm mindset. Is there an epi-brain beyond our individual or collective brains that awaits us at our request?

The central nervous system (CNS) controls most (*spiritual/energy*) functions of the body and mind. It consists of two parts: the brain and the spinal cord. The brain is the center of our thoughts, the interpreter of our external environment, and the origin of control over body movement. The autonomic nervous system (ANS) is part of the peripheral nervous system. It regulates visceral functions of the (*physical*) internal organs such as the heart, stomach and intestines. The ANS controls some muscles within the body. The biological functions of the ANS are (Psychologically) involuntary and reflexive – the beating of the heart, expansion or contraction of blood vessels or pupils, etc. We are sometimes conscious of it. The parasympathetic and sympathetic nervous systems, along with the enteric nervous system make up the ANS. The enteric nervous system (ENS) or intrinsic nervous system is one of the main divisions of the nervous system and consists of a mesh-like system of neurons that governs the function of the gastrointestinal system.

The human Aura, the Kundalini and the Chakras are responsible for the *bio electrical dynamic* life phenomenon. The transduction phenomena regulate visceral functions of the endocrine system.

The Quantity 'Quantum', Quality, (Quale-Elements) and E-nergy; Flavor or Spirit; are the three elements of Number.

Natural phenomena and their expressions are synthesized to generate flavors of consciousness. Numbers are no exception to this rule.

1 through 9 are the basic elements of quantity, quality and flavor. All expressions have their three (3) fold symmetry properties that are used to blend their elements to synthesize their states (of consciousness). The Physiology, psychology and energy (spirit) of the expression – color, matter, light, orientation along with the four (4) fundamental interactions or forces. Materiality is the basic premise of the western paradigm of modern science. This is by no means the total story.

To complete the global picture, we must include the knowledge of ancient and oriental cultures and the esoteric systems that connect them to the full complement of the physical, the psychological and the spiritual dimensions of consciousness.

The systems that are important to the expanded awareness we are developing are the seven (Hermetic) symmetry principles of the Egyptian culture and the Kundalini with the seven Chakras of the Hindu tradition. These are the basic ingredients of universal, local and individual creative processes. Nature follows these principles and applies these vocabularies to create expressions we experience in life.

There is one other significant contribution we need to add that originated in Egypt but ended up being a contribution made by the Greek philosopher Plato and engineer Archimedes. The world of three-dimensional forms is known, to western science and mathematics, as Platonic solids. They were discovered in the process of calculating the volume of the pyramids. The known Platonic and Archimedean forms follow principles of Euclidean mathematics. They are made of straight edges, flat surfaces and their multi-dimensional volumetric geometric proportions.

To this vocabulary we can now add the Non-Euclidean versions of the Platonic and Archimedean forms that I have invented and patented. The uniqueness of this Non-Euclidean vocabulary is the curved geometry employed. Curved edges and surfaces are the major features of this form language. With these expressions, we can begin our synthesis and the thought form experiments to demonstrate our understanding of consciousness. Distribution and reduction and are the basic processes applied to the creative 'synthesis processes'. The 'root logic' uses a periodic, combinatorial flavor 'blending' strategy as its synthesizing formula.

This curved geometry and its dynamic potential is more organically related to the new descriptions of our universe and how nature works. Quantitative methods are to be synthesized with the qualitative and spiritual (energy) we seam 'hell bent on avoiding.

BENNETT (CURVED SPACE) POLYHEDRA FORMS

All consciousness is consistent with and operates as the physical, psychological or spiritual symmetry principles in physical, psychological and spiritual states, dimensions, expressions et al. 'Symmetry' here is not bi-lateral or mirror symmetry. It is dynamic and can be thought of as the behavior of parts that create whole expressions naturally or make things work artificially. Symmetry is dynamic and energetic.

Language is critical to creating perceptions and concepts. A visual lexicon for ideation is critical. The smallest spatial, physical unit is called a 'quantum' (plural: quanta). It is the minimum amount of any physiological entity involved in an interaction. For quality there is 'qualia' which is the internal, temporal and subjective component of sense perceptions, arising from vibration of the senses by phenomena to produce 'sense data' and information as the product of psychological experiences or 'emotional states'. We use the term 'qualia' (singular 'quale') to refer to that accessible, introspectively phenomenal and minimal aspect of our mental lives. There is some natural phenomenology in each state of human life and consciousness in the microcosmic state that aligns with and operates with the second 'Hermetic law of Correspondence' and the 'grand macro, irreducible states of universal consciousness. Keep in mind that 'Spiritual' in our new-sense, not nuisance, is the way to our 'triadic harmony'. The context now expands and relates to thought, creative energy in higher and altered states of being and becoming as we strive in suchness and muchness to varying degrees of consciousness. By the same reasoning, we can expand the concept of consciousness into sub-conscious which is deeply psycho-logical, emotional and mental. It speaks to and about 'MIND', consciousness as normal awareness and super-consciousness at the highest end of the intelligence gauge, energy and life. Mind is the total synthesis of all faculties, dimensions and flavors of expressions.

It is not in any part or organ of the physical form. It is the quintessence of the familiar axiom of 'sums of parts and wholes'. What do we call this spiritual quantum? Let's call it what it is – 'SPIRIT'. 'Quantum, qualia and Spirit are the three 'quarks of human consciousness.

Spirit or thought uses work energy, power and intuition creatively. It is transcendental and transformative in nature. It is loaned to us by the intention and (love) of some great intelligence we are all temporarily connected to until we return to it as source always demands that all forms of energy do. In the meantime, the deal is that we should take care of it. It takes care of us. Why as humans, with all our creative expressions, have we been granted the most degrees of freedom, free-will and if we are not careful free-fall too. If we don't honor our contract, we get what we've gotten and will always get, which is ill gotten.

Does our triadic model work for basic branches of mathematics and other methods of reckoning? Here's the thought drill. Geometry focuses on the study of shapes, forms, their physical properties and dimensions. Algebra is the study of (dynamic) operations and their applications to solving (life experiences) expressed as equations that are behavioral or psychological and mental in nature.

The internal and external states of reality and mind are aligned to create solutions. Calculus is the mathematical study of change (as in the movement and vibration of states). It is used to study spiritual flavors and expressions that are metaphysical. All three are expressions of mind, intuition, reasoning (and other faculties) that can create satisfaction and joy when rules and principles are successfully applied and the task is completed. On the subject of faculties', if academic faculties used this paradigm, we might all be better served intelligently with our calculation skills which is half of the task.

Visual mathematics and geometry (ART) take care of the rest of our mental-gymnastic puzzles. How do we optimize these principles for the best results in any creative process?

THE CREATIVE DYNAMIC MATRIX

SYMMETRY PRINCIPLES	NEW PARADIGM PRESCRIPTIONS
7. The CROWN-MENTALISM: Plan for Originality of Concept and design excellence. What original thoughts or ideas can you synthesize for your life? What ideas move you? To find your voice or style, explore reading, writing, sketching, 3D modeling or internet research. Dialog with other artists and designers, participate in many forms of 'play' to invite your subconscious to the ideation process.	Ideation: mental acuity, the ability to think with clear intention and focus to achieve higher expressions of self, concepts and ideas sets the tone, with other analogs and models operating in the same realm or disciplines, with the best skills and technologies.
6. 3RD EYE: Experiment and Capture Random Occurrences. Visualization and meditation are very effective disciplines. Creative play, experimentation and happy accidents can lead to true innovation.	Imagineering is the key to manifesting thoughts, ideas, desires and needs. Feelings are critical to the connections with ideation and expressions like colors are flavored by the adjacent hues in the spectrum of light or color vibrations
5. THROAT: Communicate with many Sources of Influence and mentors. Align your findings with your vision and identity. Synthesizing multiple sources of influence will lead to more original works. Communication is a form of reality testing	Speaking to self is thought and speaking to others is considered communication. All of the energy from the principles above and below (in this matrix) are synthesized for sharing and caring.
4. THE HEART: Develop Your Passion with a Unique Artistic Vision with the power of LOVE. Part of what drives us forward is our feelings, our compassion and passion. We become interested in art to fulfill our need to share our joy and love with the world. You will learn new skills and forms of expression as you shine you light in the world through your love of art, design and the people we share them with.	All is Love: Love is All Love is the creative force in this state. It binds all in the web of consciousness. When all the correspondences are aligned, the physical, emotional and creative work begins. Energy (fuel) is needed

3. THE SOLAR PLEXUS governs energy and work. Expand your Vision and Refine Your Process and Skill Set. Some artists follow some cultural tradition, often multiple traditions. Any art-work you create might have traditions behind it, or incorporate a combination of disciplines media and beliefs.	Develop and use the purest forms of energy, fuel and nutrition for all systems to be efficient and productive. What is conceived above must be manifested below, in the real (root) world.
2. THE SEXUAL CENTER: Set realistic Goals and Confront Challenges. think we all know how to set and achieve goals. Challenges are another story. Diamonds are created with heat and pressure so are artists and designers.	I Sex and water as in reproduction is evident. Gender functions as working dynamic principles. There are male and female elements in all of nature and in the manmade world. Water is a medium with memory. It supports life in all phases. Earth, water and air are living elements worthy of our love and respect.
1. THE ROOT: with developed skills and your understanding of materials, with all due respect for mother Earth, we consistently produce high-quality original work. We achieve Inner-Direction through self-confidence and Uniqueness.	Understand and respect the organic, inorganic and inert elements, knowing their properties, characteristics and creative potential to create their periodicities and appropriate matrices
Artists search for and find their creative processes, interests, and rewarding experiences as they impact their environments positively. This leads to a vital state of Inner-direction. Originality is obtained through research, practice, and meaningful experiences such as travel, networking and community involvement. Of paramount importance is the consistent search for excellence and the reward of self-fulfillment with financial rewards.	for safe and positive uses. Respect, replenish, restore and preserve all of earth's elements, resources, environments and energies.

To transform all expressions, understanding their properties and principles allows us to correlate and synthesize them. There is continuity in every expression of consciousness and in every domain or state that it is distributed into. It goes from a singularity to a threefold distribution, then to seven and ten within the number pattern its symmetry dynamic allows. Every species, phylum or typology of form is encoded by vibration with structural, behavioral and dynamic functions, characteristics, proportions and purpose. Periodicity is also an aspect of these patterns. This is where number, behavior and energy are all interrelated and organized.

Interpreting the nature of each frequency requires a synthesis of basic elements that obeys the laws, interactions and physio-logic, the behavioral and spiritual dynamics of the family of elements or the star-stuff everything is made of. In the study of DNA, for example, we are told that vibrational differentiation (VD) establishes the environment, the context and the flavors of expression in the hierarchy of both living and nonliving forms.

This is where cause and effect enter the discussion. I preface this with a unique, almost poetic assumed proposition that is without proof as a heuristic tool for the discoveries that follow (or an axiom). *It is the quest- the question and the request all in the root 'quest'*. I use this device to deepen the thought process with the construct-'vibration'.

The quest is to discover the cause of vibration and how this knowledge affects our understanding of nature's expressions. The question is: Are there 'quanta, qualia and spiritua' (Body, Mind and Spirit elements) in the frequency itself, along with its internal and external forces and interactions, we still do not know and may never see, quantify or qualify that might be the essence of its form?

Do we accept the form 'as is' without truly knowing its deeper (physical) substance, (emotional) meaning or (spiritual) intelligence?

Are these the ingredients needed to create form vocabularies we experience when they are manifested or are born? The request would be, and I take this interpretation quite literally, can we suggest or ask for this process to be repeated consistently as systems that will endure or be preserved?

The laws of the physio, psycho, spiritual, translate to material, bio magnetic, electrical phenomena in their most elemental small-numbered ranges (1 through 9) that seem to be both where and what nature, consciousness and GOD uses. We are the ones who fall for the variations and the 'Maya' of our material (real)ity. Like DNA, does our limited understanding of the duality of 'number' have the same properties as vibration that produces the viable expressions of value and flavors that follow the same symmetry rules? Or is number a (BMS) triad as well of body, mind and spirit in its complete sense?

Minimum inventories create maximum diversities and multiple dimensions through a logical and efficient distribution of characteristics, essences and flavors as forces of nature holding them together. We seem reluctant to accept change for 'very good' reasons. We are hard wired that way. This fundamental physiologic response forms the foundation for the myth of stress as a dis-ease causal mythology. The "fight or flight response" is our body's primitive, automatic, inborn (reptilian) response that prepares the body to "fight" or "flee/fly" from perceived attacks, harm or threat to our survival. In this state we live in survival mode. When we experience excessive stress—whether from internal worry or external circumstances— a bodily reaction is triggered.

Originally discovered by the great Harvard physiologist, Walter Cannon, this is called the "fight or flight" response. This response is hard-wired into our brains and represents a form of 'genetic wisdom or intelligence' designed to protect us from bodily harm. This response actually corresponds to an area of our reptilian brain called the hypothalamus.

When stimulated it initiates a sequence of nerve cell firings and the release of chemicals that prepare our body for freezing, running or fighting. When the chosen response is activated, sequences of nerve cell firings occur and chemicals such as adrenaline, noradrenaline and cortisol are released into our bloodstream. The emotional response to the 'situation' is the cause.

ORDER
DESIGN SCIENCE IN THE NEW PARADIGM AGE

These patterns of nerve cell firings and chemical release cause our bodies to undergo a series of very dramatic changes. Our respiratory rate increases. Blood is shunted away from our digestive tract and directed into our muscles and limbs, which require extra energy and fuel for running and fighting. Our pupils dilate. Our awareness intensifies. Our sight sharpens. Our impulses quicken. Our perception of pain diminishes. Our immune system mobilizes with increased activation. We become prepared—physically and psychologically—for fight or flight. We scan and search our environment, "looking for the enemy." With the stresses of modern life, the mirror reveals who the real culprit is.

We can apply the positive effect of this natural and well-intended cause to our advantage if we are to embrace change. Stresses derived from changing beliefs and paradigms, subtle though they may seem, can be very disruptive. How can we accept spirituality when our reptilian brain is stuck in a religious mode, overpowering the other mammalian and neocortex regions and what they have to offer us for peace of 'MIND'?

How can we accept 'mind' 'consciousness' truth and reality without open dialog about these topics? The ancient and oriental paradigms are another source of downright fear, fueled by factors that are not clearly articulated again for the lack of communication. The truth about applying the keys of this creative process of expanding human consciousness is available to us through systems of dynamic principles that are natural to us through the self-regulating and self-nurturing of consciousness itself. There is an irony here that escapes us.

The lack of knowledge, regardless of its source, leads to an unkind materiality on one hand and spiritual bankruptcy on the other. They weigh heavily on our conscience. We superimpose layers, rituals, emotions and thoughts fed to us without ever using our own 'axiom' to establish our self-determination capabilities. We burden ourselves with stuff we assume and subsume to be useful.

If we break down the cultural, economic and socio-political walls, we might embrace the knowledge and beauty of universal phenomena openly and be able to change our perspectives and realities and grow. Wisdom traditions of ancient and oriental cultures build lasting frameworks and platforms for their development, calibrated in eons of time.

In the new paradigm they are to be seen as 'scaffolds of self-realization'. Though western cultures have ignored this knowledge, there is enough validity with it for us to determine how relevant and important parts of this body of work are.

We have to view this as being a global resource that is available to all. It is a living, universal record of human thought. Everyone has access to it. When it is accessed and shared, like-minded folks who receive it, with their agreement, give it value.

Seeking approval from systems that have conditioned, misguided and manipulated their citizens is quite ironic. Is this behavior (be-have-I-or not) being played out in other species and phenomena as well? The choices we make are very personal and may have more followers than we expect.

There is a pattern about this universal WIKI (Wisdom, Intelligence, Knowledge and Information) that echoes through the shifting paradigm cycles of the ages.

Spiritual experiences are familiar to people who are oriented to spiritual directions with their BMS compasses honed and pointed with trajectories that last (eternally). They are connected to source and follow natural laws. The triadic harmonies are central to many of these cultures. If this is as ubiquitous as it is, it is the best place to start with the creative processes to which it applies.

We start with the definition of consciousness or the 'All of All' as expressions of Body, Mind and Spirit. This is one number law of a set of 9 primary numbers with each one representing all expressions of nature, laws and flavors. The unique property of three (3) is that it relates to the human gauge, its realm and energies, directly. Introducing this knowledge, from a new paradigm view, begins with the law of (3) three and the harmonic dynamics representing the foundation upon which we can build our vision of the world and the contributions we make to others.

The MANDALA

The natural diversity of our 3D world is supported by a minimum inventory of fundamental elements few in number, quality and flavor. The number for our three dimensional expressions and experiences is 3. Is it because our biological nature can only allow us to operate in this range of perception and ideation? Every number between 1 and 9 represents a series of experiences that are considered laws. One is unity, two is duality, three is the trinity or the triad.

MAN is body, mind and spirit, an electro-magnetic, toroidal dynamic. Time is past, present, and future. Space is 3-dimensional: length, width, and height. The universe is space, time, and matter (energy). There is a rarity about the first three numbers with a unique metaphysical spirit or essence to them. The number four represents the tangible or physical world where the flavors of the higher creative processes are manifested for our benefit with spatial intelligence for orientation, movement and vibration. To develop the proper rituals for managing our lives in space, understanding the impact of natural forces is critical. We now know of four fundamental forces in our universe. Some like gravity and the electro mechanical forces are tangible and are experienced in our everyday lives. The set of four elements includes the four cardinal points, the four seasons etc. We have 4 Directions on the earth (north, south, east, and west), from which we get the word news, and we have 4 Seasons (spring, summer, autumn and winter). There are 4 phenomenal expressions of universal consciousness that make up the universe (matter, space, time and energy). Our current ideas about matter and energy have fused into one dynamic of energy as matter— matter now being energy.

There are 4 Major elements (earth, air, fire, and water) with a fifth somewhat esoteric phenomenon we are still to define. For the time being it is ether and etheric as are many of nature's unfolding flavors and principles we have not yet understood or explained. There are 4 Divisions of the day (morning, noon, evening, and midnight). We will explore the needs, methods and types of expansion and growth possible later. 5 is the human frequency. With 5 being at the center of the decimal system etched in our DNA, we find ourselves at the fulcrum of nature and life.

The 5 senses, the fivefold symmetry of the human form, consciousness with its new interpretation, presents its five states of being — conscious or normal awareness, unconscious, subconscious, superconscious and sacredness. Maybe we are at the fulcrum of consciousness at the place and time for reflections on the big questions. What other species or forms do this? With our big bang, have we forgotten the duality of the big implosion where we return to source and discover that everything else does and will? Is the implosion that reduces all to oneness as an internal journey, monolog or reflection of external phenomena and dynamics we may never know anything about? 6 might be the way out. 6 represents creativity. 6 is the smallest integer (a number larger than 0) which isn't a prime or a square number. Six is also the smallest "perfect number", which means that 6 equals the sum of its dividers (3). Six is the only number which is the sum of three consecutive numbers or a factorial (1+2+3=6). It's also the only even number which isn't a sum of odd cubes that are successive. There are even more 6 number symmetries and frequencies in and of nature yet to be discovered. In subatomic physics, 6 is important in describing the fundamental nature of matter, time, space and energy. 7 is our next magical number. For the purpose of looking at the role 7 plays, it can be seen as a combination of 3+4. 3 is the upper (the Above) register as in music, of natural symmetries, vibrations and (consciousness?). The four is the lower (Below) frequencies of space, matter, form and all its attributes. Time is the transitional zone experiencing every vibration between them. 7 days make a complete week; 7 colors make a perfect spectrum in our rainbows and in pigmented colors; 7 great land masses form a complete earth; 7 great bodies of water form a complete ocean and 7 notes make a perfect scale.

8 is the full octave of the musical scale; it is the 8-fold tesseract for the classic platonic form vocabularies and their transformations, all generated from the tetrahedron as is suggested by Richard Buckminster Fuller.

Nine (9) is the frequency of the completion vibration; the preparation for the new w-ave; (word construct discovery) we have the oct-ave with eight units or elements, the enne-ave with 9 units or elements as periodicity. There is the law of 'numbered-aves' from 1 to 9. What is the 'ave' of zero (0).

Is 'Ave' here holy? Nature seems to have a universal or ubiquitous combinatorial synthesis with distribution strategies that follow symmetry principles, thought or intelligent, behavioral and creative processes along with an organic structural or geometric logic starting with number (singular). Numbers are the symbols.

A number as significant as 9 operating on metaphysical levels, with deeper implications and meanings does not have its own popular 'ave' (h-ave) name. If ennead is a set of 9, then I present the 'enneave ™ as the 9th wave with its unique rhythm. 10 is the departure point for the new cycle or the next 'ave' that is repeated with zero ('0') as the transitional element.

For studying flavors there is a qualitative operation that reduces numbers to their ultimate sum. It states that the number, regardless of its value or size, will have the same flavor or vibrational symmetry falling somewhere between 1 and 9. Every number, regardless of its size, has an 'ultimate sum' in the first enneave (1-9) of (I will be bold here and say — consciousness) since it is included in the grand new paradigm theory of "EVERYTHING".

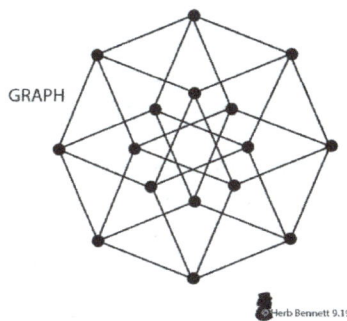

GRAPH

At the vertices (the dots) of this graph and the four central intersections of the top and bottom hexagons 19 Polyhedra can be placed. The open vertex is the null set that represents the transitions to other variations and vocabularies allowed. The TRUE boundary of the graph is the octet. The mystery of this graph is that it can be viewed as a two dimensional or three-dimensional representation.

The Tetrahedron is another tesseract or periodic matrix that can be used for ordering the features and characteristics of form and their processes. The number of generations of 3D elements could be considered fractals of n dimensional space to expand the current vocabulary of S_2 families found in the 'M' set.

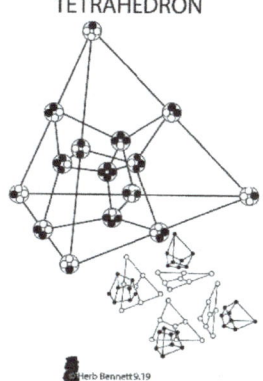

TETRAHEDRON

Fig. 13

If we reduce theories of quantum mechanics, relativity and everything to common sense, the involvement, impact or contributions of participants on experiments is completely predictable when we accept the notion that thought is the energy at work here. Relativity is about the absence of standards of absolutes and universal applications. Said another way, solutions do not apply to every situation. If there are no standards or protocols for new rituals and paradigms, heuristic methods can be used to build scaffolds of intelligence.

In time, they will become acceptable, valid, and beneficial as new (fractal) patterns in nature with number vibrations and symmetries. The process involved here is, in fact is quite simple: physical materials generally have 6-fold rotational symmetry if the arrangement of their atoms remains unchanged when rotated by 60 degrees — one sixth of a circle. The atoms in metals often order themselves in this way. However, more complicated structures with 5-fold, 8-fold or 10-fold rotation symmetry also exist. 7-fold, 9-fold or 11-fold symmetries have not yet been observed in nature. Where do we look for them and what do we look for? Do we discover realities when our thoughts are focused on them? What are the dynamic principles, rituals and creative processes involved in "making the abstract real"?

Fig.14

At the base of this all the adage of throwing enough stuff on the wall until some of it sticks comes to mind. There is no monopoly with intelligence. It's natural and free. Everything cannot be re-solved with the same approach, attitudes or equation. Is there an equation for GOD? What does the GOD particle have to do with GOD? If HIMHERIT has a particle what is its wave?

Numbers, symbols and terms are not the only standard for equating systems of value. The qualitative mathematics and the languages used to describe experiences may have no expressions, especially if we are not vibrating and resonating compatibly with the forces and states we are interacting with. Why is it that modern science still cannot describe or explain to us what the 7 hermetic principles mean or how they 'relate' (this is the key here) to every individual who, I might add, is part of the 'holy grail' theory of 'everything'? The best measure of relativity I know is this: "If you cannot describe any idea to a five-year-old child, it's not a theory". Only you might know what it is. It therefore does not help anyone else. It remains personal and subjective.

The high holy of holies of science—particularly physics, mathematics and related fields—are disciplines that describe 'us to ourselves' and our relationships to the universe, (if that is still the agenda now). Very few people truly know who they are. If we submit to the idea of our star-stuff nature this puts it all into perspective for me. What does understanding standard models, quarks and dark matter do for us if no one is 'relating' this new knowledge to life as we understood it?

The vast quantities of information and knowledge without any WIKI 'wisdom' shows a lack of spiritual and psychological consciousness or common sense, not artificial intelligence. All intelligence is natural until we remove ourselves from nature and try to reinvent systems we do not know.

There are very few opportunities and avenues for people to participate in their own lives and communities. Are participants observers too? Are they using the right light or seeing the bright light they are looking for? Creating a system with the basic elements of the three dimensions of consciousness and applying it to all the expressions of nature and life and putting it into an encompassing manageable, periodic matrix is a good start.

These are the physical phenomena we all depend on. Observers now knowing that mind does affect matter will be moved to see, and experience observed objects and their thoughts differently. They will apply their understanding of their response to nature and the behavior of internal and external subjective and objective interpretations of their own experiences with forces such as light, space, time, and gravity that operate personally and universally.

MAN, the meter and gauge of consciousness has nano, micro and macrocosmic correspondences weaving life's fabric. This offers a deeper level of living and being than we now experience. With the most degrees of freedom attainable, we do have much more responsibility.

"To whom much is given, much will be required" (Luke 12:48).

Do our new 'technology' disciples have any responsibility to deliver the good/s they promise us? Are we observing the planet in isolation, or are we participating in an open world that's truly interested in all forms of freedom (for others)? Is this threefold periodic matrix part of western 'science' or any other methodology for that matter? What are the building blocks of this new science? Let's look at what is considered science in the current paradigm. Definitions of science: the *intellectual and practical* activity encompassing the systematic study of *the structure and behavior of the physical and natural world* through *observation and experiment*.

"The world of science and technology" is a systematically organized body of knowledge on a particular subject. No mention is made of human behavior, mental acuity or spirituality.

The new paradigm definition of science:

The *practical, intellectual, mental and spiritual* activities encompassing the systematic study of *the physiology, psychology and spirituality of the physical, natural, metaphysical or the spiritual world* through community *participation, observation, (search)research and thought disciplines*; "through *design, art, science and technology*" that generates a systematically organized (ken) of knowledge, sight, insight and intuition on a particular *or multiple subjects that can be reverse engineered and/or 'synthesized' by applying related concepts, natural principles and laws with curiosity and passion now called "D_ESign Science™"*.

The central concept for this work is built on the understanding of 'consciousness' and how the knowledge can be used creatively and positively to enhance and to cause the elevation of human consciousness through a design science that can be used to manifest real solutions.

Applying new paradigm principles to our new science (not nuisance) to the subject of vibration affords a deeper understanding of ourselves, one another and the world. We are revisiting this phenomenon in light of the shifts of consciousness we are experiencing. We are searching for new ways, new forms and new symbols to express, articulate and share a constant flow of strange information we need to make familiar. This is operating on the conceptual or architectonic level. Transforming concepts into solutions is the next task. A well harmonized synthesis of principles and ideas is being developed 'to make the abstract real'. There are the intuitive, insights and *direct WIKI from source* that we attribute to sages through the ages.

Music — with Number and Color harmonize as a classic synthesis to describe nature's mysteries on levels beyond the *seven senses*. The music of the spheres is not poetry; it is real. The planets emit *sound frequencies* that have been recorded by NASA.

One of the most profound and ubiquitous of nature's phenomena is vibration. What we know more about is oscillation which is the mechanical and measurable expressions of pressures and its 'fallout' properties. The flavors that 'soothe savage beasts' are felt by motion and not description.

Vibration is at the core of ALL reality. From the law of octaves in the range of 7 (heptave) and 8 (octave), [created for this discussion is the number and wave combined to describe a range], we see evidence of cacophonous and symphonious arrangements in nature.

ORDER

DESIGN SCIENCE IN THE NEW PARADIGM AGE

The former is discordant and causes dis-ease or sickness. The latter is harmonious and creates ease and wellness. These two frequency ranges are created with the dynamics of the 3-4-7 and the 4-4-8 symmetries of consciousness. It's getting to the point where consciousness is synonymous with many more ideas such as mentalism, mind nature, life and many more that we once compartmentalized. With 'mentalized' as the root, we see (or get the picture of) division. 'Di' being two and vision being what's seen. In keeping with the patterns of unification it's possible that our language and the tones of expressions become more harmonious.

THE ANCIENT SOLFEGGIO SCALE

CHAKRA	CENTER	COLOR	NOTE	FREQUENCY
Seventh Chakra	(Crown)	Violet	Si or Ti	– 963 Hz
Sixth Chakra	(Third Eye)	Indigo	La	– 852 Hz
Fifth Chakra	(Throat)	Blue	Sol	– 741 Hz
Fourth Chakra	(Heart)	Green	Fa	– 639 Hz
Third Chakra	(Solar Plexus)	Yellow	Mi	– 528 Hz
Second Chakra	(Sacral)	Orange	Re	– 417 Hz
First Chakra	(Root or Base)	Red	Ut-Do	– 396 Hz

To continue with this discussion, I will use the thought-form experiment method to disassociate from details of physical examples and look at the process from a thought-form perspective using music as the metaphor.

There are scales in music, in the endocrinal system that maintains our hormonal life that is in synch with the kundalini, the 7 chakras, the subtle energies and the rest of the natural phenomena operating in this 'environment' as the solfeggio scale. It imbues a full spectrum.

The average of the 7 frequencies is 648Hz and at the heart it is 639 Hz?

The frequencies of the notes in each expression, across the ranges, vibrate at some level that correspond with the qualities of all the notes in many ranges, if not all, at the same frequency. The 'c' note has a color, red. It aligns with the base chakra and continues through the phenomena in whatever numbered 'w-ave' it occupies. What causes this to be as discrete as it is or to stay in its place is still a mystery. Are there phenomena in each range? What do the one, two, three, four, five, six and nine ranges 'sound' like? Or better stated, how do we experience them? Is there a marker in each note within each scale that encodes the notes and the overall range? In human beings that code is our DNA. Is the number that is associated with the frequency the marker?

One of the most popular markers in music now is the 528 'LOVE' frequency. Is the 'gematria' of the frequency (a term borrowed from the association of word and number) its quality and value or its qualitative and quantitative nature?

The rhythms and flavors of consciousness are extrapolated from a wholeness into a distributed array or matrix of quantitatively, qualitatively and dynamically energetic, interactive notes, expressions and essences. We follow the space, time, energy continuum at the levels and notes of cognition, visualization and feeling to understand and appreciate the experiences being presented or created.

What we do with this information depends on the skills we have, the passions that are aroused and the need to be fulfilled. When we are moved, we dance we sing and are joyful. In this sentence we have the demonstration of the physiological, the psychological and the spiritual.

We become finely tuned instruments to express the movement as effectively as we can. We experience the healing harmonies we strive to create.

Everything we have known, are now learning and will ever know is encoded in this creative process with vibrational frequencies of various intensities, qualities, values and flavors we align with and resonate to.

In time, we transcend the upper threefold registers of all the scales that support life, passing through the ephemeral no-time, space-less, altered-state inducing energies to 'fall' into the fourfold dimensions of *'sweating to eat bread, reproducing and devouring the world'*.

The dimensions in the new paradigm can and will invite people to shift to another mentality with experiences that are aligned, as we were meant to be, as higher conscious beings. Is the music we hear created by others and fed to us, or are we creating and living our own?

Let's look at the word *'Intensities'*: intensity, in-tense and intention and its root *'tension'*. It is understood as the measurable amount of a property, such as force or a magnetic field. Tension is a creative state. For there to be a flawless, colorless diamond, heat and pressure create tension in the rough stone, in the lapidary and in the owner of it eventually. Brilliance, in all forms of light, is exponentially proportional to skill, effort, focus and intention.

The next word is 'resonate': It means to be filled with a deep, full, reverberating (vibration) not just sound but in all consciousness, life spirit and soul. At some level these are all the same.

We resonate to the tension they create in us. Resonance is produced and/or exhibited with tension and intention to levels of intensity for others to respond to all (our) expressions as if by resonance, presence, sense, acceptance and agreement and all else that is warm and fuzzy. We create rituals and repetitive patterns that resemble resonance and resonate harmoniously or in 'chaos' to what we experience. *Re-son-ance; d-ance, accept-ance, rom-ance, clear-ance (focus).* Reason is another related term to be put into the mix here: meaning,

ORDER

DESIGN SCIENCE IN THE NEW PARADIGM AGE

purpose, benefit and value come to mind. These two concepts; in-tension and rea-son (reality created) in all their forms and cases are essential to manifesting 'culture'. The New Paradigm (NP) definition of culture is the blend of the physical with the psychological and the spiritual. This applies on all levels of consciousness and could even shed some light on consciousness itself.

It works in the 3-4:7 octave and all others. It is especially important in the 7- fold frequencies where according to Gregg Braden in *The GOD CODE* he references the relationship of man to GOD, whom I refer to as *'HIMHERIT'* to clear up any gender issues and avoid the host of names we feel uncomfortable using. We have a *'HIMHERITANCE'* we do not respect!

"He [humankind] unites both heaven and earthly qualities within himself…. [HIMHERIT] and will create man to be the union of the two …." Here is an eloquent reference to the 3:4:7 'Heptave'. Does any of this relate to the Brain-Mind Dialogs we've been having all along? Here is the framework for the dialectic.

We have too many words with diverse meanings built on old scaffolds of un-consciousness, with too little clarity, no 'overstanding' and no consciousness that we can experience or have dialog about. Someone ate the nuts and left us the shells. There are several theories about how man came to be and evolved to 'being'. Regardless of the veracity of any of them, we are here and are concerned with becoming. I was. I became. I am now becoming—three sentences with presence in mind. Have we ever noticed the patterns of the BMS-STEP qualities in the word we use to communicate? Do linguists know that there are body words—nouns, mind word connective devices and spirit words—verbs in all languages of the world?

We might be able to reverse the 'Tower of Babel (now social network Babble)' effect on the world. If we did, we might begin to get along.

We have a brain and very often make reference to it as our mind. Here we are, some seven billion people and counting on the planet, divided physically, emotionally, behaviorally and spiritually. All seven billion people are entitled to their opinions, their space and freedom, supposedly. For this discussion, there are two major divisions of importance.

There is one word I propose to be the umbrella to get to the gist of the matter at hand— the confusion between the word 'brain' and the word 'mind'. Please, let's leave Mr. Webster and his friends out of this dialog. Thank you. They seem not to be keeping up with our evolution.

We just added a few more people by this point of our meditation. It's when we share this that it becomes the dialog we are lacking.

The adult human brain weighs about 3 pounds. Our adult human brain is about 2% of the total body weight. The average human brain is 140 mm wide. The average human brain is 167 mm long. There are approximately 100 billion (100,000,000,000) neurons in the human brain. There are 200 to 400 billion stars in our galaxy. People enjoy enormity. We focus on the simplicity here though with the number three (3) representing the three parts of the brain—the limbic, or reptilian, brain, the mammalian brain and the neocortex. The Mind is physical. Where it is located and how it works is not clear. The word for this thought process here is 'heuristic.'

It means 'fake it until you make it'. In offering ideas about the mind, we look at the complex of organs, systems and processes that form the 'mind's portal'. The brain, the Spinal column and spinal cord with their neurons, the endocrine system and the organs it supports (the largest organ being the skin), the skeletal structure and the cells are constantly being replaced in much less time than we imagine. These replacement cycles are functions of the quantum mechanical dynamic. The physical parts mentioned are the western culture's knowledge of human anatomy.

In the west, discussions about the mind start with the brain. In some cases, the brain is considered to be the mind. The oriental paradigm, for some time, has had concepts close to and aligned with the quantum mechanical theories, experiences and descriptions of the spiritual and electrical life through physiological, psychological and energetic dynamic sub-atomic physics recently discovered. The path of the mystic has been the living laboratory for exercises and mental disciplines by participants who are investigators, gaining access to a holistic and organic knowledge-base that unfolds through 'pure' living. While some (western) scientists, in both hemispheres, are alternating between measuring and observation, they experience the quantum magic at work and do corroborate their findings with the wisdom traditions developed centuries earlier. When amputees have sensations where their limbs used to be, what faculties are involved with that experience? Is there an invisible subtle body, still intact, that is functioning in an altered state of higher dimensional consciousness, or is it simply memory?

The aura (subtle bodies with vital functions outside the physical body), the kundalini with the seven (7) chakras that are operating at a deeper level than the endocrine system, the psychic abilities and other functions of the 'spiritual complex' do not relate to religious traditions. If they do, they are the mystery and esoteric traditions that are tightly guarded. Mind, in the 'oriental' context, is a holistic experience. It includes all the physical, psychological and spiritual aspects of life. The vibrational range of this life force or the 'chi' goes a lot deeper than what a 'brain alone' does.

SUBSTANCE: Solidity is a result of the negatively charged electron, wave/particle: particle/wave, orbiting around the cell's nucleus at approximately the speed of light in sync with (the eternal, ever present, timeless-spaceless) transduced super-consciousness. The wave particle, stimulated vibrating, cell wall interaction produces a 'Solidity Effect' that's transmitted through the body and regulated by the brain and the nervous system. Is this how we develop our sense of Space, Time and Energy? Is this cell-vibration interaction, a force, or simply a dynamic ritual? Is it a bio- electro-magnetic energy, one of the four fundamental forces now known to sub-atomic physics? The 'bio' quality seems to be excluded from the forces.

In the Hindu tradition, creation is a dynamic of three fundamental forces symbolized by the three gods: Brahma the creator, Vishnu the sustainer, and the transcendent Shiva the destroyer. The correspondence of these three principles (creation, sustenance and destruction)

ORDER

D_ESIGN SCIENCE IN THE NEW PARADIGM AGE

in our daily existence is to be found in birth, life, and death. They occur not only at the physical level, but at the psychic and spiritual levels as well.

They represent the universe, in its continuous becoming. The eight-fold way is another bridge between physics and oriental philosophy. The rhetoric represented in this east west dichotomy is no longer relevant. The truth of the energy is that so called primitive (first) peoples, ancient scribes of scriptures including disciples in the bible and Jesus himself taught the mystical wisdom to those who were in tune with the Christ consciousness. This tradition was the charge of the Egyptian priesthood.

The Hopi's idea of the *Eternal* and ever present Thought and the presence of oneness is the essence of natural law "*The Hopi* Prophecy continues…Until, suddenly…from the stillness, the *Eternal* and ever present.

Thought (presence)had the Will to move, that surrounds it, so too was Man, blind to the perfect *oneness* of God, into which he had been born…and that every being, and event in every moment of *existence*, provides nourishment for the soul".

Pythagoras and Tales knew that matter was psychic. It was awake and aware of its environment and obviously of itself. This sounds like intelligence to me. Modern material science also knows this.

Geometric forms obey basic intelligent principles of *sacred geometry* now called TORIMETRY™.Thecommunal behavior of plasma and gasses (star stuff) separates impurities from their environments. In the vastness of the multiple universes, Energy (Thought-ether) is the only way to hold itself and the cladistics' energies of every other expression of thought form in harmony. Death is the transition to source where there is no conscious-ness, only love. Life is the 'fall'. Death is the door to a-'rising'.

Other Game-changing paradigms include Einstein's Photoelectric effect. Electrons emitted from metal surfaces cause electric currents to flow. Schrodinger and de Broglie discovered the fundamental wave particle's inter-transformative properties. Heisenberg'sprinciple of uncertainty, with its lack of simultaneity, cooperation and unreliable expectation, would set measuring positions or reference points off.

Creation Myths: Gurdjieff's 'Heptaparaparshinokh',from BLZ Bob's tales told to his grandson for the polarization from one to two and three dimensions. The Great common-cosmic Trogoautoegocratic-process is actualized always and in everything on the basis of the two fundamental cosmic laws, the first of which is called **Heptaparaparshinokh**,the'Fundamental-First-degree-Sacred-' and the second **Triamazikamno**the 'Fundamental-First-degree-Sacred-.' "And so, my boy, the Omnipresent- Okidanokh obtains its prime arising in space outside of the Most Holy Sun Absolute itself, *from the blending of these three independent forces into one*, (synthesis) and during its further involutions.

It is correspondingly changed, in respect of what is called the 'Vivifyingness of Vibrations' according to its passage through what are called the 'Stopinders' or 'gravity-centers' of the fundamental 'common-cosmic sacred **Heptaparaparshinokh**.' We can translate these terms to speak to Mr. Gell-Mann, the father of 'quarks'

Murray Gell-Mann's eightfold way resonates to Buddhist philosophy with his Baryon octet theory or (w) 'ave' of numbers or periodicity, as it is also found in our DNA and other natural gauges, scales, energies and vibrations. Murray Gell-Mann is an American physicist who is credited with the introduction of the concept of quarks.

He won the 1969 Nobel Prize for physics for his groundbreaking work on the description and classification of subatomic particles. *Gell-Mann* turned his attention to some particles that behaved particularly strangely. He called them "*quarks*" with a nod to James Joyce's novel, *Finnegan's Wake*.

"Three quarks for Muster Mark! Sure he hasn't got much of a bark and sure any he has it's all beside the mark".

Chromodynamics (color as force) in the subatomic scale creates cacophonies and symphonies of cosmic music. At a certain point, this journey transcends the physical and scientific dialog. Its genius becomes qualitative; art, music, storytelling and poetry to nurture our thirsty and hungry souls. When the fun is over, rigorous work begins. *HIMHERIT* is the genderless a safe name for what anyone holds very sacred. It is the grandest form of epi-consciousness operating as *SOURCE*. Names have too many shadows, says Chief Seattle. Are we Wave, Particle or Both; Chamaeleonidae Class: Reptilia (Reptiles)? Gravitation effect might be particle. Electro-magnetic is wave?

THE AGENDA:

1. The Hermetic philosophical principles are, in fact, principles of consciousness that can be articulated into real world applications.
2. The Bio energetic, magnetic electrical dynamic is a significant element for the nano, micro and macro cosmic creative development processes. It can transform life support, maintenance, healing and wellness protocols, systems, technologies and professions.
3. The Euclidean and Non-Euclidean systems of geometry and related disciplines set the tone for new identities and aesthetic expressions for the built environment. They hold in suspense nature's unfolding mysteries.
4. With great economic value, having new forms to define new concepts and vocabularies of 'Form' and identities for branding this epochal shift is of paramount importance and global cultural significance.
5. The intellectual property technology will impact new material sciences, production and engineering technologies, offering significant added value and exciting opportunities. The knowledge component of this science, apart from being constructively disruptive, is 'epochal' and exciting.

6. The transformation of conceptual, intellectual and natural logic structures will create new developments in computing science, in calculation, design and manufacturing, management systems and qualitative technologies. New systems for modeling the new paradigm and a new world view will impact the quality of life significantly.

7. Transforming these concepts into economic opportunities and enterprises can be pursued with the applications of diverse business models, each chosen to do the best.

8. This rich knowledge base will prepare professionals and entrepreneurs, through education and training programs, for generations to come. The quality of life design professions, include, and are not limited to the built environment, with emphasis on occupational shifts to emerging technologies and opportunities for community development and wellness sectors.

9. The *New Paradigm Research and Development* model will focus on future applications of all emerging technologies, expanding knowledge bases and cultivating new opportunities and technologies through collaborations and other mutually beneficial relationships.

10. Esoteric technologies and further research will help pursue future development of concepts beyond boundaries of known technologies to transform knowledge that continues to evolve. This will be done in collaboration with other New Paradigm Scientists and all who support the vision of a positively transformed world.

11. Transforming concepts into solutions is the next task. Developing a well harmonized synthesis for principles, ideas, resources and applications with all the marketing strategies, collateral and sales systems in place 'to make the abstract real' is essential. The idea bank is created with in house opportunities and properties and with other developers and entrepreneurs.

12. A Praxis for the next generation of empowered personal development is needed to cultivate the proper mindset needed to embrace emerging opportunities from the level playing field the new technologies are offering us now. If we are serious about equality this Praxis is a mandate. [Man has a date with destiny and fate.]

"Difference that's unfamiliar does not necessarily make the genius but true genius can make the difference familiar."—inspired by Hugh Lendrum

CHAPTER 4 TRINE C
MIND

(Individual, collective and universal minds.)

'**THE INTERCONNECTED ONE COMMAND CENTER**' for this creative process is the MIND. What is mind? 'Occam's razor' informs us that it's in the brain. This is the simple and quieting resolution of an otherwise complex (key clue) construct that touches all of consciousness and its expressions in my humble opinion.

MIND: noun: mind; plural noun: minds: The element of a person that enables them to be aware of the world and their experiences, to think, and to feel; the faculty of consciousness and thought.

The evolution of human knowledge and consciousness

The MIND is NOT the BRAIN; as we are often tempted to believe. The mind is one of many complexes in the 'thought, emotion [CONSCIOUSNESS]continuum' that enables humans to follow all natural (and manmade) laws, symmetry principles and disciplines that govern the creative processes needed to survive in our external world.

We connect with MIND internally. This complex blends the essences of the threefold elements or consciousness, namely the body with its physiology, the mental and emotional faculties and the spiritual or energy components. They permeate all that exists, even the subtle and energetic realities. Density is a frequency illusion. It is an inherently multidimensional (threefold) micro-component linked to the universal source of all information, knowledge and wisdom along with the adherence to the laws that govern all reality.

This micro and macro connection is the mind dynamic process of consciousness. It is not found in any one region of reality or for us non-reality. It is another flavor of universal consciousness in its Non-linear, Non-Euclidean triadic form.

We use our brain (the circuit control panel) our senses and all elements of our finer (thought) fuel, subtle energies and base electrical life to correlate with this threefold triadic [Body, Mind, Spirit] harmonizing consciousness dynamic and its symmetry principles to align with a S.(space), T.(time), E.(energy) Periodic (new paradigm) MATRIX of quantities, qualities and flavors in a sub, super and normal conscious dynamic complex for encoding and decoding impulses and sense data with these micro tools that afford us access to the (macro) universal MIND or source of ALL.

MIND

D_ESIGN SCIENCE IN THE NEW PARADIGM AGE

The Law of 3 or the number three plays a significant role in this synthesis of the triad as the extrapolation of flavors, quantities and qualities are distributed into manifestations, feelings and thoughts. The purpose of MIND is meant, intended, willed to be creative. It is Physical, Emotional and Spiritual here to mean all forms of energy related-ness are involved with mind. The disciplines and methodologies are Physiology, Psychology and Spirituality. Ask yourself these questions: in brain-death where is the mind? Where does it go? See the "flavor machine" as the synthesizing system.

We are beginning to discover many other more subtle forms of expression and forces with qualities and behaviors not previously known in our 'paradigm-based inflexible methods' of interacting with (knowing) the inner and outer worlds we deal with. Dark matter, the standard model of particle physics and the quark theories are all part of the etheric makeup of the *'micro-macro mind dynamic'*. Of the 3M Dynamic; the micro mind is that aspect we have control of or should be able to use as our compass to guide us back to the source of the universal mind, taking back the evolved information and refined essences we have worked on to the source of all arising.

This is the purpose for and of life for natural expressions, experience, desire and design. All of nature's expressions operate with this triadic dynamic with qualitative and quantitative ever-present characteristics harmonizing processes of Body, Mind and Spirit in synthesis and on multiple dimensions in simultaneity, unlike our linear, binary brains.

Body, Mind and Spirit are holistic, omnipresent and omni-potent processes.

The goal is for the triad to be in harmony and in synch with the universal mind. This complex uses the characteristics of the MICRO-CONSCIOUS levels of being, where humans operate, to harmonize its internal dynamic synthesis. This same interaction is taking place in every other expression, phylum and form of life, thing, place and energy. Humans do not have a monopoly on 'living'.

We make little effort and are not aware of our true potential or the benefits of aligning with our inner and outer-ness. We are not being guided by, nor are we applying universal laws and principles to our lives. If we were to redefine the concepts that have evolved in the emerging paradigm, we might have a better chance at participating in a more realistic and sustainable way. Nature, Consciousness and Man are Expressions and Flavors of super-normal and sub conscious expressions. When the universe in its vastness emerged, did what we know as nature, grow slowly over time? Was it unfolding to laws to reveal its hidden potential that we were not aware of? Do we understand what nature is? The living and non-living are all parts of nature.

Nature (nurture) : is the collective physical world; including plants, animals, environment, other features and products of the earth, as opposed to human creations since. We have removed ourselves from nature with our own version of 'Human nature' that's neither natural nor human. The Egyptian 'neter' or GOD comes full circle to add light to the subject. The physical force regarded as causing and regulating these phenomena are part of nature. When we talk of phenomena, are we talking about light, energy, space and all the 'extraterrestrial' forces known and unknown, but yet to be known?

"The audacity of man to remove him-herself from NATURE is arrogance worthy of the state of ignorance, confusion and lack of growth we inherit for doing so. The dominion given was mistaken, evidently. We are not aligned with nature according to this current paradigm. It is a passport used to abuse nature and inadvertently and by repercussion, self in the process. Can Nature be MIND? The physical force that's inaccurately associated with 'nature' is the greater force of creation and the cause of nature that creates expressions governed by principles and laws of the universe that connects all things. "Laws of nature" are immutable.

Do all nature's expressions, in the new paradigm, belong to what we know as consciousness or do we know that this is strictly a human experience?

When Symmetry principles, laws of nature and forces like Physiology, Psychology and Spirituality are appropriately, quantitatively and qualitatively apportioned, balanced and harmonized through the expressions and thoughts of consciousness, reality is manifested. This definition can apply to many other creative fields. It is ubiquitous and an evident quality of oneness.

To look at the components of consciousness its flavors and essences, we must look at the laws of numbers. Here again we need to adjust the paradigms of numbers. There are many characteristics of numbers. The two major types are qualitative and quantitative. Suchness is the essence of quality. It conveys meaning. Number is the qualitative gauge for value also.

Muchness is the essence of gauge and measure. It gives expression to counting and articulating space. We seem to be stuck in using numbers strictly for keeping score. We do not know the deeper qualities of number or form that are created by measure, proportion and scale for that matter. There is a subtle difference between NUMBER as the phenomena or principle and NUMBERS in the plural sense that conveys all properties related to the physicality of quantitative expression for space and the use of numbers for counting. The qualitative and spiritual or creative use of number is different.

'NUMBER' is a dynamic phenomenon of nature's narrative or storyteller that is not geometrically nor quantitatively defined the way we think.

'NUMBERS' are used for counting, keeping score and for defining Euclidean and Non-Euclidean space. The periodicities of both number and numbers can be synthesized into a system that allows us to express the typologies and phyla of phenomena. We understand nature to gain knowledge that can be used to not only address immediate needs but also to prepare for deeper meaning and sustainable futures.

The idea of 'things returning to the source of their arising' [TRSA]: [STAR] is not a part of our thought process or comfortable conversations. We can add this to the taboos of sex, religion, money and politics in contemporary culture. Wordsmithing: 'STAR' Spirit Truth Ascended and Returned (home). We are in fact 'star matter, in-form (astro-torimetrically) and energetically' informed and transformed perhaps only as conscious beings. As pure energy we are probably of less use to ourselves or to others.

MIND

DESIGN SCIENCE IN THE NEW PARADIGM AGE

Our creative purpose demands that we raise the consciousness of everything around us as we add value, purpose and meaning to highest levels of self and life. Having the HOLISTIC attitude of everything being part of the ONE, paves the way for the new paradigm.

Are we engaged in the process of evolution or is it a hands-off process that we have no control of? With this mentality are we being responsible and are we preparing to deal with the responses that nature and its self-regulating dynamic seem to exercise when its stresses become too great. Humans are part of the self-regulating dynamic of nature. This is the dominion we find in the gene of Isis- or the book Genesis.

NATURE, CONSCIOUSNESS AND MAN

NUMBER	MEANING	WORD
0	CONSCIOUSNESS	ZERO
1	UNITY	ONE
2	DUALITY	TWO
3	THE TRINITY OR THE TRIAD	THREE
4	THE CARDINAL DIRECTIONS	FOUR
5	BALANCE	FIVE
6	CREATIVITY	SIX
7	THE FLAVORS EXTRAPOLATED FROM THE TRIADIC EXPRESSIONS	SEVEN
8	THE OCTAVE	EIGHT
9	THE ENNEAVE	NINE
10	ONE WITH ZERO AS THE CYCLICAL AND VIBRATIONAL ELEMENT	TEN / ZERO

THE EIGHT MAJOR CANONS

ORIGIN	PHENOMENA	DESCRIPTION
HINDU	KUNDALINI THE SEVEN CHAKRAS	THE MICRO AND MACRO ENERGETIC COMPLEXES IN MAN AND THE UNIVERSE

WESTERN MEDICINE	THE ENDOCRINE SYSTEMS IN THE DUCTLESS GLANDS OF THE HUMAN BODY WITH THE HORMONES AND ORGANS	THIS CORRELATES WITH THE CHAKRAS AND NOT KNOWN IN WESTERN MEDICINE
AKASHA	ALL KNOWLEDGE PAST PRESENT AND FUTURE	ACCESSED BY HIGHLY CONSCIOUS HUMAN MINDS
EGYPT	THE HERMETIC PRINCIPLES OF HERMES TRISMEGISTUS	HERMETIC PHILOSOPHY
NATURE'S EXPRESSIONS	LIGHT, ORIENTATION, COLORS, NUMBERS, AND ALL FLAVORS EXPRESSED BY NATURE	TO SYNTHESIZE REALITY WITH THE EXTRAPOLATIONS AND DISTRIBUTIONS OF THE ELEMENTS OF THESE EXPRESSIONS
FORM GEOMETRY	GAUGE THEORIES AND SYSTEMS OF GEOMETRY AND FORM	EUCLIDEAN AND NON-EUCLIDEAN FORMS AMORPHOUS AND GEOMETRIC
MATTER	EARTH, WATER, FIRE, AIR, ETHER [PLASMA]	THE ELEMENTS
THE TRIAD	BODY, MIND AND SPIRIT	THE BASIC ELEMENTS FOR CREATING THE QUALITATIVE AND QUANTITATIVE MATRIX IN THE PERIODIC

"If I have ever made any valuable discoveries, it has been owing more to patient attention than to any other talent."
—Sir Isaac Newton.

HIGHER DIMENSIONS OF PHYSIOLOGICAL, PSYCHOLOGICAL AND SPIRITUAL, CONSCIOUS EXPRESSIONS.

THE CROWN	THE ENDOCRINE SYSTEM	INTELLIGENCE	THE SPIRITUAL DYNAMIC
THE THIRD EYE	The pineal gland lies deep within the brain and produces melatonin.	NEOCORTEX THOUGHT IDEATION	influences your connection to the divine, higher source

THE THROAT	PITUITARY influences on the whole body	VISUAL ACUITY	Your Intuitive Chakra, insight, knowing, visualization
THE HEART	THYROID producing thyroxine,	THINKING TALKING TO SELF: TALKING TO OTHERS AS COMMUNICATION	responsible for your self-expression, use your own voice, speak your truth, be authentic, listen
THE SOLAR PLEXUS-	Relates the thymus to the healing properties of the body	LOVE BINDING FORCE	influences your relationships LOVE, Gratitude better relationships
SACRAL	ADRENALS: The pancreas secretes substances for the digestion of food, such as insulin.	WORK ENERGY SUN POWER TRANSFORMED INTO FOOD	Power Center, creative energy, Powerful purpose
ROOT CHAKRA	TESTES: Estrogen and progesterone	GENDER FORM AND FUNCTION FOR CREATION AND REPRODUCTION	influences your sexuality, creative expressions, healthy self- image
	At the top of the kidneys are the adrenals with several hormones including adrenalin, used for "fight or flight"	MATTER USED TO CREATE PHYSICAL FORM AND REALITY	responsible for your self-esteem, family, money making, healthy empowerment

The fear-based conditioning, aggression and inhumane oppression of self and others is eroding our humanity. Only when we expand our consciousness will we get back on the path to civility, respect and our humanity.

The East West dichotomy with its cultural, religious quarrels and atrocities that MAN is engaged in, is also taking its toll. This knowledge that is being shared now can open our hearts to our higher and better selves with discipline and a minor shift of awareness. It offers practical solutions and the means of developing real skills to create whatever we desire on our path to freedom and wealth. It gives clues into the psychological composition of the basic principles of how the universe works and how we can mirror that behavior.

The spiritual-scientific understanding will stay clear of the religious dogma to keep us on a path to holistic growth and overall strategies for wellness, peace and harmony.

We can all achieve our destiny to live our lives with the principles shared in this message. It is a message that helps us clean up the 'mess of our age' to ensure a better future for ourselves.

The key element missing from the understanding of the Kundalini and how it affects us is our knowledge of the three Nadis. They work with the seven chakras of the Kundalini energy. They are the Ida, the Pingala and the Sushumna. We know about the Sushumna indirectly because this is the channel along which the chakras are located.

The characteristics of the paths are much different than the chakras or centers of energy, also known as vortices. The adage of 'the whole being greater than the sum of its parts' comes to mind here.

In essence we have a decimet made of three nadis and the seven chakras. This becomes a tenfold 'tesseract' corresponding to the basic 'distribution matrix' used to describe the flavors of nature. This is the model used to represent the fundamental synthesis of consciousness which employs the three basic elements of Body, Mind and Spirit in a threefold dynamic or continuum where we experience expressions of nature, the universe and life. Here is a profound shift that will help us make the transformations needed for evolution and our expansion of consciousness. We will embrace new paradigms and value systems to create new realities, habits and energies. Our languages, forms and heightened and evolved mental and emotional lives will be positively impacted.

Forms of expression of consciousness have an inherent threefold set of dynamic elements of Body, Mind and Spirit in them. They are encoded and identified by their geometric properties and names. Every word used to define the structural experiences of all forms are expressions of that one singularity we know of as consciousness. Words represent the physical, psychological or behavioral and spiritual flavors of consciousness.

Every culture and language require parts of speech—Nouns which are Physical and verbs or action words which are dynamic and Spiritual. Emotional expressions and mental constructs are Psychological. The term 'singularity' defines consciousness as unity or source.

Where there is singularity, by extrapolation or extension, we find multiplicity and exponentiality. This same threefold quality applies to consciousness itself with consciousness as our 'normal vibration' awareness, sub-consciousness vibrations operating at a deeper level and super-consciousness at the highest level of vibration.

That they are all expressions of energy is clear. Consciousness is that state of unity that is scattered into the three major qualities of suchness and muchness that obey natural LAW. This LAW is the LAW of three or the TRIAD.

In looking at the nature of the Nadis we find the TRIAD in a similar form, even if the words that describe it are taken from other cultures and languages expressing the fundamental triadic nature of consciousness.

MIND

DESIGN SCIENCE IN THE NEW PARADIGM AGE

Western culture does not embrace true understanding. I believe we are short-changing ourselves and knowing who we are and how we can live higher and better lives in a more organic and harmonious way. All phenomena are expressions of consciousness in its threefold potential. If we can accept the premise that an impulse, in some future time, can become an original thought or idea with related experiences associated with it in the mind of the creator of the thought or idea, storing that experience as a memory we will be on our way to sustainable growth.

Once that initial event is over, it is the past. This thought goes through the three life cycles of its experiences. There is the future or pre-manifestation phase where stimuli are transformed into sense data. The Pingala is the Nadi (right para sympathetic) corresponding to actions and planning, as well as mental and physical activity. It terminates at the ego which gives the "I-ness" This is where the Chakras spring into creative and productive action as each center can then support the overall creative process needed to manifest, create or transform the idea into form. This is the birthplace of identity. This identity is used for naming the thing, expression, habit or ritual.

There is a distinct vibrational frequency attached to the thought, the thing, the name and all other extensions of it. Is there one frequency for all of the expressions of the same idea, or does every expression have a different frequency? This is where ancient cultures used numerology to identify the qualities of expressions of reality, emotions and actions.

The Ida (left sympathetic) corresponds to the past, emotions and desires. It terminates in the superego—storehouse of all habits (PARADIGMS), memories and conditionings.

This is the part of our lives that offers us the opportunity to evolve. It requires making changes that allow us to align with the vibrations that are continuously changing. Change is the most natural attribute of our universe we seem bent on defying.

The negativity that emerges from this defiance causes stress and disease. When we get into the flow, the rhythm of consciousness, the LAWS and forces or energies of nature, we can be in harmony with our environment, ourselves and others.

The Sushumna (para-sympathetic) or the autonomous nervous system is the NOW or Present. It is the channel of ascent. It sustains our evolution and guides us towards the higher awareness. I propose that this is the source of the super-conscious. All its expressions mirror the GRAND creative process of Consciousness that governs all things, actions, desires and needs of everything in the universe (one –verse).

The three channels in the system, described above and their relationships to life are not part of western medical knowledge yet. The Ida and Pingala functions are juxtaposed and opposite. The Ida and Pingala cross at the brow chakra or the Ajna. This crossing is found in Egyptian Metaphysics and its Spiritual Sciences as well.

The Ida Nadi looks after our emotional life and our past. It creates our past. The subconscious mind receives information from this channel. The subconscious mind has an age-old, subconscious collective mind.

Everything in the past since creation is in the collective subconscious. This contains all that is dead, collected and stored in the evolutionary process. Whatever is gone from one's subconscious mind goes into the collective sub-conscious.

The right-side channel— the Pingala Nadi—is connected to the front of the brain. Here is the supra-conscious mind which creates the future.

Thoughts about our future are recorded on this right side and it also has a collective supra-conscious. This has all that is gone that resulted from over-ambitious, futuristic personalities, aggressive animals or plants.

The Shushumna Nadi, through which the Kundalini passes, pierces through the Fontanelle bone area (Little Fountain or Brahmarandhra) to enter into the subtle energy of the all-pervading power. This power is the power creator or the SOURCE of all consciousness. This is where self-realization and actualization emanate.

First the hands feel at the fontanelle bone area and on the fingertips, the cool breeze of the Holy Ghost. The hands are steady, they do not shake, and they look normal.

The seeker feels the ripples of the cool breeze. For the first time we feel the existence of the all-pervading, POWERFUL, allknowing, being and becoming consciousness in all of its expressions, energy centers and nodes in the cyclical paths of the dynamic principles in the human bio, energetic, magnetic, plasmic complex. They are ubiquitous, infusing information and knowledge through the vortices and intersections of systems into the gross and subtle bodies to stimulate and resonate to the universal vibrations of conscious action and appropriate paradigm building meant to serve mankind. There is a direct correspondence with this knowledge and all other traditions.

That we have removed ourselves from nature, as we have pointed out earlier, causes us to disconnect from the source of this ubiquitous conscious power, that we are blessed with, leaving us to depend on our rational and intellectual reasoning and illogical constructions of illusions that lack the harmony of the physical, psychological and spiritual foundation upon which we can build sustainable and meaningful lives, societies, countries, nations, and eventually civilizations.

Civilization building is the next level of evolution people are supposed to be pursuing. To begin to align with the deeper organic knowledge, through inner inspirations, motivations, intelligences and wisdom gained from the information and disciplines of proven esoteric and cultural traditions unfamiliar to us, often through our cultural bias, we need to see the world as a super conscious model of oneness, not only of 'i-ness'. We need to redirect our focus and efforts to manifest a bigger vision of inclusion and compassion towards a higher purpose, where justice, peace and love for ourselves, the planet, our creator, by whatever names known, along with our brothers

MIND

D_ESIGN SCIENCE IN THE NEW PARADIGM AGE

and sisters become possible again. This is the paradigm shift being offered here to be attained through following this creative process outlined here. We can acquire the sense of introspection and meditation to begin to experience the insights and knowledge from within that would unfold as we engage in the meditation that thinking about these ideas offer.

There is much interest in and studies on the subjects of dark matter and melanin. They are beginning to shed light, literally, on energy functions of the vital internal organs that the endocrinal system made of the network of ductless glands and plexes manages. Melanin is detected on the surfaces of the organs that produce an 'inner light'. Is life electric? Is believing this sufficient to cultivate our divinity or do we have to experience or know it?

Here again we look at the Hermetic axiom of the Law of Correspondence— "as above so below" coming full circle to address the question: what is mind? We think of this inner light as the micro mind, corresponding to the above of the universal mind and super-consciousness. If we accept the

laws of thermodynamics keeping conservation in 'mind', as that expression instructs us to do symbolically, the perpetual quality of mind and light are energies that are neither created nor destroyed.

Are they the same energy? Our goal is to evolve as we return to the source of our arising to the 'Source of Oneness with The ONE. We have a covenant with the creator to be the extensions of the universal energy, given degrees of freedom we seem ready to surrender in exchange for creature comforts.

If we agree that mind and light could be the same, we can accept the idea of the presence of a sustainable continuum that's always at work, perpetually changing and transforming all of consciousness itself through time, space and matter with the universal power. It is the same source that regenerates itself perpetually. We go in and out of this consciousness over intervals of time and on all levels in periodic spans of lifetimes in the triadic definitions of physical, mental, emotional and spiritual expressions of energies and flavors much greater than ourselves. These are described as holographic or binary on–off episodes. My question is: is the binary system adequate for our time, given where we are now in our development as a species in relation to all others that are found on levels of 'consciousness vibration'?

Levels of vibration include animate and inanimate forms of expressions— people, trees and forests, rocks, mountains, creatures, animals, LAWS, forces and elements. We are evolving to what could be appreciated as the third level man (CHRIST) consciousness.

This is a level of consciousness, known back in Egypt that few have achieved and the rest have not yet accepted.

As time goes by, more people are experiencing this awakening. We seem to be stuck in the perception that time, space and energy stopped and we have too. If our store of intelligence has run its course then this may be the case. What follows is the New Paradigm Age and the next level of human consciousness, with everything the future will deliver is in the balance.

The mass impact of human will power has grown exponentially. The thinking power that precedes and is also translated into computing power keeps growing according to Moore's law. It is facilitating problem-solving and decision-making beyond our binary brain and mental capacity.

The profound impact of this exponential growth of power, on all levels, includes physical—where work is done with its unique energies to support namely human creativity—ideas and thoughts. These all reflect the full spectrum of the body, mind and spirit continuum corresponding with physiology, psychology and spirituality along with space, time and energy, of which thought is our highest form. Space is pure extension. Time is pure duration. Spirit is pure energy. Extension, Duration and Energy are 'charged' with Pure Consciousness or Universal MIND.

The 'holographic projections' fuel the micro mind through the SOUL. This continuum then extends to all the expressions in an alignment that follows this threefold symmetry or TRIAD. The goal is to harmonize all of these expressions, flavors and energies for there to be transcendence weaving between and beyond the realms, attainable through these states as 'portals', as it were.

We might believe that the binary dynamic we have been using is adequate and it is to varying degrees very useful. It is dualistic and relates to the realm of the intellect and is just enough to manage our materialism orientation. In a relative sense duality could be very unstable, but still be useful, as a pendulum. This may be fine for the pendulum and the paradigm we are in now which is based on physical and psychological essences with a harmonized intellect as the mediator of the mind and spirit faculties.

Energy and thought related to physical and creative efforts comprise the extent of the "Spiritual" element of a deficient and non-harmonized triad. Religion alone does not account or compensate for this 'short fall'. The gurus who offer 'milk to babies instead of meat to men' do not know nor help the cause either.

A totally dedicated "spiritual science" that embraces all expressions of the dynamics of life, faith, Consciousness and even religious knowledge is required if we are to achieve that state of third level consciousness, which we can, and were promised. By decoding the systems of creation and contemporizing them we participate in our evolution, destiny and divinity.

What does this have to do with creative, responsive and conscious beings? With this 'blueprint', we can ART-iculate new ideas and solutions for our environments and our lives with an ever evolving and expanding aesthetic reality that captures our imagination and the essence of the constantly unfolding paradigms to keep us alive as creatively, emotionally, environ-mentally and spiritually responsible human beings.

The dominion we were given in the 'Gene of Isis' could be and is probably being revoked, as it appears to be today, given the quality of life and inhuman conditions we are experiencing around the world in general.

MIND   D_ESIGN SCIENCE IN THE NEW PARADIGM AGE

In looking at the Egyptian civilization, its Pantheon, The *Ogdoad*, *Hehu* or Infinites, *'celestial rulers'* of the cosmic age, the Spiritual Science and wisdom, at the root of the word 'nature' is 'neter'. The links between cultures of Egypt and India also relate to the root of the word Shu, or the 'neter of the past' as this too is used in the Shu-shu-mna Nadi. Is this significant? We will look into this further but a little later. Through the interaction of time (Shu and Tefnut) and space (Nut and Geb), both light (Ra)(now described as light energy) and darkness (Thoth) (now dark energy) come into existence. Ra and Thoth are the first two children of Nut and Geb, and they correspond to different aspects of human awareness and intention. On the *coherence meter* this registers as pure Science.

Ra is the neter of the light, represented by the sun, whilst Thoth is the neter of the dark, represented by the moon. These five children are Osiris, Isis, Set, Nephthys and Horus the Elder.

The story of the next five children of Nut and Geb is a description of what goes awry in human development, and the work that can be done to redress the balance, not so much to heal the wounds but to reframe and include them. These five children are Osiris, Isis, Set, Nephthys and Horus the Elder.

Osiris and Isis are best known as the animus and anima, the masculine and feminine aspects of the human psyche. We need to look beyond the symbols.

Set is the shadow, set about with the difficulties blind emotion and unconscious action brimming with the possibility of redemption.

Nephthys is the dark feminine, sometimes a dreamer, out of touch with aspects of reality, sometimes the woman of insight and vision. Horus the Elder, her male equi-valent (power), is sometimes the carrier of the seed of potential, on both physical and psychic levels.

There are five of these children just as naturally as there are five fingers on a hand. The sixth finger (sixth sense) that can count the original five is the foundation of all human under-standing, and the offspring of Osiris and Isis, known as Child Horus. The story of Child Horus is the story of our coming to know ourselves or self-realization through accepting responsibilities of limitation and power, restriction and love. The story of his coming into full adulthood offers hints for the next step in the collective human story. Indeed, some versions of the 'Age of Aquarius' describe it as "The New Age of Horus." The five elements with Five platonic forms representing them.

All these neters are voices of consciousness, reflecting universal mind, calling us to remember their deeply rooted 'es-senses' within ourselves. They offer a reminder that through our understanding of their significance we can understand who we are and how to find our truth. Through an understanding of the story of the neters and an attempt at the practical application of its implications 'makes the abstract real and readable'.

The ancient Egyptians founded the greatest civilization of the ancient (world), a civilization that lasted for many millennia.

The implications of what such an understanding offers us at this time of worldwide change are immense. We are the efterlife they planned for in the continuum of constant creation and eternality.

The first step is for us to realize that every move we make is endowed with meaning and clearly so, both individually and collectively. We then become able to hear the call of the neters (qualities of suchness and muchness) and follow their guidance, to hear their resounding call to us to become something other than no-thing or Divine'. A more serious state is the no-mind and no-spirit. Civilization building is not in our vocabulary, or on our MINDS. The highest state of consciousness modern cultures have reached is being nations. A nation is a long way from becoming a civilization if there are no consciousness compasses to show the way (with a Dao Design).

"The Song of Consciousness: Ah Rising at/that lasts"

Consciousness is arising in every dimension
Not surprising all who are conscious.
Catalytic change abounds against de-mentions. Higher frequencies are more profound
Not so evident to the whole of life spectrum
Still stuck in stress and deep chaos-ness.
The price of un-resolved increase is steeply rising Depleting our vital energies completely while we sleep, As the Earth and Cosmos change reality to illusion.

Be able and be ready to embrace inevitability Contribute to catalyzing transformations willingly. Be not resistant to its immeasurable power.

A Dao Defined methodology of awareness in order Occurring in our time to trigger greater healings Releasing resolutions of the past we embrace
Our destiny has a new humanity emerging paradigm.
In S.T.E.P.(space, time, energy, paradigm) with *SOURCE?*

We are in a time of critical mental and spiritual growth. Transformations occurring; personal powers changing both Exchanging paradigms for myths of times gone on by. Autonomous selves realize more wholesome parts
In harmonious configurations of our inhumanity.
We precipice jump stepping over into worlds anew,
A new paradigm, a new Reality, for mother Earth's fold.

It is time to make the leap up from our deep sleep. To ground ourselves in a New Earth we all can keep. To fully participate in it, and in its new becoming. Collaborators, and co-creators on this journey all Await Earth's alignment with us if we heed its call.

Thriving versus surviving, in a new way, is the choice. So few of them express their own true dimensions, And flavors of our focus for participants like us.
In transformative, extraordinarily mental spaces,
Not yet, grounded in meaningful realization of grace,
To harmonize ways of being and living stress-less-ly in time
Where we manipulate and create the matter-energy.

 *"Optimism is a strategy for making a better future. Because unless you believe that the future can be better, it's unlikely you will step up and take responsibility for making it so. If you assume that there's no hope, you guarantee that there will be no hope. If you assume that there is an instinct for freedom, that there are opportunities to change things, there is a chance you may contribute to making a better world. The choice is yours."* —A. Noam Chomsky.

Study the way all technological developments will affect the emerging culture. Carefully consider how people's attitudes and modes of thinking are changing. One change is the rising expectations and desires when observing how wealthier people live. This is a product of media and communication. If they can have it, why can't I?

Principles of Ethics: 'Ethical behavior helps protect individuals, communities and environments, and offers the potential to increase the sum of good in the world. As 'D$_E$Sign Scientists', making the world a better place is our mission.

We should avoid (or at least minimize) doing long-term, systematic harm to those individuals, communities and environments...' (Israel and Hay, *Research Ethics for Social Scientists,* 2006)

The three principles of ethics include informed consent, confidentiality and avoiding harm to do good. Informed consent is important. Those participating in the research understand its aims and objectives and ensure that informed consent is given, for research that is carried out with children or vulnerable adults. It is essential to acquire informed consent from a parent, guardian or responsible adult.

Confidentiality
Confidentiality needs to be considered - how will confidentiality be maintained? Is it always appropriate and applicable
(i.e. criminal activities, if someone is in harm...etc) Avoid harm and do good.

Ethics can go so far as to suggest that research need not only avoid harm, but to ensure that its purpose is to do good...how might this impact on the methodology of the research and its impartiality?

MANIFESTATION

Design is a skill that uses Affirmations & Creativity to manifest ideas. Writing or inscribing thoughts is powerful employs words. Using any Media to record thoughts is highly recommended to enhance one's Creativity and connection to higher levels of creativity for imagery and Imagination. A journal format helps to visualize, ideate and author One's desires. Affirmations are the follow-up habits that reinforce the Desires and visions, with focused intention and attention, revised as Needed, to manifest whatever we focus on by taking action. This Format is highly recommended. Love is the reality tester for our Passions and creations.

"The deepest longing in the human breast (heart) is the desire for appreciation." —William James

THE BENNETT TENETS for the New Paradigm Age

The First "Bennett Tenet" in the Synthesis FORMULA recognizes Consciousness as Body, Mind and Spirit (Creative Spirit, thought, work energy or effort.)

Questions come from a much deeper place than answers which are buoyed in a sea of materialistic and mythic conditioning and thoughts. Of all questions we continue to ask, on our quest, without satisfactory or clear answers, the most salient ones to me are: "Do we have the appropriate language to describe who we are, our place in the universe, our true purpose and how do we relate to these fundamental aspects of consciousness?"

Especially when we rely on confusing concatenation posing as truthful communication, we do not upgrade many aspects of knowledge and information to keep up with paradigm changes, thus rendering our language somewhat obsolete. In looking at the definitions of words in our lexicon, I find some not relevant to our time. Who are the wordsmiths responsible for the accuracy of physical, psychological and spiritual experiences and communication? We would be quite surprised to know what forces invent our languages.

If consciousness is defined and accepted as Body, Mind and Spirit— the symmetry principles of living—this would set the understanding of this notion of 'movement' (of the human spirit, mind and body) into rapid and inspired motion. This motion moves in different directions, synthesizing information that in turn, is correlated with Body, Mind and Spirit in an ever expanding and continuous pure extension, pure duration and pure energy or spirit.

This 'Formula' permeates everything we *think, see, say and create*. This is a 'new' way or (Dao Design) of looking at and applying an evolving design and aesthetic intelligence to a practical manifestation strategy to align with natural symmetry elements of culture and life itself as the 'consciousness' core, leading to higher states of being and becoming...

MIND

DESIGN SCIENCE IN THE NEW PARADIGM AGE

I attribute these qualities as evidence of a paradigm shift and this movement we need to activate NOW. We all need to be on board with this new agenda.

The Second "Bennett Tenet" is the 'East-West Dichotomy'. This is where the energy systems of the ancient wisdom traditions among various cultures that, if we are open, reveal links to 'modern physics, quantum theory', subatomic physics and many other disciplines offered to us by a Paradigm that shifts our basic nature.

I would imagine this impacts our DNA as well as our neurogenetic makeup. Forming the relationships to share this knowledge and information to make it more available must be part of the conversation about the new paradigm. Is there a grand paradigm with multiple sub paradigms within it?

I would propose the Consciousness be Grand Expression of Infinite, normal awareness and sub-consciousness which then permeates the filters and densities of manifestation into our material world. "Yesterday's mysteries become today's wisdom, knowledge, information and technologies.

It interesting that in the realm of real-ity, four becomes apparent as the symmetry of nature and manifestation. This aligns with the four forces, four directions and many other examples of the Law of Four (4). This number idea will be explored later as part of the Law of Numbers.

The Third "Bennett Tenet" of the New Paradigm Movement through synthesis is the foundation. It relates (relies on) ancient wisdom traditions, metaphysics, other esoteric knowledge and new interpretations that change constantly. When the correlations with cultural information align, awareness is confirmed and there are connections that bind human understanding.

The Fourth "Bennett Tenet" synthesizes tenets 1, 2 &3 into a praxis for 'making the abstract real'. Time changes as the patterns of life repeatedly transform old methods, processes and energies into new technology.

The Fifth "Bennett Tenet" Exploiting a new FORM vocabulary of Non- Euclidean curved 3D geometric forms is next. This is the intellectual property asset in the idea bank, the Intellectual Property agency and all services and products to be developed that are available to capable, creative professionals through some novel means of technology transfer, under development.

The Sixth "Bennett Tenet" is the idea bank that will keep us busy and prosperous for a long time to come. To create an avatar for this movement, we can imagine Steve Jobs as Body, R. B. Fuller as Mind and Mohandas Karamchand Gandhi as Spirit, fused into one BEING. How could their synthesized consciousness, intelligences and qualities inspire, motivate and help us create this movement?

The Seventh "Bennett Tenet" is represented by my Research and Archi-tectural (D$_E$Sign Science) practice/s. It now focuses on transforming shipping containers into habitable structures, among other modular systems and construction technologies for holistic communities as a wealth building strategy. This is an earth-shattering paradigm shift of its own, redoing traditional approaches in some circles. The reason for this message is to share this idea of exploring how to create and implement a strategy for the promulgation of, not just my work, but the wider ken of knowledge other designers are currently exploring. We need to redefine the role design plays in our lives to communicate how we add value to lives.

These *Tenets* represent a definite economic, material value potential that needs to be assessed, accessed and realized. Realization is the goal of innovation. Innovation is the synthesis engine. Doing this evaluation with the old paradigm methodologies is not the highest and best approach to arriving at the quantitative measure and the qualitative gauges the new paradigm thinking and methodologies can offer or need.

."To understand the whole, it is necessary to understand the parts. To understand the parts, it is necessary to understand the whole. Such is the circle of understanding."   Ken Wilber, *Eye of Spirit*

THE AFTERWORD

I MUST SHARE MY IDEAS AND joy for what I believe in and do creatively that is critical to our survival as human beings in a world that needs solutions. Here is a mechanism for creating solutions that can transform our lives and our economies. This is what SOURCEcompelled me to do but forgot to tell those who might need my help that I even existed. With the many times, avenues and opportunities I presented myself and my goods, I was dismissed or not heard.

How can newly discovered information become accessible and useful? The issues we encounter on our journey do not belong to us per se. If we buy into them, we have surrendered. Integrity is not to be relinquished or taken for granted. It resides in the collective soul. The fire can always be re-kindled and acted upon to become the bridge to a shared, loved and passionate vision for a sustainable future.

The goal is to reveal the knowledge, and the hidden principles and sources of information to inspire other creative designers, material scientists, producers and developers to recognize their own evolution and heightened consciousness giving them permission to adopt the new Paradigm ideas as viable solutions. Everyone who recognizes this quality in them has a voice, an expression and a flavor to offer the world and worlds to come. We are also developing certain segments of this strategy. My voice is the tone for three dimensional curved geometric forms. Knowing the logic structures that are the principles of how nature works cannot be monopolized by the Ivory Tower High Priests of an entropic western thought-generating system that isolates itself from the rest of the planet's cultures, wisdom traditions and peoples.

Value 'engineering', visioneering and imagneering are the quantitative, qualitative and creative spiritual essences of form generating through "synthesis". It's how we experience Harmony. This supposedly abstract process helps create uses for ALL forms, created or not. From this we can derive the value of the ideas for those who need them.

Once this exchange is completed and all parties are satisfied, economies are created. DO this enough. Do it repeatedly at levels of excellence and your authority will be cultivated. D*on't be late, or hesitate. Create a greater destiny for you, loved ones and the world!*

D$_E$Sign Science: gives us keys to The Unfolding, The Awakening and The Trans-forming of the New Paradigm Movement affecting our lives NOW. Design Science is the grand synthesizer of all arts, sciences, knowledge and information evolving from the infinite consciousness or source now being art-iculated as an epochal shift of human consciousness in and through our space, time and energy continuum. It gives us a much deeper understanding of "CONSCIOUSNESS",ourselvesand all of our expressions of that life-giving force that connects us all to SOURCE. We attain higher states of being, becoming in harmony with all the principles and laws we seek (to create our lives), systems of support for life and sustainable processes needed to pursue our desires, live and be happy.

D$_E$Sign Science involves applying multidimensional thinking to use the existing resources we have to 'create' original Ideas, Knowledge and Information that align with universal laws, strategies and principles of Body, Mind and Spirit to synthesize holistic solutions, expressions and flavors of space, time and energy to get more for our investments and efforts. D$_E$Sign Science allows us to access and harmonize the three states of normal, sub and infinite consciousness which we extrapolate into the physiology of matter (things) the psychology of all dynamic behaviors, feelings and the spirituality of thought creativity, direct knowledge, energy and (work) effort, are balanced with natural forces.

"The musician is very close to mysticism, far closer than the philosopher...because music is meaningful without any words; it is meaningful simply because it rings some bells in your heart creates a synchronicity between you and itself, when your heart starts resonating in the same way, when you start pulsating in the same way." Osho, Philosophia Ultima

D$_E$Sign Science involves a totally harmonized and balanced praxis™ that manifests, articulates and expresses solutions, ideas and thoughts through the use of the right materials with the proper applications of creative disciplines and the correspondences of spiritual Laws to create, support and attain higher states of creative excellence, optimized living and self-realization for the freedoms we enjoy.

D$_E$Sign Science uses all media, technologies and creative processes in the manifestation of all of the above that we bring below as true Design Scientists. The oneness of our vision and purpose, from now, on makes this our sole profession. Ownership of old paradigm definitions now disappear. Who am I?

I am a Design Scientist inviting you to celebrate our evolution and freedom revolution in a safe space, with abundant resources, free creative expressions and right actions, thought, energy and lasting unconditional love.

There is a schism that can only be bridged by teams of like-minded, conscious, professionals who are experiencing and have survived their own transformations. Consequently, they can align with this vision and mission. This team is the personification of transition in a "Matrix of Use" that can move towards imple-mentation of the tenets and other policies, principles, value engineering, currency and financial capital formation needs with operations, management functions and marketing intelligence. On the social engagement side, networking with influencers, connected high network folks who are committed to this movement is a (preferred) asset unto itself.

Such a collaboration would be incentivized by an autonomous type and level of partnership that goes beyond equity, debt or any other transaction and compensation or remuneration found in the old paradigm.

NOTES ON THE CANONS

 **O**NE OF THE MANY GOALS of this work is the establishment of a *'body, mind and spirit map'* for the journey of self- discovery, self-effort and self-knowing. We can transcend all the artificial divisions we encounter to enhance our lives. In this case a *'body, mind and spirit map'* is needed. We need to establish fundamental principles and natural laws of the cosmic being in the DNA in us for example, that's ready to unfold and no longer be dormant. The awakening is long overdue.

The Dao De Jing was referred to as a canon that inspired the 'Dao DeSign' (system). It is used as an oriental harmonizer for the *'body, mind and spirit'* triad that, in principle, is part of a wider swath of oriental wisdom traditions. 'Vasistha's yoga', like the Dao De Jing, is the second canon used to inspire the meditation and thought processes from the Hindu tradition. This storehouse of wisdom by Swami Venkatesananda"provides the means to eliminate psychological conditioning".

The next canon is the 'Temple in Man' and the 'Temples of Karnak' by A. Schwaller De Lubicz. This is a three-volume series focusing on the study of the geometric, spiritual Design science of temple and celestial architecture. This sets the tone for my Non-Euclidean Geometric inventions and patents.

Gauge theories involving the proportions of man as the meter, with space and measure in the western form tradition is art-iculated with the canon of proportions for the human body with the Vitruvian Man by Leonardo da Vinci. The transition from the pharaonic era in Egypt to the Christian or Piscean age employs one of the key canons of mathematics and geometry for temple building—placing man in a hexagon described by the radius of a circle. In so doing "man is placed under the sky of the temple". In the second canon, "man is placed on the sky of the temple as the radius of the circumscribing circle".

I arrived at a similar two-dimensional geometric expression by exploring and modeling, with cardboard curving 'interstitial spaces' centered in the voids of spheres in various stacked configurations, starting with the four spheres of tetrahedra. I later tested this 'paradigm-shifting thought experiment' by transforming right angle cones (dixie-cups) into extensions of curved form vocab-ularies conforming to the Non-Euclidean Geometry of Gauss, Bolyai and Lobachevski

I received utility and design patents for these inventions. I was more familiar with Schwaller De Lubicz's 'number theory' before discovering these two canons corresponding with the two dimensional, curved triangular resolutions of space that were similar to my work. This research continues to generate insights and innovations in fields beyond my expectation and knowledge.

As an artist *first* and an architect I have become an open and curious *'at it dude'* (I misspelt attitude and recreated myself) is who I have become.

(My subconscious is smarter than I am.) As a going 'at it dude' there is no monopoly with knowledge I am attracted to. All fields are open and fair game—especially when I recognize and can interpret visual content, I find using my trained 'eye' or visual intelligence like I did with the Egyptian canons and my other research methods and findings.

REFERENCES

-A-

Edwin a. Abbott: flatland
w. marsham Adams: the Egyptian doctrine of the light born of the virgin
d. g. Adler: the finding of the third eye
nur ankh Amen: the ankh: african origin of electromagnetism
rocky richard Arnold: the smart entrepreneur
khaled Azzam, keith Critchlow, prince of wales's institute of architecture.
Study in the geometry of the arch in Islamic architecture (visual, islamic & traditional arts department, benjamin bold): famous problems of geometry and how to solve them

-B-

Richard Bach: jonathan livingston seagull.
michael F. Barnsley: fractals everywhere
roland Barthes: image, music, text
herb g. Bennett: co-author with brian Tracy: transform.
Itzhak, Bentov: stalking the wild pendulum, a brief tour of higher consciousness
william, Blake: poetical works edited by william rossetti, george bell & sons, london, 1891.
karl Blossfeldt: art forms in nature
gregg Braden: the god code
e. a. wallis Budge: the Egyptian book of the dead
brendon Burchard: the motivation manifesto
herbert Busemann: the geometry of geodesics-: convex surfaces

-C-

Fritjof Capra: tao of physics.
Joseph Chilton Pearce: from magical child to magical teen robert Cialdini: pre-suasion
deepak Chopra: the seven spiritual laws of success

george s. Clason: the richest man in babylon-amazon reprint ishi press
paulo Coelho: the alchemist
andrew Collins;'gobekli tepe; genesis of the gods'
theodore a. Cook: the curves of life
richard Courant: dirichlet's principle, conformal mapping and minimal surfaces
dr. stephen r. Covey:The 7 Habits of Highly Effective People
h.s.m. Coxeter: Projective Geometry, Regular Complex Polytopes,
keith Critchlow: islamic patterns, into the hidden environment, time stands still: the hidden geometry: k. Critchlow, Jon Allen: the whole question of health

-D-

The 'Dao DeSign'– inspired by the Dao De Jing the classic Buddhist canon,
Leonardo da Vinci: Vitruvian Man.
edward De Bono; lateral thinking: creativity step by step
schwaller De lubicz:'temple in man', the 'temples of karnak' and a study of numbers.
c. a. Diop: Pigmentation of the ancient Egyptians
Dr. Joe Dispensa: you are the placebo
clayton w. Dodge: euclidean geometry and transformation
peter Drucker: the social age of transformation

-E-

Tarek El-Bouri, Keith Critchlow, Salmá Samar Damlūji: islamic Art and Architecture:
hans, fischer, Ernst: geometry of classical fields

-F-

Joseph pierce Farrell: manifesting michelangelo
timothy Ferriss: the 4-hour workweek: escape 9-5, live anywhere, and join the new rich
richard buckminster Fuller: nine chains to the moon 1938, synergetics 1975, and it came to pass 1976, critical path 1981.

MIND   D*SIGN SCIENCE IN THE NEW PARADIGM AGE

-G-

Jeremy Gray: janos Bolyai: Non-Euclidean geometry-geometry   and the nature of space. (Non-Euclidean geometries).
Carl Frederick Gauss (1777-1855),Nikolai Lobachevsky   (1792-1856),Janos
Bolyai (1802-1860),and Bernhard Riemann (1826-1866).
matila Ghyka: the geometry of art and life
samuel i. Goldberg: curvature and homology

-H-

Ernst Haeckel: kunstformen der natur: art forms in nature (lithographic halftone prints)
graham Hancock: magicians of the gods.
kenya Hara; designing Design
walker evan Harris: the physics of consciousness.
herman Hesse: Siddhartha.
Asa G. Hilliard III, Larry Williams, Nia Damali (Editors): The Teachings of Ptahhotep (The Oldest Book in the World)
alan Holden: shapes, space, and symmetry. Photographs by Doug Kendall ernest Holmes & willis Kinnear: thoughts are things-Ernest
Holmes: creative mind and success-the ernest Holmes papers.

-J-

James p. Jans: rings and homology
roger A. Johnson: advanced euclidean geometry

-K-

jerry King: the art of mathematics "Touch [es] the mathematical grandeur that the first geometers contemplated." — *Publishers Weekly*

-L-

haresh Lalvani; : patterns in hyper-spaces
solomon Lefschetz: algebraic geometry marc Levinson: The Box.

204

-M-

john Maeda; the Laws of Simplicity (Simplicity: Design, Technology, Business, Life)
edward Malkowski; the spiritual technology of ancient Egypt. john Martineau: a little book of coincidence.
e.a. Maxwell: deductive geometry
bruce e. Meserve: fundamental concepts of geometry
kōji Miyazaki: An adventure in multidimensional space: the art and geometry of polygons, polyhedra, and polytopes
t. owens More: the science of melanin

-N-

Neugebauer: the exact sciences in antiquity don Norman; the design of everyday things

-P-

Joseph Chilton Pearce: from magical child to magical teen
m. scott Peck: the road less traveled psychiatrist
dan Pedoe: geometry a comprehensive course, geometry and
penney Peirce: leap of perception
luther Pfahler: coordinate geometry
peter Pesic: beyond geometry the visual arts
manfredo Perdigao: riemannian geometry
daniel Pink: Drive. the surprising truth about what motivates us
alfred s. Posamentier: geometry; its elements and structure

-R-

James Redfield: the celestine prophecy
tony Robbins: awaken the giant within: how to take immediate control of your mental, emotional, physical and financial destiny!
Anne Rooney: the story of mathematics joe Rosen: symmetry discovered
don miguel Ruiz: the four agreements: a practical guide to personal freedom.

MIND

DESIGN SCIENCE IN THE NEW PARADIGM AGE

-S-

Harold Scott, MacDonald Coxeter: the beauty of geometry: twelve essays marc Seifert: transforming the speed of light.
lee Senella: the kundalini experience, kundalini.
rebecca Skloot: the immortal life of henrietta lacks
blake Snyder: save the cat.
barry Spain: analytical conics
lewis Spence: ancient egyptian myths and legends
saul Stahl: geometry from euclid to knots
shlomo Sternberg: curvature in mathematics and physics
robert R. Stoll: set theory and logic
d. m.y. Sommerville: the elements of non-euclidean geometry

-T-

John Thakara: how to thrive in the next economy.
eckhart Tolle; 'the power of now' published by new world library, a new earth and stillness speaks.
brian Tracy: transform
amos, Tversky, David, Krantz, Suppes, Luce: foundations of measurement

-V-

Swami Venkatesananda: Vasistha's yoga.

-W-

Warren k. Wake: design paradigms: a sourcebook for creative visualization
edward t Walsh: a first course in geometry
d'Arcy Wentworth Thompson: on growth and form
herman Weyl: symmetry
ken Wilber: the eye of spirit
harold e. Wolfe: Introduction to Non-Euclidean geometry
c. r. Wylie, Jr: foundations of geometry
marianne Williamson: return to love "a course in miracles".
h.g.Wells: world brain.

-Y-

Paul b. Yale: geometry and symmetry
paramahansa Yogananda: autobiography of a yogi.

-Z-

Gary Zukav: the seat of the soul.

PARADIGM HOOKS:

Paradigm 1 All Wisdom, Intelligence, Knowledge and Information (the WIKI) come from source.

Paradigm 2. The 'WIKI' with the BODY, MIND, SPIRIT, is the prime life support system formula.

Paradigm 3 Truth and integrity are critical to accessing and sharing the formula.

Paradigm 4 Transforming knowledge through collaboration into the WIKI for communities.

Principle 5. Needs, passion, imagination and Love drive our current external knowledge. Solutions come from within. With our focus, attention and will we manifest reality.

Paradigm 6 Engagement and Empowerment are keys for growth.

Paradigm 7 Respect for life is respect for self, others and source

CAREER RESOURCE GUIDE
NEW PARADIGM OCCUPATIONS

Designers	Need
Augmented Reality Designer-ARD	As technologies for augmented reality evolve, they will allow for new information to be layered over the physical world in seamless ways.
Avatar Programmer - AP	Our celebrity clients will need help in representing themselves best in virtual scenarios such as VR, mobile games, and movies.
Chief Design Officer or Chief Creative Officer - CDO-CCO	The CDO or CCO will be a position in every company, overseeing the design of a business's every touchpoint and solidifying a fluid visual narrative that can maximize efficiency and purpose.
Chief Drone Experience Designer CDED	As companies such as Amazon deploy unmanned drones in their businesses, there will be an increased demand for the design of the entire service experience
Conductor: Creative Technology Researcher	Extending the musical analogy, design has typically been preoccupied with creating new instruments.

Cybernetic Director	Cybernetic directors will be responsible for the creative vision and autonomous execution of highly personalized media services.
Fusionist 'SYNTHESIZER'	While still expertly versed in classical design skills, the fusionist will mix those skills with a "generalist" approach to technology, working across disciplines and interest groups. In many cases, the fusionist may feel like an outlier.
Human Organ Designer	Human organ designers will be experts in bio-engineering and design, fitting newly created organs and artificial limbs to humans.
Intelligent System Designer	The intelligent system designer doesn't design discrete objects or experiences. Instead, he/she focuses on designing the software systems that make possible the design solutions of others.
Cybernetic Director	Cybernetic directors will be responsible for the creative vision and autonomous execution of highly personalized media services.
Director of Concierge Services	Retailers will harness the power of big data to give their most valuable customers a higher level of service than that of the general public.
Embodied Interactions Designer	This role is expert in interface pattern languages and touch-points that have largely been considered alternative or merely subservient to screen-based GUIs.
Intelligent System Designer	The systems this person designs will integrate multiple domains, and those domains will themselves be the product of designers, artists, and technologists.
Interventionist	As organizations and their challenges become more networked and complex, it will be harder work to help them digest new ideas and build towards a better future.
Machine-Learning Designer	A machine-learning designer's job will be to construct data models and algorithms that allow companies to create artificially intelligent products.
Program Director	This person is a business strategist. He/she understands the "who," "what," and "why" behind a project/product; have a deep understanding of what it means to be a designer and a developer, and also has a track record of effecting change and influencing the end product.
Real–time 3-D Designer	Virtual and augmented realities are on the forefront of design and technology explorations. Interaction design and game design will collide and integrate.

Sim Designer	The sim designer integrates customer data, behavioral models, and statistical models to design simulated people that can be used to help predict future customer behavior.
Synthetic biologist/nanotech designer	We're already on the path to creating customized medicine, and within five years synthetic biologists will be designing treatment that ties to the DNA of the patient. These medicines will be designed in software and printed on 3-D biological printers.

CREATING COMMUNITY

Our goal is to mine the WIKI and grow a prosperous community worldwide with like minds, shared values and vision. "Design Science" pays homage to Richard Buckminster Fuller who gave us this idea in 1957. The evolution of art, science and technology impact all we can now relate to and the many Creative Design disciplines of Art, Architecture, engineering etc. They are becoming more complex and it seems that synthesizing the 'MATRIX' of elements into a 'Design Science' is a logical step.

This allows us to distill new wisdom, intelligence, knowledge and in-form-ation (a WIKI) to transform the world with more organic solutions and experiences in harmony with the pace at which human consciousness, needs to and in some cases, has evolved. This bridges the gap between those who are aware and need to be, to level the 'living fields' or work, play, self-realization and community.

This 'Design Science' synthesis distills and simplifies (Simple-Fi) the new knowledge and information to create a holistic (easy to grasp and apply) set of ideas, tools and technologies for the new paradigm™'. Simplicity is still a viable goal that nature loves, it seems. This discipline gives us a robust 'Design Information Processing, Management, and Application System' that is a profound transformational technology which will enhance our vision, creativity and life.

These creative principles have inspired innovations through decades of research studies, testing applications and planning in applying new ideas and form vocabularies to architecture art, sculpture and industrial design etc.

I have invented a set of new three-dimensional forms, which to me is a clear indication of this New Paradigm Expression of an emerging future, full of new possibilities, we need to embrace. Sharing this knowledge and information will inspire the global community as we seek the visual, verbal and cultural languages for the necessary communication and unification. Knowing and trusting the source of this (DₑSign Science) WIKI is critical to all the arts, sciences related fields of endeavor and the people who see these original and important life changing innovations as gifts to empower themselves to tap into our deeper states of becoming as we define, refine and enhance our (constant) creative freedom.

D~E~Sign Science is developing a Design Information System DIS™ platform with access to the expertise-building knowledge and information publishing portal, a constant design and creation research base for an innovative conscious community. What we have attained will lovingly be offered to inspire and motivate others to gain their own expertise with the right perspectives and vision for their destiny.

This 'New Paradigm Movement' will be with us for some time to come, if the past cycles are any measure. It is therefore necessary to also have a legacy component in place with succession in action. We must make our contributions to its expressions by each 'one teaching one' to control their destiny, regardless of disruptions and distractions. DIS™ gives us all advantages and opportunities during the transform-ations we might normally not recognize or be conscious of. This is powerful. It's worth the price of admission to DIS™ Future we are creating. Our community loves these new habit-forming disciplines that enhance creativity while we live in a strange world, we can eventually make familiar. In DIS™ community, learning is a shared lifestyle.

All quest-ions reflect our quests and are seen as highly respected requests for directions to help others form their cross pollination of ideas, opportunities and relationship building in true community with adherence to sound Body, Mind and Spirit principles.

Design professionals need to engage in opportunities to enroll and invest in our educational and training programs, buy our books, consumer products and information products branded with this new paradigm aesthetic, identity and JOY.

All currencies, including equity of any kind needed and invested, are to be considered on the basis of their worth, equitable value and added or appraised potential. "MONEY" does not speak above all other voices in this cacophony of harmonious sound that resonates from the He-art to all the key components of Consciousness with its Body, Mind and Spirit dimensions in rhythm with the universe. This knowledge is encoded in our ances-story, saved for us to tell our version now.

It includes all that is now known and verified, considered as the New Paradigm and its movement. Real, talented 'actors' have to be identified as activists and action-takers to fill these roles and others that by the nature of transition and change will be needed or be replaced to fill all needs. This is a working team in flux that remains fresh, always moving in cohesion and toward effectiveness to manifest this long-term development plan to the best of our abilities.

Develop a "matrix of use" for all sectors of the economy where the plan could be and/or will be applied.

The Null Set	Provider From	Each	Sector With	Specific talents	Resources
Need					
Food					

NEW PARADIGM OCCUPATIONS: D_ESIGN SCIENCE IN THE NEW PARADIGM AGE

This all gets put into a space, time, energy continuum and developed into a computer system.

The new paradigm movement™

Neuroplasticity evolutionary wisdom paradigm movements

A knowledge economy based not on old paradigm values that are 'obso-less-sent' but the new paradigm opportunities.

New paradigm knowledge is now available and user friendly. The transformation of data (organized/designed) into information is the key "innovation strategy"; "using care instead of fear to do good"

The question for this quest is: What is **"CONSCIOUSNESS?"**

1. The Triad of Consciousness: The law of Three (3) and the number system
2. Periodicity and the transformation matrix
3. Ancient wisdom traditions, Sciences and Traditions with alternative interpretations of life forces and their Operating Systems
4. The Kundalini vs Western Philosophical Frameworks
5. The Flavor Machine, Ancient 'Archeo-Celestial or Architectural Sites as in 'Gobekli Tepe' South Eastern Turkey.
6. The classic Euclidean Geometry and the Polyhedra vocabulary— the Non-Euclidean.
7. Form vocabularies and their applications to design science and technologies
8. Cultural aesthetic expressions, Ubiquitous Architecture and holistic communities with the emphasis on wealth-creation through housing
9. Lifestyle transformations, principles, sciences and technologies
10. Creating an educational system based on new paradigm knowledge
11. Andragogy: the method and practice of teaching adult learners; adult education.

"Much has been written about *Andragogy—the method and practice of teaching adult learners (adult education)*, in general education circles over the past fifty years," but there is no organized system to develop and provide it. Pedagogy is obsolete.

The State Transformation Triad with Universal Consciousness and Symmetry Principles

BODY	MIND	SPIRIT
Stimulus	State	Results
Goal	Desire	Outcome
Statement	Intent	Meaning
Thought	Emotion	Passion
Scene	Mood	Act
Space	Time	Energy
Physiology	Psychology	Spirituality
Vision	Visualization	Imagine
Was (Tense)	Being	Becoming
Expression	Feelings	To Experience
Words	Articulation	Communicate (Vocalize)
Form	Tension	Formulate
Dominion	Personal Power	Create (Creative Energy)
Thing	Balance (forces)	Harmony (Flavors and Essences)
Event	Quality	Flavor
Voice	Tone	Essence (Vibration) (Resonance)
Reflection	Observation	Intuit(ion)
Declaration	Confidence	Faith
Message	Exchange	Resonate (Sharing Values)
Knowledge	Comprehension	Will
Motion	E-Motion	Movement
Reasons	WHY	Evaluate
Concept or Idea	Experience Value	Think (Fulfill Need/Desire)
Meditation	Clarity	Evolve
Brain, CNS, Kundalini, Chakras, Endocrine System, Aura	Living	Self-Realization
Paradigm	Insight	To view

NEW PARADIGM OCCUPATIONS:

Concept	Perception	To Conceive and Realize
What is said	Why it is said	How To Say it
Aura	Clarity	Knowledge vs Faith
Intuition	Sense	Wisdom
Awareness (Conscious)	Subconscious	Superconscious
Intellect	Intelligence	To Know
Task, Deed	Accomplishment	Being Satisfied
Life	Integrity	Happiness

Continue developing this matrix to explore other threefold relationships in the triadic harmony with the following concepts.

Hallucination, Delusion, Agonizing, Hesitation, Indecision, Premeditation, Procrastination.

COLLABORATION OPPORTUNITIES

THE VEHICLE FOR THIS IS a new paradigm Prize, a gift to conscious creative inventors for the world. This is how it works: Establish a "New Paradigm Pri$e" for "The global recognition of excellence through practical creative efforts, collaborations and contributions in D$_E$Sign Sciences and Visual

Intelligence' disciplines responsible for innovative breakthroughs, Philosophies, strategies and concepts. This will create ideas, exponential and/or disruptive technologies and designs that can transform creative processes, design solutions, technologies, materials and computer technologies and systems for the development, creation and management of any aspect of the inventions. They need to add exponential value to the Quality of Life, preserve the environment and be energy efficient. This aligns with any field of human endeavor, regardless of the patentability of any invention under consideration for "New Paradigm" recognition.

This extends to qualified individuals, stage one startups, entrepreneurs and educational institutions, worldwide.

THOUGHTS: If ancient oriental cultures could believe that destruction was a principle in natural law (and WAR became a phonetic accident), why did western cultures misinterpret destruction as WAR and not see it as being an organic creative aspect of growth? Could history have pivoted into another direction on this notion?

Exploring Breakthrough Paradigms:

To understand consciousness and our higher selves to build better relationships in the human family and all manmade environments.

To redefine consciousness, as the body, mind and spirit continuum as the inspiration for making abstract thoughts, natural principles and technologies real.

To reclaim and share the emerging creative, intellectual and spiritual capital to be free and totally fulfilled personally, professionally, in community and be on higher purpose.

To collaborate and accelerate transformations to harmonious futures for a new world and its peoples embracing the most natural universal attribute of all—change. Do so with courage and vision!

NEW PARADIGM OCCUPATIONS: D~E~SIGN SCIENCE IN THE NEW PARADIGM AGE

The new imperative is to add value to all human endeavor, with honor, respect and gratitude to all forms of 'design sciences' and arts disciplines with all technologies, present and future, with deeper 'ubiquitous architectures' encoded with richer identities, new form aesthetic flavors and breakthrough technologies now being and continuing to be manifested and articulated for the greatest good".

In "The Sciences of the Artificial by polymath", by Herbert A. Simon, *the author asserts design to be a meta-discipline (metaphysics) of all professions. It is a science.*

Everyone who creates courses of action aimed at changing existing life situations into preferred ones is a designer. (Original 'non-existing' situations?) The intellectual activity that produces material artifacts is no different fundamentally from the one that prescribes remedies for a sick person (needing healing) or the one that devises a new sales plan for a company or a social welfare policy for a community.

Design, so construed, is the core of all professional training; it is the principal mark that distinguishes the professions from the sciences.

Schools of engineering, as well as schools of architecture, business, education, law, and medicine, are all centrally concerned with the process of design." Are courses of action affected by designers only?

Courses of action that cause themselves are organic or natural or can be caused by man's interaction with the environment and systems.

Healing is a form of design. The *meta-discipline for design professions* is a spiritual science. *Evolution* is either a manmade or paradigm shifting preferred course of action. Where is "need" in this definition?

THE BENNETT CULTURAL ECONOMIC DEVELOPMENT MATRIX

		APPLICATIONS	
CONCEPT	OLD PARADIGM	NEW PARADIGM	TECHNOLOGY
Logic Structure	Gobekli-Tepe	The x-z & z-x Flavor Machines	Celestial Architecture Computing Systems O.S and Higher Level Qualitative Reckoning
Philosophical and Esoteric Concepts		Metaphysics and Consciousness Theories	Intelligence & Creativity Enhancement
Geometric Form Inventions	Platonic & Euclidean Polyhedra	Bennett Non-Euclidean Polyhedra	

Architecture and Construction	Ubiquitecture™ in other technologies	ISBU Autohomes and Communities	Housing, Energy and Commercial Space
Industrial Design	Household Accessories Food Forms, Tools Kitchenware ™	New Form Technology applications	New Materials and Forms
ART; production, Publishing & Distribution	Sculpture, Paintings	Digital Images and mixed Media works	
Educational	Systems and Devices	Pedagogy	Andragogy
Literary and Technical Publishing			
Fashion and accessories	Trilliant™ Watches Optix™ Eyeware	Chronotecture	Bespoke Chronotex
Healing & Wellness			Vibration (Sound) and other media
Wisdom, Knowledge & Information	Publishing	Visions & Ideas	Self-Publishing
Paper Engineering			
Toys, Games, Puzzles	Communication Devices	GEOMIFORMZ™ Media Cubes	
Real Estate	Development		Wealth Building
Environment Organizing Systems		The File Carrier Systems	
Studios and Affiliate Networks	Global Design Studios ™	Global Studio Designs™	
Media Production and Distribution			Product Development
Marketing Research & Sales	Internet-Analog-Word/Mouth-WOM	Network Affiliates	e-commerce & Digital
R&D-Licensing and JV	Stealth	Stealth	Intellectual Property
Capital Formation	Crowdfunding	Crowdsourcing™	Cultural Development

The Lotus River flows between the high mountain and the low delta carrying life from birth to death. In our Piscean story, named after our present epoch, various 'vesica piscis' or fish forms live in its stream. Some, like the salmon, swim against the current, upstream, to reproduce, answering nature's calling. The bottom feeders are floundering in blissful nescience concerned about meals they missed. The predators, the salmon and the flounders are all in the continuum of 'who eats whom' and are all in/on their DAO to their inevitability.

NEW PARADIGM OCCUPATIONS: DᴇSIGN SCIENCE IN THE NEW PARADIGM AGE

Are there fish in heaven from all the fishing that's been going on since the original creator of fishers of men did his magic? I am sure Noah saved two, from his mysteriously symbolic genetic cargo, one for himself and one for 'HIMHERIT'.

In the Hindu triumvirate (or Triad) Brahma is the creator of the universe. Vishnu is the second god responsible for the upkeep of creation and Shiva is the destroyer of the world. Consciousness, the all omnipresent, omniscient cosmic being in it omnivibrational essence, causes Vishnu to arise. From the cosmic being's heart entire worlds arise.

All arisings have the ability to preserve themselves through Vishnu. Out of Vishnu arises Brahama who in turn gives rise to the four expressions of animate and inanimate things—sentient and insentient form. This is all prior to the dissolution.

At this point Shiva dances to the music of life and death; ease and dis-ease; pain and suffering that is played out on the lower register's realm. Here men conjure desires in their hearts and build air castles in their minds. The three hearts—the physical, the emotional and spiritual hearts with strong desires and illusions—are rendered onto Shiva because the rewards of little or no self-effort and no right action are Shiva's tools.

Self-effort is the result of knowledge from the good books, instructions from wise teachers and one's own passion, focus and will. Here is an equation: Fs x Es=Iy x SE; Fruits of endeavors equal the intensity of self-effort. Right actions create positive outcomes.

Looking further we read: "Kundalini is the Goddess of speech, (language, symbols, words) and is praised by all. When awakened she offers illumination (light), the source of all Knowledge and Bliss. She is pure consciousness; the Supreme Force, the Mother of Prana, Agni, Bindu, and Nada. It is by this Sakti that the world exists. Creation, preservation and dissolution are in Her. Only by her Sakti the world is kept up. It is through Her Sakti on subtle Prana, Nada is produced. While you utter a continuous sound or chant Dirgha Pranava! (OM), you will distinctly feel the real vibration starting from the Muladhara Chakra. Through the vibration of this Nada, all the parts of the body function. She maintains the individual soul through the subtle Prana. In every kind of Sadhana the Goddess Kundalini is the object of worship in some form or the other".

This system represents the deepest level of our knowledge of the gross nature and fuels of human physiology without the chemical processes, without the electro-magnetic forces, the color, vibrations and the host of flavors involved in the human experience we call life. The Chinese were isolating sex and pituitary hormones from human urine and using them for medicinal purposes by 200 BCE. In 1849 Arnold Berthold pioneered this research. In 1902 William Bayless and Earnest Starling continued the development.

In the western world knowledge feeds our voracious materiality. Prayer is strictly for supplication and revelation is a book in the bible few truly understand. Of all the sentences in this work this is the most dispassionate. Entire libraries have been dedicated to how to do the right thing, leaving us on a trajectory to oblivion. From a spiritual (NOT RELIGIOUS) view every word in this text is a practical, emotional and super energy generator to create the lives we were meant to live.

Here is another dedication to the library of human failure celebrating Shiva's triumph.

Experiments that are mechanical are STEM (See, Touch, Estimate and Measure). They no longer work. The Thought STEM is now (See, Think, Energize and Meditate) with observation and participation.

The search for truth and freedom has an upside and a downside to it. Even if in the study of the nature of life we do not find truth or freedom, the process of seeking could have its rewards. What we discover could soften the pain as changes in life are encountered. Discovering truth and freedom could be the bonus. Wisdom could be gained in either scenario, like paying attention, which does not cost anything, except when it is not paid attentively. The search for wisdom and freedom costs much less and the gain is exponentially greater.

Physiological, psychological and spiritual transformations follow the eternal creative principles outlined in this work. The goal of this work is to establish a *'body, mind and spirit formula'* for the synthesis process as The Dao of (self-discovery, self-effort and self-knowing) elevating 'DESIGN' to a science.

On second thought, maps already exist. Others with broader shoulders have left us their wisdom to help us transcend the artificial diversions we encounter as we continue to enhance our lives. For this, a *'body, mind and spirit'* paradigm is needed. Fundamental principles and natural laws of the cosmic being in the DNA in us for example, that's ready to unfold can no longer remain dormant. This awakening is long overdue.

We now bring out the big 'canons' to help us fight our spiritual battles. The Dao De Jing was referred to as first canon to inspire the 'Dao DeSign' (system). It is used as an oriental harmonizer for the *'body, mind and spirit'* triad that in principle, is part of a wider swath of oriental wisdom traditions.

The 'Vasistha's yoga', like the Dao De Jing is the second canon used to inspire the meditation and thought processes from the Hindu tradition. This storehouse of wisdom by Swami Venkatesananda "provides the means to eliminate psychological conditioning".

DESIGN DEVELOPMENT:

1. The "Book" Title—D_ESign Science-in the New Paradigm Age This is the first in a series of publications devoted to the promulgation of a movement that informs and gives access to all 'designers' in this movement to understand what D_ESign Science is and how it inspires our mission and defines our goals and purpose from a holistic view.
    a. Our intellectual assets come directly from *'SOURCE'* to inspire the highest and best creative expressions that serve our environment for mankind to nurture human growth through body, mind, spirit and energy development.

b. We have synthesized a new aesthetic (identity) for all our creations in keeping with the 'Body Mind Spirit' principles and the Space, Time Energy Paradigm or STEP formulae.

c. From the synthesis of these disparate elements in traditional business models come the 'oneness, cohesion and simplicity' we 'enjoy' and are grateful for sharing. We Simple-fi our vision and mission and will continue to do so as we grow.

The Theoretical Premise: We define the 'BMS' formula as the 'synthesis of consciousness' as our "New definition and ART-iculation" of 'culture'. All creative Systems, technologies, intellectual properties, assets and activities become the 'holistic foundation' and 'guiding symmetry principles' to support all our creative, social and entrepreneurial endeavors.

This is our New Paradigm model that 'moves' the research, creation and dissemination of the Direct Wisdom, Intelligence, Knowledge and Information (WIKI) 'using these universal principles we access from source. As creative and respectful spirits, we honor all life that's in pursuit of self-realization and higher consciousness.

We advocate for all creative, social, economic, cultural and development activities, thoughts and expressions through our research, publishing and production, and the dissemination of information, consumer products, industrial designs, architectural and building technologies, media and communication systems to include but not be limited to the following:

2. Information products in print, digital published media will be made available periodically.
   a. 3D form vocabularies with new aesthetic identities for consumer products, objects and electronic devices, architecture and Art and other inventions yet to be developed.

3. All intellectual properties will be made available through 'agents', to developers, joint venture partners and clients to develop opportunities not aligned to our mission and agenda.

4. The people aspect of this campaign becomes a global initiative to explore possible exchanges needed to expand our reach and creative contributions worldwide.

5. This is a cultural development and entrepreneurial movement with a development agenda dedicated to creating business opportunities and models of production, distribution and service delivery related to the new paradigm WIKI technologies. We believe that the future depends on D$_E$Sign Science for the infusion of innovation to create the industry growth and expansion for the prosperity and wellness needed now, for The Good of All (FTGOA). "Design Heals ALL" is our motto. "Making the Abstract Real" is our 'secret sauce'.

6. The book with the WIKI, the business and its agents, with the collaborators, form the model to create and share the knowledge meant to promote opportunities that further the cause, growth and prosperity of this vision and movement for the good of all (FTGOA).

7. The 'ticket' is the acquisition of the book. With proof of purchase, readers become chartered members of this movement and affiliates of the 'Centerpri$e'. They may choose various levels of membership according to their skills, professional and business acumen and needs.
   a. The social currency aligns with the marketing trends we now engage in.

   Supporting the vision and mission is not mandatory but highly recommended with all benefits offered to the 'agency and membership'.

8. The book represents the body of work I have distilled that's now being shared as the process, resource and product of a synthesis of many creative professions I have enjoyed.
9. The future of design will involve a harmonized blend of Science, Art and Mathematics (SAM), to manage the complexity that continues to unfold from the new systems and disruptive technologies we will now be prepared to handle with this business model.
10. Visualization, and Meditation are the two recent contributions made to the western world that have had significant impact on self-development, starting in the fifties. This is the first step to resolving the East West dichotomy that could bring peace and prosperity to the world.
11. I believe these are the tools for thought processes (not experiments) that can be used to connect to Source.
12. The exponential value of this 'creative sector' will be significant, according to all the currency gauges we have.
13. There are 7 tiers of participation, activation and collaboration in this model.

Non-Euclidean forms become the new aesthetic vocabularies to be exploited in developing all possible applications at different scales and sizes in different materials for uses in different industries and markets.

"STRUCTURAL PHILOSOPHY"

purpose: author/s: channel/s that gain access to 'direct knowledge' from Source and is in the flow of constant creation and creative manifestation while obeying 'natural laws' using intuitive, creative and spiritual disciplines with 'design' as the core science or other methodologies we create.

This matrix can be expanded to meet the growth needs and implementation processes.

	THE TIERS	CREATIVE TALENT	DISCIPLINES
1	Founders	Finance and Capital Sources	Operations Managers
2	The Agency	Multi-talented talent searches	Data Bases and Associations
3	Consultants,	Vendors and Suppliers	Distributors
4	The 'heart' membership,	Professionals	General audience; Students
5	Technology Inventors	Developers	Operators
6	Creatives:	Planners, Artists	Producers; Fulfillment
7	Joint Venture Partners	Clients	The Market Niches

AUTHOR-ITY: Is an organic and natural energy enhanced in the group dynamic rather than with the solo 'expert'. Design as an authority, is a ubiquitous discipline. When exercised it commands attention which confirms the 'authority' inherent in its creative process. I am now synthesizing Art, Architecture and some of the sciences into a 'D$_E$Sign Science'.

These principles form connections and core elements using the new visual intelligence, intuition, metaphysics, knowledge and experience in art, science to create inventions going beyond the boundaries of the classic '3D form consciousness'.

This is then used to create a MATRIX with a quantitative and qualitative periodicity that could organize vast amounts of information and data. Sooner rather than later we are going to need new systems to process this data.

We exploit all forms of 'AUTHORING and AUTH-ENTICATION: This comes from creating viable applications and solutions for various industries, markets and individuals open to new ideas, opportunities and methods of creating prosperity and good works for their clients and themselves in the transformed and emerging world *economy*.

Contrary to the non-standard definition of economy as 'the study of the lack of resources', this new economy is one of a-bun-dance, open and available to all who can connect to SOURCE and are in the flow of the WIKI with values to be shared and exchanged.

A profound transformation is taking place on every level of life and what supports it now. This turns into a spiritual dimension as our consciousness expands to align with all the changes taking place.

AUTHENTICITY: I am secure in my abilities and confident in my connection to SOURCE and the flow of the 'WIKI' which keeps me humble, compassionate and profoundly grateful.

INTEGRITY: is the major system of value exchange. Intellectual property is our currency. The following tables show the shifts between the old and new paradigms:

OLD PARADIGM	NEW PARADIGM
EFFECT	CAUSE
STIMULI	SENSE DATA (EARLY STAGE INFORMATION
STRESS	TENSION
FOCUS (DISTRACTED)	ATTENTION (ATTRACTING ENERGY TO ACTION)
MEANING	INTENTION
HOARDING	GIVING UNCONDITIONALLY
LOVING SELF	LOVING OTHERS

OLD PARADIGM	NEW PARADIGM
SELF DEVELOPMENT (ENABLING)	SELF-REALIZATION (EMPOWERING & LIBERATING)
PEDAGOGY	ANDRAGOGY
SELF HELP	EMPOWERMENT
ENTREPRENEURSHIP	ARTREPRENEURSHIP
QUANTITY	QUALITY
A JOB FOR LIFE & (A GOLD WATCH)	CREATIVE FREEDOM
DEFERRED LIVING	ACTUALIZING DREAMS
GIVING THANKS	GRAMMERCY (PROFOUND GRATITUDE)
NUCLEAR FAMILY	COMMUNITY
SALT OF THE EARTH	SALTING THE EARTH
EGO & SHEGO: ME, MYSELF AND I	CONNECTED TO SOURCE & IN THE FLOW

Here are some issues we need to develop that relate to the Intellectual Properties in this work:

1. The protection and legal issues must be addressed with systems in place to assure the proper and legitimate use of any and all of the ideas disclosed. Publications can be cited in patent application, but they are by no means as effective as official patents and copyrights.
2. The relationships will include, but not be limited to, outright sales, licensing, and other forms of co-creating and partnering on a project basis. They include agents, developers, marketers and manufacturers among analog and digital makers in creative sectors that are form intensive and wanting to be part of this Non-Euclidean aesthetic (movement) and any of the brands we develop.

3. Prepare and make available as a follow up with 'proof of purchase' (POP) of the book for clients to obtain documents and agreements upon request.
4. Trade secret agreements and provisional patents would be the first level forms to consider.
5. Patents will be applied for if and when 'the assignment of rights' is required as part of the memoranda of understanding.
6. The Special Opportunities Division will manage the annual Enterpri$e Programs for designers to enter an RFP process that will focus on innovative and feasible applications of ideas from the 'Gallery of illustrations' in the back-matter and the "Idea Bank". A supplement related to the RFP will then be released. The prize: the winner becomes the co-creator of the idea as its lead developer (terms to be negotiated).
7. Membership will be granted upon paying a one-time membership fee and the book will be complementary. Other technical information will be available when published. Putting thoughts into action is the exciting part of this movement creative designers might be looking to collaborate with. Innovative ideas and opportunities are available.

PROVERBS & PROFHERBS:

"The future of design will involve a harmonized blend of Science, Art and Mathematics (SAM) to manage the complexity that continues to unfold from the new systems and disruptive technologies we are not now prepared to handle". It must become a 'D$_E$Sign Science' if we are serious about our evolution.

In the New Paradigm Age our major challenge is keeping pace or ideally overtaking the 'pace of Progress'. Progress is now 'undertaking' us!

"Synthesis" is a way of getting from many to one not with the pain of isolation, but in community.

Through D$_E$Sign Science the fundamental synthesis of innovative 'design' ideas uses the canons and symmetry   principles of nature. The challenge we face is reframing the mental scaffolding or old paradigm that does not support the new building blocks we are all co-creating. The New Paradigm Dynamic (NPD) is a collective energy effect we are all participating in as we create. Words, Images and Actions are driven by Will and creativity. This may seem strange to the 'egoic' isolationist and materialist. Here is a candidate for extinction if there ever was one.

Design is a 'spiritual awakening process', a renaissance it was called, meant to restore and regenerate all that is and will become naturally. This speaks to a kind of 'ubiquity' at the very core of life which is internal with the potential to be expressed in the creative world.

There is a cyclic motion that controls information and innovation that inspires growth. In one phase of the cycle the external environment inspires us. The power of the thoughts that conceived all of it is what we absorb and process.

This is what sustains us, doing more good than food, clothing and shelter does for our Body, Mind and Spirit.

Is this a paradigm we subscribe to now? What would this idea do for us if we could then process this 'collective internalized thought energy', reframe it with the new (NU) flavor and share it with the world?

Our life support systems now have major gaps that seem to be widening in almost all aspects of life. Shifting our mindsets just a few degrees could make a difference. Difference is what we do not handle properly as a mental principle. Similarity is the comfort zone we guard without regard for embracing the value difference makes.

Design is our ability to create whatever we align with, *not want nor desire*. Science is the method of doing it for ourselves with materials, tools and gifts we already have but have not 'loved' ourselves enough to try u-sing them. Love is a universal force that holds all the multi- verses together.

You may call it light, gravity, the weak or strong force, but in the oneness of infinite consciousness it is LOVE. The life force is love.

Life must love us to keep us in its flow of the three energy fields that 'synthesize' it for us.

They are the physical (Eros) the mental (Philos) and the spiritual (Agape). We seem to be clueless about doing it ourselves. Here again we see the imbalance and the focus on the physical that consumes us. If we use the marketing metaphors in the self-development world, this idea of a design science would bring dimensions to new creative levels we can all begin to explore.

Supporting ourselves by loving the life that loves and takes care of us, regardless of the state we have designed for ourselves, is the first step.

Our hi-story, my-story or future and the present or the gift we are given needs to be repaid This is more crucial than paying off the multitrillion dollar US debt.

Though the currency is different, it will more than compensate for our intransigence. Paying attention is one of the currencies we do not understand. Attention is focused consciousness. It is what directs our energies and our creativity to attract the 'scientiam recta', direct knowledge we have access to.

It is the key to designing our lives. Everyone can afford to pay it (attention). It is one of those powerful gifts that on the surface, seems to cost nothing, so why can't we afford to pay it? It causes all the pain we suffer.

Cycles of life change along with the expressions of the space, time and energy that is encoded in it every 1,000 to 2,000 or 3,000 years.

NEW PARADIGM OCCUPATIONS:

D_ESIGN SCIENCE IN THE NEW PARADIGM AGE

Is there anything about our space, time energy continuum worth keeping? Let's make a time capsule and move on with our new mind agenda and begin designing our new lives. D_ESign Science will help us access the Wisdom Intelligence Knowledge and Information (WIKI) needed. The new forms and skills we 'I-earn' will ART-iculate the new aesthetic reality with the identity that will 'brand' our time and our contributions to humanity in this new era known as the 'new paradigm age.' We have a level playing field opportunity for inclusion into community like we have never seen or experienced before.

All of these ideas are the seeds of our time that's been lying fallow too long. It is spring— time for planting new seeds. Are we going to continue what we are doing now with the same results, or do less with more or do nothing at all and atrophy when we are given (or always had) opportunities to empower ourselves with the ease of an (awkward) awakened consciousness. All it costs is paid for with attention and love.

We need to put design into its most powerful and purposeful context to be the connection to source which, ironically, we are already experiencing, but are not aware of.

There are two spiritual principles to which the west was recently introduced in our recent past that have infused our consciousness with methods of developing the human mind and spirit. They are meditation and visualization. These are the disciplines that are the portals to our destiny—the one we create especially for those who are prepared to shift their paradigm and embrace the new WIKI about our reality as spirits on a physical eternally conserved journey. They are the cash registers and the score-keeping media for new age wealth.

Meditation is 'free' and thoughtless awareness is its reward. All it costs is paying focused attention. Visualization is mindful and focused visual creative thinking. Meditation opens the portal and visualization receives the signs that inspire de-signs we process to grow and be healthy.

Meditation takes us to the hidden dynamic behind everything, everywhere in spiritual no time, no space but in all energy. There may be realms of 'no energy' if we acquiesce to the quantum theories. Visualization operates in physical space and psychological time and in spiritual space with creative human effort.

We get to an intersection of Mentalism and Visual acuity where thought and action cohere in intelligence activated by meditation (thoughtless awareness) with visualization and all other harmonious 'threefold systems in place' to create 'synthesis'.

Do we create synthesis or anything for that matter? Are we instruments responding to the grand orchestration of the universe and are being betrayed by the 'quality' of our ego, mind and emotions?

There is another state with methods, expressions, form, skills and power aligned with will and passion being used to help support the life force which is the ultimate generative, regenerative and eternal dynamic we are privileged to experience. This is the same force that holds multi-verses together. Why are we not in tune with it?

There are some key principles needing enhanced focus, attention, clarity, imagination and thought, to name a few that D$_E$Sign Science offers. Design on all levels is in this unfamiliar intersection of Meditation, Visualization and Attention fueled by thought, imagination and intuition. Let's extrapolate these two fields of information in a matrix to expand our awareness.

The questions are about relationships. How do the column elements relate to the row elements. What is the product of the two terms in 1-intersection and 2 for other ('symmetry') behaviors we define or are observing?

THE MECHANICS OF CONSCIOUSNESS

	MEDITATION,	VISUALIZATION	ATTENTION
Meditation	Thoughtless awareness	Undesirable distractions Guided of unguided thoughts	Return to Thoughtless awareness
Visualization	Thought Processing	Imagination-Innovation	Observation
Attention	Focused Thought Insights	Thought Experimentation	Intense Focus Clarity

	Imagination	Intuition	Thought
Meditation	Creation	Inspiration	Conceptualization
Visualization	Visioneering	Dreams	Cognition
Attention	Creativity	Source	Expression

Every human being is capable of expressing this human dynamic because it is already a part of us and we a part of it. There is no rocket science here. The lack of awareness of this idea comes from our unrealized state of being in existence and stress, not true living.

Design is about connecting to source, being in the flow and being the channel for all the goodness that we sidestep. This first habit to be absolved is the 'ego'. Knowing how to balance positive and creative aspects of it with all else requires skillful mental work.

NEW PARADIGM OCCUPATIONS: D_ESIGN SCIENCE IN THE NEW PARADIGM AGE

Man's ego (and now shego) does not 'pair' with Source, nature and self. Many of our current paradigms confront these phenomena under a pretense of dominion. We still do not get the messages that mother earth sends us, for example, with storms, chaos and 'psychic imbalances'. Native Americans and other cultures have much better ideas about 'Mother earth'.

Implementing these ideas to support human life with all its desires, needs, wants and wishes requires a methodology that is designed with physical, mental and spiritual harmony in heart and mind that is in 'equilibrium' with the symmetry principles, laws of space, time, energy in correspondence with consciousness on all levels. D_ESign Science does this for us. It is meant to give us more than things. It might just return us to ourselves before our 'empty containers' return to the source of their arising.

Body, Mind and Spirit are three distinct vibrations of universal energy.

TRAITS AND HABITS OF A DESIGN SCIENTIST

BODY	MIND	SPIRIT
DESIGN	VISION	MENTALISM
Formulation/Formation	Polarization	Ideation
Imagination Clarity Incision Form Ex-tensionTraction Tension Electricity XLF (7-8hz) The Physical Heart (Eros) Solar Plexus De-Cision Sexual Center and Gender Symmetry: male and female elements in all things The root Matter and will Spirit making the abstract real and with 'thought alone' in ALL three Spaces	Visualization Thought Visual thinking Focus Decision Division Re-tention (memory) Attraction Distraction Spirit making the abstract real and with 'thought alone' Spirit making the abstract real and with 'thought alone' in ALL three Times.	Meditation Thoughtless awareness Attention In-tension Cision Magnetism Spirit making the abstract real and with 'thought alone' in ALL three Energy fields.

Historic ages are cyclical. Europe in the 18th century 'cultivated' ages of Enlightenment and Reason. Many writers and thinkers questioned established beliefs, the authority of kings and Church, looking for reason and scientific proof. Their desires and wants were met but they lacked spiritual alignment. Entropy prevailed. It does not care about material wants it needs proper *spiritual* energetic alignments.

DEFINING (DESIGNING) SPACE TIME ENERGY PARADIGMS

Before we create anything, we need to understand the simple elements we use and define them and what's behind them. Defining them is the first S.T.E.P. Space is pure extension that can be perceived and understood by position and dimension.

It can be measured against an established and consistent gauge, a ruler. It can be viewed in terms of displacement in time. There are three types of time—an objective (or spatial) time, a subjective (or emotional) time and a spiritual time which is timelessness. Time is physical displacement, change and motion of objects (in space or pure extension), and is calibrated by a standard gauge. The experience of internal transformations and changes of state in humans and the events we experience are emotional expressions of 'subjective time'.

It is the flow that follows the freedom of thought or maybe no thought and needs no gauge because there is no-time to tell nor ringing bell.

Spiritual temporality is the ascended bliss that is neither objective nor subjective. It's paradoxical but drastically transformative.

Energy "is" space; space "is" energy. Without energy there is no space and without space there is no energy. Three types of energy correspond with three spaces. They are the physical me-as-sured Space, the emotional feeling State-Space and the Spirit-Space which is epi-dimensional; Substance is vibrational. Likewise, substance changing and moving "creates" time. Place is a well defined and localized

space. Vacuity is the complement or polarity of place.

Sub-stance is *presence* with *heavy* vibrational (gravity) characteristics, properties (muchness) and qualities (suchness) like form "mass", resistance, in keeping with the laws of symmetry. Density and integrity are aspects of consciousness. All is vibration which implies movement, in time-space and energy, in waves and or particles that switch states to correspond with the environmental conditions they are in.

Light, mind and thought (and naturally observers and participators) are important elements of reality. Power is the mechanical advantage and leverage to do work.

The primary element of reality is form; the behavior of the materials that give it its integrity are its psychology. The flavors of its energies are "colors" (visible and not), aesthetics and identity. Matter or energy: particle or wave are expressions of various energies of the "infinite" space, time and prime energy.

NEW PARADIGM OCCUPATIONS: D_ESIGN SCIENCE IN THE NEW PARADIGM AGE

What 'tricks' us into 'thingifying' space, time and energy and reducing its 'purity' are our materialistic mental proclivities based on the immediate sensorial relationship/s we have with our bodies and the immediate 'false evidence appearing to be real' sensations we experience in space with our bodies. Our friendly, overprotective and conditioned responses to the fight or flight limbic warnings overwhelm our immune system, leading to stress.

There is a strong positive correlation between materialism and several mental and physical maladies. In other words, people who pursue money and things at the expense of relationships and other meaningful endeavors are more likely to suffer from these stresses. If they are not managed properly, they lead to disease and chaos or at least confusion. Living in stress leads to dis-ease. What does this have to do with design you might think?

Just look at the following list of Pain points. Not being recognized, appreciated, respected and rewarded while dedicating one's life to sharing one's creative talents and gifts with others can lead to: 1. Unhappiness. 2. Envy and jealousy. 3. Depression. 4. Social anxiety.

5. Passive-aggressiveness. 6. Short attention span. 7. Poor self-control. 8. Feelings of failure. 9. Mistrust of others. 10. Tendency to mistreat others for personal gain. 11. Shorter, more conflicted relationships 12. Feelings of social alienation. 13. Exclusion based on Cultural, Social and Political differences. 14. Less generosity. 15. Narcissism. 16. Egoism.

The list goes on…! Every one of these stress points can be healed by corresponding design aesthetic or creative spirit with its unique vision and discipline. Some are more general and are in the realms of being physical, psychological or spiritual, all requiring forms of knowledge talent and skills energy and thought formulated into methodologies we call 'science and more directly D_ESign Science.

Design here is used as the great interactive opportunity for self-assessment as we all explore the relationships with the stress points as we 'design' the Paradigms that can transform our lives. The design professions have an advantage in being connected to source, skills and energies. These are needed for adapting to shifting 'PARADIGMS' with many of the correlations to the principles. Of course, correlation does not suggest causation. The correlation is essential nonetheless, and it's easy to see how synthesis does more to perpetuate than remediate the problems on the list.

The goal of this work is to take the positive path by resetting the mental scaffold, to first design and build good habits and healthy paradigms of and for ourselves before we project our creativity onto the world.

Summary

There are three dimensions (states) to everything in all of consciousness. They come on the 'quixotic 'waves of energies and packets' of interchangeable and transmutable physical things, mental and emotional states experiences and feelings with essences, energies, thoughts, flavors and spiritual expressions defined (and designed) as Body, Mind and Spirit. We interpret the stimuli and inspiration through Physiology, Psychology and Spirituality as the tools of synthesis of culture and the comprehension of consciousness to make connections to attain higher forms of ourselves with the proper application of creative energy, attention and thought.

We use these as the operational dynamics in direct correspondence with space, time, energy and the power of thought, the fin-est fuel we know, with all the symmetry principles and natural laws we use to design our lives, the life support systems.

With artifacts and environments we need to live not in but with the LOVE Design and the "Scientiam Recta" or direct knowledge brings to our families, our creative communities and to the world. This is D$_E$Sign Science's purpose and whoever aligns with it and adheres to its principles is a 'D$_E$Sign Scientist'. The beauty of these principles lies in a compassionate DIY mentality.

Welcome to the New Paradigm Age!

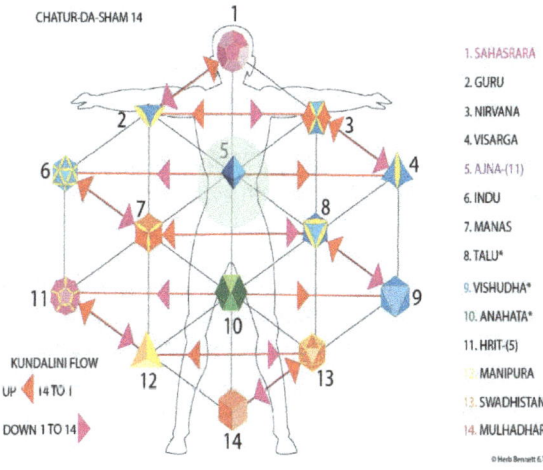

Fig. 15
Mapping the Polyhedra onto the Hexagonal - Cubic Matrix

"Creativity gives rise to the limited out of the limited, to sanity out of madness, to the valuable out of the priceless, to abundance out of nothingness, to the original out of the familiar and to hope out of despair" -Wallace Huey

Chatur-Da-Sham-a means 14 and *Sapta*-is 7 in the Sanskrit language.

NEW PARADIGM OCCUPATIONS: D_ESIGN SCIENCE IN THE NEW PARADIGM AGE

*The VISHUDHA chakra represents Purification. It is part of the threefold dynamic called the Kundalini, made up of: 1- Psyche (Body) faculties and Powers regulate the physical body (health and wellness) the social life, energies and psychic effects. 2-Mental faculties and powers regulate, talents, creativity and the mind. 3-Spiritual faculties and powers regulate the mind and the psyche (body).

The spatial geometric expressions of the chakra faculties are defined by three 'regular' systems of geometry—a straight line or edge and flat surface version, we call Euclidean, an imploding (inwardly curving) curved edge and 'compounded' curved surface version and an outwardly expanded (outwardly curved) compounded curved surface as the third formal type. Other variations and combinations exist. The 14 'expanded' faculties can be assigned the qualities of the Euclidean variety for the 7 we know from our popular understanding and the second 7 from the newly invented Non-Euclidean curved space varieties

Thanks to the wisdom and guidance of Ra Un Nefer Amen of the Taui Network located in Brooklyn, New York USA, and the international Khamitic community, the kundalini in its holistic nature, the popular knowledge is expanded by seven chakras for a total of fourteen (14). The *extra-po-lation* of an additional seven (7) chakras, reframes the wisdom, intelligence, knowledge and information (WIKI)we can apply holistically, in a new synthesis of our body, mind, spirit towards an exciting and deeper understanding and lifestyle creation to know the true meaning of our human potential, our purpose on earth and the god-man/god-woman transmutations and harmonizing of our consciousness rising we are realizing now. The new Aquarian age is defined as 'spiritual'. The shift of consciousness from the Piscean to the Aquarian age is consuming cultures around the world. Knowledge of our truer nature and how we can empower ourselves is available in the life force of the kundalini dynamic. It's no longer hidden from us or adulterated in the seven centers or abridged iteration of such a powerful constant creation 'spiritual technology and science.

*Vishudha purification interactions: 1- psyche (body) faculties and powers regulate the physical body (health and wellness) the social life, energies and psychic effects. 2-mental faculties and powers regulate, talents, creativity and the mind. 3-spiritual faculties and powers regulate the mind and the psyche (body).

Syncretism: There are two forms of syncretism. One is the amalga-mation of different religions, cultures, or schools of thought, and the other, the merging of different inflectional varieties of a word during the development of a language are used here to show the veracity of "oneness" among people. It speaks to the beliefs we have and the myths created with the language "word" we use to express them, not for manipulation or control.

The spatial geometric expressions represent the *chakra faculties* and are defined by three 'regular' systems of geometry—a straight line or edge and flat surface version, we call Euclidean. It's an imploding (inwardly curving) curved edge and 'compounded' curved surface version and an outwardly expanded (outwardly curved) compounded curved surface as the third formal type. Other variations and combinations exist. The 14 'expanded' faculties can be assigned the qualities of the forms to the 7 energy centers we know from our popular understanding and the additional 7 of the Egyptian tradition. How do the newly invented non-Euclidean curved space varieties relate to these two systems?

We can assign 'gender symmetry' qualities to both sets of 7 and 14 and they would both would be relevant. An analogy for this is the program that runs in the background of our computer's operating system. Euclidean could be male and the Non-Euclidean female according to the Law of Gender as in Hermetic philosophy.

There are systems within systems too numerous for us to discover, especially if searching for them is not high on our priority list or we are unaware of them in the first place.

Our periodic Matrix expands as a result of the 14 faculties, we must now experience and incorporate into the universal WIKI as the 'Mystery Tradition' for our self-realization and DIVINE nature to be enhanced. When the Student is ready, teachers arrive in the extra-sensorial world.

On the inside, and through discipline, being one's own master and connection to SOURCE comes with self-realization. The temple we are that was built at birth is a constant creation project.

Sahasrara, Guru*, Nirvana*, Visarga*, Ajna, Indu*, Manas, Talu*, Vishudha, Anahata, Hrit*, Manipura, Swadhistana, Mulhadara. The asterisks * are the expanded 7 Egyptian faculties that align with the kundalini language, 'spoken in Egypt, India and China with their own symbols and expressions. This is the language of life in each culture, nurtured by rivers and the fertile planes they truncate. They vitalize their spiritual and creative visions, leaving legacies we still do not know. A fundamental phenomenon as our electric life defies our carnal knowledge and has left us in the dark for millennia. Until my meeting with a remarkable teacher, Ra Un Nefer Amen of the Kamitic tradition here in New York and, by extension, the world, I would still be in the darkness about the 7, not knowing about the 14 with the 7 higher dimensions of self-realization and divine connections they offer.

Archaic (Early Dynastic) Period (c. 3100-2686 B.C.) King Menes founded the capital of ancient Egypt at White Walls (later known as Memphis), in the north, near the apex of the Nile River delta. The capital would grow into a great metropolis that dominated Egyptian society during the Old Kingdom period. The Egyptian tradition was/is based on the Ennead and its Spiritual Science Traditions.

In Mesopotamia, Egypt, Indus River, and China and the Yellow River civilization there are many rivers including the Indus, Ganges and Brahmaputra. The Deccan plateau juts into the Indian Ocean. The Deccan Plateau is a large plateau in western and southern India.

It rises to 100 meters (330 ft) in the north, and to more than 1,000 meters (3,300 ft) in the south, forming a raised triangle within the South-pointing triangle of the Indian subcontinent's coastline.

The Hindu evolutionary story of India is still being debated as to its influences and civilization building. Was it influenced by the Aryan invasion or did it evolve internally from the east to west migration that was supported by the spiritual traditions and cultural interactions?

NEW PARADIGM OCCUPATIONS: D_ESIGN SCIENCE IN THE NEW PARADIGM AGE

The knowledge of Kundalini we have inherited is the (New Cardinal Concept) of a *Septa-7* Chakra (soul quality). This expands to the 'Chatur-Da-Sham or 14 in Sanskrit and predates the abridged version.

In China, the Zhou dynasty (1046 BC to approximately 256 BC) was the longest-lasting dynasty in Chinese history. By the end of the 2nd millennium BC, the Zhou dynasty began to emerge in the Yellow River valley, overrunning the territory of the Shang. According to some, Taoism formed into a religious system within the lands of China sometime around the 4th or 3rd century BCE. Being the first to receive the inspiration of the Tao, some cite Lao-tzu as the first Taoist philosopher and the author of the Taoist texts known as the Tao-te Ching. The I Ching or "Yi Jing" is one of the oldest known documents in the world. This "Classic of Change" can be traced as far back as 3000 years in written form, and the Chinese claim that it was passed down, as oral traditions often do, for two thousand years prior.

The extended *Chatur-Da-Sham* or 14 Faculties is the synthesis of the three dimensions of consciousness harmonizing man's ascension to higher states of consciousness or being 'Divine' with greater fidelity. The Tao that can be told is not the eternal Tao speaks silent volumes.

All can know good, as good, because of its polarity only ... evil. The Tao is an empty vessel; it is used, but can never be filled.

The human story unfolds with the rise or fall of our *KUNDALINI* of which there are many in number, quality and flavor, but 7 or 14 work.

To balance each faculty polarity keeps us in equilibrium and in peace if we obey natural laws and work to enhance our lives.

It is our electric life, coursing through our physical body, charging the subtle and electro-magnetic fields of energy in our physiology to vitalize us and prepare us for the cycle of 'decay' and rest before we return. So, when 'His-tory' tells us of Egyptian Pharaohs becoming GODS, we need to look at who is telling the story and check the source and motives of the story-teller.

As an artist and an architect, metaphysics, design and science are skills with very wide ranges of comprehension and application inspired by the primary, if not only dynamic, worth remembering here:

"To the ALL, All is ONE [GOD which is energy. Form Space, matter etc.] To the Many, They are the Many [to the few there is no space no time] As to the Pure [spirit], All is Pure [spirit].

A few if any know this

As natural Law [and no one dares to update it for our PARADIGM].

In this ONENESS all is consciousness and will. In states of Constant Creation man can, through transformation and Transmutations, become the ONE we're sent to ascend and return to.

For Humans this One is all CARBON…the life element. (The Author)"

The 14 Faculties are the *SAHASRARA, GURU*, NIRVANA*, VISARGA*, AJNA, INDU*, MANAS, TALU*, VISHUDHA, ANAHATA, HRIT*, MANIPURA, SWADHISTANA, MULHADARA*. Instead of taking the psychological journey for healing or spiritual growth, this story is all about creation—Constant and Synthesizing Creation.

The corresponding *SAHASRARA* faculty in the Hermetic principle is

'Mentalism'. It is thought of as the Neurological transduction of pulses and stimuli into sense data. In other words, it generates concepts and ideas into life support systems to satisfy needs. Spirit is wonderful, and meditating on our navels is peaceful, but we need to ACT on our covenant with GOD, Nature and our human family to create our destiny and to manifest our purpose (the VISARGA) on earth.

It is Spiritual. *Chaturdasham*: thought paths to *KUNDALINI SOUL SYNTHESIS* we all dance to.

The GURU* faculty is the first of the 'qualifying' centers that can direct the more overt actions in the creative process that is ubiquitous and universal. Our binary polarized hemispherical brain is the fulcrum for/of our equilibrium. The major qualities here are our connections to SOURCE-GOD, AKASHA and PEACE. We are naturally at ease until stress, tension and disease set in. KUNDALINI and its 14 Faculties heal and build according to the grand designs of the Great Spirit and LAW.

The term 'qualifying' adds flavor and gui-dance to the music of the polarizing process of 'cision' (dividing and cutting) or (dividing and multiplying matter) as in decision and precision needed for the realization of aesthetic expressions and materials used to create. We Dream in the sleep and the awakened state. We imagine think and visualize our creations, expecting insights, intuitions and gut reactions to inspire us to plan. It is Spiritual.

NIRVANA* is the next qualifier for ALL Growth of Body, Mind and Spirit [BMS]. It is the faculty for natural co-creation and pro-creation process or the harmonizing of the environment with matter and energy as our creation. Here we find a similar concept to the Hindu Triad. The god Shiva is part of the Hindu Trinity, along with Vishnu and Brahma. He is considered to be everything by those who worship him: creator, preserver and destroyer. In Shiva, the opposites meet.

(Extremes are the same phenomena to different degrees) Shiva, the destroyer, is a necessary part of the trinity because, without destruction, there can be no recreation. To fill the bucket, it must be empty. Lots of buckets are filled with old paradigm stuff, subconscious conditionings and pain. Some buckets need to be kicked. Kali however is the force or dynamic that is helping to make the changes of state in the inter phase evolution in life.

NEW PARADIGM OCCUPATIONS:
DESIGN SCIENCE IN THE NEW PARADIGM AGE

Chaos, Dissonance and Incoherence are her tools. In our creation we must program growth into the process for sustainability and proper function. Our new normal will best be Spiritual.

VISARGA* is the faculty of/ for Spiritual Purpose. Entraining truth, filtering useless attainments by and from other faculties on the path to SAHASRARA and divine realization. In the intervals of the Sapta (7) system, between the 'Mother' energy wave we call KUNDALINI, between the Sahasrara and the Ajna, the Ajna and the Vishudha with one 'tone' between the Anahata and the Manipura we find the Sapta (7) qualifying Faculties in a three (3)-(3) and (1) sequence along the chaturdasham (14). What does this sequence mean, and are there reasons for their positions?

The phrase 'energy wave' is a hint to the western science quantum theory that is 'too embarrassed to admit' its connection to 'KUNDALINI'. Concentration is the skill this faculty uses for automatic flow of consciousness. It is Spiritual and can work for us in creation. Trance is the effect of focused concentration in Dhyana and Samadhi.

AJNA* is the 'Assimilator portal' of self to the divine, residing in the Sahasrara, the Source of Pure Consciousness. Vitalization of self through initiation helps to achieve Spiritual Goals. Jesus, initiated into the Egyptian temple and given the title "The Christ", is an Ajna faculty experience. It is Spiritual. Hrit is its opposite. Ajna is the synthesizer while Sahasrara is the harmonizer.

We realize pure consciousness in that intersection. This is the aesthetic that is expressed in what we create. It is the self that is manifested. Hrit (heart). Look at the words inh(e)rit and Ajna (mind). They have a vital link similar to the Ajna and Anahata, North-South, prolate poles of the ANKH or the "crux ansata", the ankh, an ancient Egyptian symbol. Coming from crux ansata or cross with a handle from crux, cross + feminine of ansatus from ansa, a handle, it is an ancient Egyptian hieroglyphic ideograph symbolizing "life". The Egyptian gods are often portrayed carrying it by its loop, or bearing one in each hand, arms crossed over their chests. The ankh appears in hand or in proximity of almost every deity in the Egyptian pantheon. The East-West oblate axis traverses the Indu and Mannas faculties. It aligns with the ankh's loop and the cross.

The terms prolate poles and oblate axis refer to the toroidal dynamic found in all electro-magnetic fields. Every form is a Torus. In the Sapta System, the known (7) edition, the third eye, the Ajna is replaced by the Guru faculty of/for visualization. It flows two ways, but they all do. Ajna interacts with number 11, the Gatekeeper Hrit.

The INDU* faculty governs virtues, collectivity, social interactions and, by extension, 'Communty'—Holistic community. It is here we refine our social graces. This faculty is key to the planning of our creative projects. It provides mental discipline and control of the auto-harmonization qualities and flavors to achieve 'SYNTHESIS' through order and symmetry. Symmetry here is about 'the behavior of parts that make things whole and functional'. The reality testing of Spiritual Truth overlays this process. Faculties support processes and obey laws for creation. Nothing just happens. The correspondence of as above so below and as below so above applies.

Conviction to the 'word', the word that was spoken at 'in-tention time', can get us into de-tention if the MANAS and BUDDHI (higher mind) faculties are not aligned. The above register of consciousness controls the below levels.

Our logical reasoning needs to be direct, honest and true. The Indu or Buddhi faculty is Spiritual.

MANAS*— this faculty is the bridge between the self and the body. It is the seat of imagination and verbal intellect with a background program in communication. The integrity and truth of our ideas align with intentions.

Being in the state of meditation or Samadhi leads to balance, harmony and synthesis. The limbic brain is the detractor here with its emotional paradigms and conditionings. Beliefs afford transcendence of the self-image. It is an extinguisher of the worldly presence for God-ness and adherence to the 11 laws of MAAT. It is Mental [DHARMA: DIVINE LAW-]

TALU* is the modulator of the Psyche or BODY. It can be purified by the VISHUDHA. The Talu chakra, is also called Taluka or Lalana chakra.

The Lalana chakra is a minor chakra associated with the throat chakra or Vishudha. It is the energy center that governs our speech and creative expression in the world. Talu chakra is described in the sacred teachings as the secret chakra taught by spiritual masters to their disciples. It is considered that by reciting the beej (seed) mantra "hangsah", the spiritual devotee makes the kundalini energy pass through this secret chakra while traversing Sushumna Nadi. This chakra radiates twelve pathways or thought channels which are divisions of time by our orbital relationship to the Stars and Sun in the ecliptic dynamic of our universe. Furthermore, when the disciple reaches this chakra, a sweet nectar starts dripping on the tongue. When the throat chakra is inactive, this sweet nectar runs down into Manipura chakra and is consumed, resulting in physical degeneration. With the khechari mudra (considered the king among the mudras) the nectar can enter the vishudha chakra, where it is purified to become a nectar of immortality. Khechari Mudra is an ancient yoga technique used in the practice of Kriya Yoga. It is taught by Yogananda and his lineage of Kriya gurus.

It has also been practiced by yogis and meditators for perhaps thousands of years, due to its wonderful benefits. In the Song of Solomon (sun and moon) this verse is mentioned: "Your lips, my bride, drip honey; Honey and milk are under your tongue. Yes! my Beloved, to my sight Shows a sweet mixture, red and white:

The fairest of ten thousand fairs; A sun amongst ten thousand stars". Key words: are Honey-Comb, Lips, Milk, Nectar, Scent, Smell, Spouse, Sweetness and Tongue.

VISHUDAH* is the purifying filter FACULTY for the body or psyche. Its 16 petals are thought paths to the dance of the KUNDALINI MOTHER. Purification helps to achieve the sensitivity needed for the subtler higher register chakras. Purification is attained through diet, yoga, meditation, and exercise. Translation: Pure ("Poison Removing")

Bija Mantra: HAM.
Sense: Hearing.
Color: Blue.

Element: Ether.
Organs: Thyroid/Vocal Organs/Ears/Skin.

Spine: Cervical.
Outer Body: Throat/Neck.

ANAHATA*—faculty of the heart is the reality tester for creation. LOVE is its energy with an ample share of polarities we see around us too clearly. Thoughts and ideas that are processed by the higher register must encounter this gatekeeper. It is more ubiquitous and powerful than its complement, the Hrit faculty.

It interacts with the ten upper and four lower faculties (including its self). LOVE—emotional and conditional, Divine and unconditional and the plethora of Greek expressions Eros, or sexual passion. ...Philia, or deep friendship. ...Ludus, or playful love. ...

Agape, or love for everyone. ...Pragma, or longstanding love.
...Philautia, or love of the self are what's available. Quite a menu!

HRIT*—Hrit (or Hridaya, "heart"), with eight petals, hridaya chakra, hrit padma, hridaya padma, hridaya kamala, hridaya-amburuha, hridaya padmakosha, hritpundarika, hemapundarika. Hrit chakra is sometimes known as the Surya (sun) chakra, which is located slightly to the left below the heart. Its role is to absorb energy from the sun and provide heat to the body and the other chakras (to Manipura in particular, to which it provides Agni (fire). We can use the HRIT faculty to transform the de-generative mind into a generative or regenerative consciousness for creation to transform our lives and the world. Through initiation, we can avoid aviyda—not knowing self and being about our father's business which we can inherit. Holism is this faculty's force. It is sun energy that is life giving and interacts with the Manipura chakra. The Gatekeeper lives here and with the body-mind continuum, higher vibrations get through. Described only in the Shakta tradition of Tantra, the Hrit (Heart) Chakra, which is variously described as white, gold, or red in color, has eight petals, and is located just below the Anahata. The most distinctive quality of this chakra is the mythical Wish-Fulfilling Tree represented in the center of the pericarp, the part of a fruit formed from the wall of the ripened ovary…

MANIPURA* The animal designated to represent Manipura is the Ram. The corresponding element is Fire, therefore it is also known as the

Fire or Sun Centre. The fire element manifests in the body as heat in the Solar Plexus. The Manipura Chakra is the centre of vitality. The Manipura Chakra contains many precious gems such as the qualities of clarity, self-confidence, bliss, self-assurance, knowledge, wisdom and the ability to make correct decisions. *The third chakra is the one that gives us the sense of complete satisfaction and contentment. It is the center which makes us peaceful and generous, and also sustains our spiritual ascent. When enlightened by the Kundalini, it expresses as righteousness and inner sense of morality, and it gives us balance.*

"These life skills are needed to design and build communities with life support systems, inventions and innovations.

	USING THE KUNDALINI AND 14 CHAKRAS AS THE CREATIVE PROCESS	
1	SAHASRARA	KUNDALINI is the essence of desire for Divinity. Ease is the state we achieve through self realization and connection the divine mind.
2	GURU	Peace gained from manifesting creative solutions st-art with impulses thoughts and desires. KUNDALINI is a universal design process we use.
3	NIRVANA	The creative process goes through growth cycles, evolution and the elevation of higher states consciousness to shape our lifestyles.
4	VISARGA	Purpose is material, psychological, emotional and spiritual states of mind, laws and principles we connect to and use to stay on course.
5	AJNA	Being able to visualize solutions, create technologies to ART-iculate them requires visual intelligence, in all (B.M.S) states of dreaming.
6	INDU	Mental Discipline and Control leads to Auto-harmonization and excellence. There's power in words used to define our thoughts.
7	MANAS	Truths and Spirit control all 'animal' faculties in the Limbic Brain, with its Paradigms and negative conditionings we call habits.
8	TALU*	Modulation of the physical form is done with Vishudha purification* LAWS used to Extinguish Self Image; creates the 'Worldly Presence'
9	VISHUDHA*	When we speak to ourselve we think. When we speak to others we communicate. The medium or material needed is explored here.
10	ANAHATA*	The heart is the 'reality tester'. If the tought is loved it inspires us to create and share the eternal LOVE with generosity and compassion.
11	HRIT	The heart-hrit link is the love-logic balance seeking dynamic. It is the SELF and the HOLISTIC faculty. Through Initiation it create identity.
12	MANIPURA*	This is the power plant with energy from the sun used for all creative effort, work and vitalized by the vishudha purity and nirvana synthesis.
13	SWADHISTANA*	The creative center for co and pro creation. It is the gender faculty for symmetry principles to express the 'male and female' nature.
14	MULHADHARA*	The (heart-earth link) aligns measure matter, form, energy and thought (thing) that's manifested until it's energy is depleted.

Fig. 16   Fig. 17

MULHADHARA —destiny lives here, imagination and verbal intelligence are in the mulhadhara crucible for crystalizing the GOD/good stuff. Processing concrete information on the lower mental level is what makes 'the abstract real'. Matter and energy have their physical, behavioral, thought, energy and LOVE sensors wired to this faculty. This is the final stop (temporarily) for the law of correspondence. What was prayed for, created processed and synthesized is delivered and approved by quality control. For the creative spirit, immortality

NEW PARADIGM OCCUPATIONS:

DESIGN SCIENCE IN THE NEW PARADIGM AGE

could be attained through works that endure in harmony with all the forces. [Profound thanks to Ra Un Nefer Amen and the Taui Network Community, in Brooklyn, New York USA and the world.

THE SUCHNESS OF METALS, SYNTHESIS OF PLANETS, METALS AND THE CHAKRA ENERGY CENTERS IN MAN

Planetary Body:	Metal:	Western Chakra correspondence:
The Sun (Sol):	Gold	Heart Chakra
The Moon (Luna):	Silver	Brow Chakra - Third-Eye
Mercury:	Mercury (original, I know)	Crown Chakra
Venus	Copper	Throat Chakra
Mars:	Iron	Sacral Chakra
Jupiter	Tin	Solar-Plexus Chakra
Saturn	Lead	Root Chakra

THE SUN BEHIND THE SUN, OSIRIS, AND THE GREAT PYRAMID

The Principle of All Things: Beyond the Sun in the direction of the Dog Star lies that incorruptible flame or Sun, Principle of All Things, willing obedience from our own Sun which is but a manifestation of its relegated force.

The existence of the Sun behind the Sun has been known in all ages, as well as the fact that its influence is most potent upon earth during that period every 2000 years when it is in conjunction with the Sun of our solar system. Then gathering to itself the power of its own Source and transmitting it through our Sun to this planet, it is said to send the Sons of God into the consciousness of the earth sphere, that a new world of thought and emotion may be born in the minds of men for the stimulation of humanity's spiritual evolution. Such a manifestation marks the beginning or end of an epoch upon the earth by the radiation of that divine consciousness known as the Christ Ray or Paraclete.

To the Egyptians, the Sun behind the Sun was known as Osiris (and also as Amen-Ra, The Hidden Sun), said to be the husband of Isis (Nature) and the parent of Horus (the Sun), symbolically represented as a hawk because that bird flies nearest the Sun.

This ancient people knew that once every year the Parent Sun is in line with the Dog Star. Therefore, the Great Pyramid was so constructed that, at this sacred moment, the light of the Dog Star fell upon the square "Stone of God" at the upper end of the Great Gallery, descending upon the head of the high priest, who received the Super Solar Force and sought, through his own perfected Solar

Body, to transmit it to other Initiates. This added stimulation for the evolution of their Godhood. This then was the purpose of the "`Stone of God,' whereon in the Ritual, Osiris sits to bestow upon him (the illuminate) the Atf crown or celestial light." "North and South of that crown is love," proclaims an Egyptian hymn. "And thus, throughout the teaching of Egypt the visible light was but the shadow of the invisible Light, and in the wisdom of the ancient country the measures of Truth were the years of the Most High (Marshall Adams, The Book of the Master," page 141-2)."

Modern science partially confirms these facts about the significance of the Great Pyramid, but lacks the key to them. Dr. Percival Lowell, in a recent essay entitled "Precession and the Pyramids," says, "The Great Pyramid was in fact a great observatory, the most superb one ever erected," and "The Great Gallery's floor exactly included every possible position of the Sun's shadow at noon from the year's beginning to its end. We thus reach the remarkable result that the gallery was a gigantic gnomon or sundial telling, not like ordinary sundials, the hour of the day, but on a more impressive scale, the seasons of the year."

Excerpted from the Comte de Gabalis, originally by the Abbe N. do Montfauconde Villars (1670)

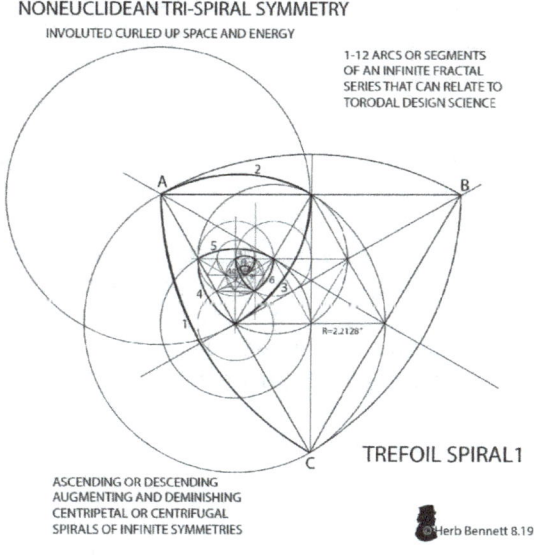

Fig. 18
A TREFOIL SPIRAL SYMMETRY

NEW PARADIGM OCCUPATIONS: *D$_E$SIGN SCIENCE IN THE NEW PARADIGM AGE*

Here is an interpretative, non-descriptive geometry with another premise that is not about *'SPACE'*. It is a synthesizer of thought quantities, qualities and flavors that can generate and predict results of formations, combinations and formulations using the principles of the threefold symmetry (of nature) in polarization, Ideation and formation to arrive at a transformative phase of creation as thought processes found in D$_E$Sign Science:

In the current paradigm Descriptive geometry's primary function is to translate an object in three dimensions into a two dimensional representation of that object. Each such representation is called a view or paradigm.

With 3D modeling, however, this becomes irrelevant to the visualization and realization processes since the "view" is not needed. New definitions and parameters are needed. The ideal is "the holistic and instant manifestation" of 3D form with access to generations and variations of the vocabulary following strict symmetry rules. What type of "metry" is this? Al·lom·e·try: is the growth of body parts at different rates, resulting in a change of body proportions. Morphology is related to this function. A holometry with roots in holism and hologram could be a candidate for this instantaneous manifestation of form.

This 'Triadic Maat-rix', the essence of a *visual mathematics, logic structure and other systems yet to be Maat or Ma'at (Egyptian m^{ʕ}3t), refers to both the ancient Egyptian concepts of truth, balance, order, harmony, law, morality, and justice, and the personification of these concepts as a goddess regulating the stars, seasons, and the actions of both mortals and the deities, who set the affairs of the universe from chaos to order.*

This is the canon for a new geometry beyond what we call sacred. It is holistic and a 'HOLOMETRY'. They go beyond the traditional 'Geo (physical) Metric' principles and gauge theories we now use to synthesize new holistic reckoning strategies and methods. The evolving phenomena being discovered now require a different level of reckoning. It is the method of

SYNTHESIS in the discipline of D$_E$Sign Science of all creative fields of Wisdom, Intelligence, knowledge and Information— past, present and future.

Body: The most familiar expression is its role in counting and keeping score and for settling accounts.

Mind: It is a person's view, opinion, judgment, evaluation, estimate which all relate to the idea of "paradigm".

Spirit: Reckoning is the action or process of calculating or estimating something based on observations and thought processes that would harmonize the Body, Mind, Spirit triad and the calculation methods we know.

EPI-GEOMETRY: REALMS OF CONSCIOUSNESS BEYOND [NON EUCLIDEAN] GEOMETRY [TORIMETRY is a ubiquitous Gauge]

"A Dream Deferred" by the Harlem Renaissance poet Langston Hughes, written in 1951, was the inspiration for Lorraine Hansberry's classic play *A Raisin in the Sun*.

What happens to a dream deferred? Does it dry up like a raisin in the sun? Or fester like a sore—And then run? Does it stink like rotten meat?
Or crust and sugar over—like a syrupy sweet? Maybe it just sags like a heavy load.
Or does it explode?
Langston Hughes

D$_E$Sign Science:

The tone and the quest implied in this poem resonate with the story of my search for the Non-Euclidean Geometry and the vision I have for sharing it with the world. The deferment of the dream, between the development stage and where we are in the new paradigm age (renaissance), is basically the same range of emotional states ART-iculated here. These questions are derived from those who are in touch with the ideas of their time and choose to express them in their voice as they seek and speak to our human values.

The story of life can be told as a 'design story' with time as the rhythm of events and accomplishments we participate in. We do not ask for risks. We take them and are emboldened by the courage they offer us when we connect to Source and are in the flow of the energy that coalesces into the synthesis of our life and purpose through our vision. Geometry is the voice that tells the *cosmic* story. We are the instruments that must be connected to the source to be in tune with the wisdom to encode the message. The response to the message is the world we create.

The expressions are best described by geometry. It echoes more than materialistic sensibilities and values we get trapped in otherwise.

The Language of form started with the recognition of physical space. Once thought to be rendered by straight lines, flat surfaces and fixed, it turned out to be (a space-time- energy dynamic) in a curved space redefined by general theory of relativity, such as was dramatically shown by the 1919 solar eclipse measurements that corroborated all assumptions first recognized by the giants of Non-Euclidean geometries— Gauss, Lobachevsky, Bolyai and Riemann. Their rigorous application of mathematical possibilities developed new paradigm ideas that transformed geometry into an elaborate branch of generalized mathematical concepts in the nineteenth century. Disciplines such as astronomy and astrophysics pointed to the possible geometrization of physics and the many emerging disciplines we see today. Up to this point there was no tangible, constructed proof of any of these theories. Nothing was built or created with it, still amorphous and philosophical.

The diffusion of this innovation inspired fields of scientific investigation (scientification) that was influenced by the prevailing ideologies and even the religious dogma of the day. Albert, not believing that God did not roll his dice, is one example. What was the dream deferred

NEW PARADIGM OCCUPATIONS: D_ESIGN SCIENCE IN THE NEW PARADIGM AGE

that to this day still is not realized?Non-Euclideangeometry has a rich aesthetic potential to transform the world. There could be no bigger dream than this. There has never been such a profound transformation on this planet for very logical reasons, the major one being the 'Tower of Babel' syndrome we are still affected by. The metaphor used here is meant to include all dimensions of division and confusion derived from basically the collective ego and 'shego' over time, wrapped in one convenient and powerful symbol.

In astronomy Friedrich Wilhelm Bessel, Born on July 22, 1784, in Minden, Germany believed that the geometry of his day was incomplete, needing correction that disappears when the sum of angles in a plane triangle = (equal) 180°. He thought that "Non-Euclidean geometry would be the *true* geometry, while the Euclidean would be the *practical expression*, at least for figures on the earth." But earth was not the only realm that these ideas would relate to. This reflects Plato's ideas about the purity of Polyhedra, and the symbols of the five elements in the syncretism of elementology.

The 'dreamers' of non-Euclidean geometry were Hungarian mathematicians János Bolyai and the Russian Nikolai Ivanovich Lobachevski, both of whom (contrary to Gauss) published their own discoveries that *a geometry different from and as valid as Euclid's is possible*. While Bolyai's sole work on what he called "absolute geometry" dates from 1831, Lobachevski's first study was from 1829, followed in 1840 by a booklet in German, *Geometrischen Untersuchungen zur Theorie der Parallellinien*. Although working independently and in almost complete isolation, the two theories were remarkably similar. Synchronicity is the name of this concept.

The ideas of Gauss, Lobachevski and Bolyai circulated slowly in the mathematical community. They gained attention when the Italian mathematician, Eugenio Beltrami in 1868 presented that the Non-Euclidean *paradigm* and its geometries had truly entered the world of mathematics. It then resulted in a geometry revolution. Though we no longer apply it to land surveying this moniker is etched in our consciousness.

The British mathematician *and philosopher* William Kingdon Clifford *May*

*1845– 3 March 1879)*translated the lecture into English in 1873. It came to be seen as a visionary address on the possible 'geometrization' of physics. Riemann's thoughts also became known to the English-speakingworld through articles by Helmholtz that appeared in *Mind*, a new quarterly journal for philosophy and psychology, founded in 1876.

In 1870 Clifford introduced Riemann's ideas to a British audience and wrote, "There are very *different kinds of space of three dimensions;* and that we can only find out *by experience* to which of these kinds the space in which we live belongs." He extended Riemann's ideas by speculating that physical phenomena could be fully reduced to properties of space curvature varying between one portion of space to another.

Heat, light and magnetism might be mere names for 'tiny variations in the curvature of space', he boldly hypothesized. That curvature I call "Toroidal".

It is the most ubiquitous phenomenon in all of nature from the subatomic to the intergalactic and cosmic dimensions of space, time and energy expressions and creations.

Clifford pointed out that within the framework of Riemannian geometry, *the association (correlation) between limitedness and finite extent* was invalid.

He emphasized, as earlier contributors to Non-Euclidean geometry had done, *that the 'geometrical structure of space' was a question of empirical facts and not of metaphysics. He was the first to suggest that gravitation might be a manifestation of an underlying geometry. In his philosophical writings he coined the expression "mind-stuff". Was he intuiting what could be 'Toroidal Dynamic geometry or Torimetry'™?*

Here is another synchronistic observation that is related in acoustics. The Chladni vibration models are Non-Euclidean Geometry elements. For roughly the next 140 year this paradigm-shifting event in geometry remained an academic 'ivory tower' event. There were sporadic attempts at ART-iculating these ideas in real world applications in philosophy, technology, science itself, and the design professions in art and architecture. *"Non-Euclidean geometry is a true practical geometry with a 'real' system of form generation, for figures on the earth that obey all natural laws and symmetry principles of space, time and energy in the Body, Mind Spirit continuum of consciousness of life itself as well."*

In Egyptian temple architecture canons, reducing three dimensional forms to their two-dimensional geometric patterns of building component was a major *'design science strategy'* for simplifing solutions of complex temple forms. This two-dimensional pattern-generating process is used to generate a vocabulary of forms from three-dimensional Non-Euclidean geometry now.

Flat S_2 two-dimensional blanks are created from a basic threefold pattern to create blanks that are folded into complex structures that would ordinarily require computer modeling, 3D technologies and advanced mathematical knowledge. Simple methods create complex, innovative solutions that can then be used in various fields of design, engineering and production.

The vocabulary that's created expresses a unique identity and a resulting 'aesthetic' with curved spaces as the predominant feature of the forms. The classic 'Polyhedra vocabulary' serves to 'reality-test' this Non-Euclidean form theory. In the Euclidean Polyhedra, using a cube for example, the edges are straight, the faces are flat and the vertices are 'mostly' equidistant. In the Non-Euclidean vocabularies, edges are curved and doubled to form 'digons', faces are imploding or exploding and vertices coincide with those of the classic vocabulary.

Polyhedra were first invented by the Egyptian temple builders who needed to calculate the number of blocks needed for their pyramids. This knowledge was then taken to Greece by Plato to be the 'Platonic solids'. The materials used to build structures using Euclidean form designs are generally rigid framing systems and flat sheets or modular units like bricks and stones.

NEW PARADIGM OCCUPATIONS: D_ESIGN SCIENCE IN THE NEW PARADIGM AGE

This invention was a paradigm shift that would take time to find its niche in the post, 'post and lintel' technology employed around the world. Richard Buckminster Fuller, the American Architect and visionary, championed the technological advancements. In 1957 he was the original proponent of 'Design Science' that inspired social and cultural movements in the 60's with his geodesic dome home, dymaxion house and automobile. The dymaxion is now featured in Torimetry.

The relationship between the observer and the observed goes beyond the physical space or location. It involves the psychological, emotional (time) and spiritual or energy (dimensions of consciousness) operating in and around both the observer and the observed in space, time and energy. If the observer is located at Papua New Guinea, central location on the planet, the geometry perceived will be relative to the height of the observer and the curvature of the earth that is displacing the prime space of the entire universe. The Egyptians had this 'perspective' factored into their understanding of the world and their 'strategic' location on it.

The premise for Non-Euclidean geometry started in the same place and with the same idea—*constructing a 90-degree angle*. It is my opinion that there was a major east-west paradigm shift in the application of this development here, and sides were chosen, as it were.

Each side in the East-West dichotomy represented the meaning of what this idea represented according to its philosophical, cultural and religious traditions. This divide paved the way for each part to create traditions that its design, science and mathematics would then lead it to. Euclid stayed in the '90-degree construction' realm and exploited the iterations of 'his' technique and the emerging technology that followed and spread to the world.

Oriental cultures integrated their systems into their lifestyles in keeping with the aesthetic traditions of their ken. They both expressed their rhythm, faith and belief in the Body, Mind Spirit expressions of 'consciousness' either knowingly, viscerally or spiritually that related to religion or religious belief according to their guiding principles which informed many, if not all, their 'canons'. There were time differences during which the growth and development took place along with interactions and exchanges and some were not very peaceful.

What was handed down to us has not yet been resolved on many of the levels needed for the bridges to be built permanently and peacefully. A number of new actors have encroached on this cultural axis, making matters more complicated. The term East-West Dichotomy is a cultural metaphor with many dimensions not needed for this demonstration and argument.

The genesis of Non-Euclidean Geometry: The intersection of circles used in some oriental fabrics represent the "Harmonic Expansion" of *Riemannian geometry* with smooth manifolds and a Riemannian metric. It is the inner product on the tangent space at each point that varies smoothly from point to point for Riemannian Space patterns in all dimensions. The next series of forms with the intersection of circles represents the "Harmonic Contraction" of the *Bolyai, Lobachevsky geometry*. János Bolyai or Johann Bolyai, was one of the founders of non-Euclidean geometry along with Lobachevski. They created a geometry that differs from Euclidean geometry in its definition of parallel lines to define complementary spaces found in the Riemannian Space.

Between the 90 degree angle and the trefoil pentagon construction lies a curved triangle also known as the Reuleaux Triangle, a spherical triangle when mapped on the surface of a sphere. The polyhedra approximates creating spheres using available flat materials before modern forming techniques were available to artisans.

The world of sacred geometry was considered the highest form of endeavor to engage in man's early development.

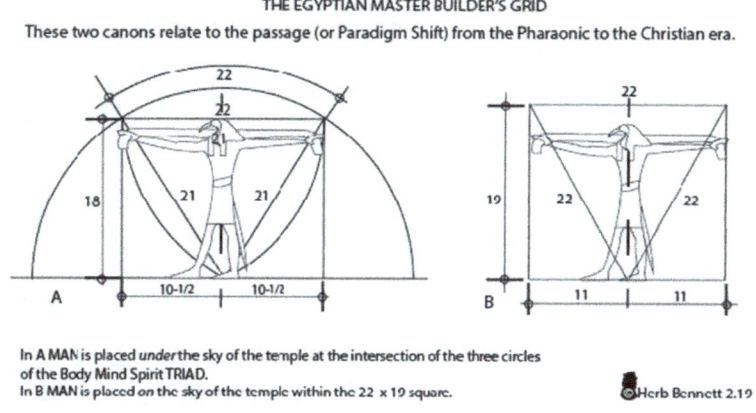

Fig. 19

BOOKS ON CREATIVE THINKING:

The Design of Everyday Things by Don Norman
The Laws of Simplicity (Simplicity: Design, Technology, Business, Life) by John Maeda
Fab: The Coming Revolution on Your Desktop–from Personal Computers to Personal Fabrication by Neil Gershenfeld
Designing Design by Kenya Hara
Universal Principles of Design by William Lidwell, Kritina Holden and Jill Butler.
Cradle to Cradle: Remaking the Way We Make Things by William McDonough and Michael Braungart.
It's Not How Good You Are, Its How Good You Want to Be: The World's Best Selling Book by Paul Arden
The Love marks Effect: Winning in the Consumer Revolution by Kevin Roberts *Small Is the New Big: and 183 Other Riffs, Rants, and Remarkable Business Ideas* by Seth Godin.

NEW PARADIGM OCCUPATIONS: DESIGN SCIENCE IN THE NEW PARADIGM AGE

Design (Tom Peters Essentials) by Tom Peters.
Journals from the Design Management Institute by DMI members.
The Creative Priority: Putting Innovation to Work in Your Business by Jerry Hirshberg
Designing Interactions by Bill Moggridge.
Lateral Thinking: Creativity Step by Step by Edward De Bono.
What They Don't Teach You At Harvard Business School: Notes From A Street-Smart Executive by Mark H. McCormack.
The 48 Laws of Power by Robert Greene.
The Art of Innovation: Lessons in Creativity from IDEO, America's Leading
Design Firm by Tom Kelley.

BOOKS ON CREATIVE PROCESS:

Design Secrets: Products 1 and 2: 50 Real-Life Product Design Projects
Uncovered by Lynn Haller and Cheryl Dangel Cullen, and edited by Industrial Designers Society of America.
Process: 50 Product Designs from Concept to Manufacture by Jennifer Hudson.
Manufacturing Processes for Design Professionals by Rob Thompson.
Biomimicry: Innovation Inspired by Nature by Janine M. Benyus
Product Design and Development by Karl T. Ulrich and Steven D. Eppinger.
Managing the Design Factory by Donald G. Reinertsen.

BOOKS ON CREATIVE DESIGNER SKILLS

Presentation Techniques by Dick Powell.
Creative Marker Techniques: In Combinationa with Mixed Media by Yoshiharu Shimizu
Sketching: Drawing Techniques for Product Designers by Koos Eissen and Roselien Steur.
Architecture: Form, Space, & Order by Francis D. K. Ching.
Elements of Design: Rowena Reed Kostellow and the Structure of Visual
Relationships by Gail Greet Hannah.
Basic Visual Concepts and Principles For Artists, Architects And Designers by Charles Wallschlaeger and Cynthia Busic-Snyder.
Digital Lighting and Rendering (2nd Edition) by Jeremy Birn.
Thinkertoys (Michael Michalko)
The Creative Habit: Learn It and Use It for Life (Twyla Tharp with Mark Reiter)
Geometry of Design: Kimberly Elam

248

The Industrial Design Reader: Carma Gorman
Design Basics: S. Pentak and A. Lauer
Design in the USA (Jeffrey Meikle)
History of Modern Design (David Raizman)
Design Studies: A Reader (Hazel Clark and David Brody)
Design as Future-Making (Susan Yelavich and Barbara Adams) Product Design (Rodgers and Milton)
The Design Process (Karl Aspelund)
Toward a New Interior: An Anthology of Interior Design Theory (Lois Weinthal)
Graphic Design: Now in Production (Ian Albinson and Rob Giampietro) The New Basics (Ellen Lupton and Jennifer Cole Phillips)
Digital Design Essentials Rajesh Lal
Don't Make Me Think, Revisited Steve Krug
About Face: The Essentials of Interaction Design Alan Cooper, Robert
Reimann, David Cronin, Christopher Noessel
The Best Interface Is No Interface Golden Krishna
Designing Interfaces Jenifer Tidwell
Simple and Usable Web, Mobile, and Interaction Design Giles Colborne
Evil by Design Chris Nodder
Designing with the Mind in Mind Jeff Johnson
UI is Communication Everett N McKay Serious Creativity, Edward de Bono Cracking Creativity, Michael Michalko
A Technique For Producing Ideas, James Webb Young
Making Ideas Happen, Scott Belsky Applied Imagination, Alex Osborn The Art of Innovation, To Kelley
The Power of Positive Deviance, Richard Pascale & Jerry and Monique Sternin
Biomimicry; innovation inspired by nature, Janine Benyus
Patterns in Nature: Philip Ball,- Why the Natural World Looks the Way It Does
Black Hole Blues and Other Songs from Outer Space: Janna Levin
Mapping the Heavens: The Radical Scientific Ideas That Reveal the Cosmos: Priyamvada Natarajan
Welcome to the Universe: An Astrophysical Tour: Neil deGrasse Tyson, Michael A. Strauss, and J. Richard Gott.
Hidden Figures: Margot Le Shetterly
The American Dream and the Untold Story of the Black Women
Mathematicians Who Helped Win the Space Race
Rise of the Rocket Girls: Nathalia Holt
The Women Who Propelled Us, from Missiles to the Moon to Mars
The Only Rule Is It Has to Work: Ben Lindbergh and Sam Miller
Our Wild Experiment Building a New Kind of Baseball Team
The Invention of Nature: Andrea Wulf; Alexander von Humboldt's New World

NEW PARADIGM OCCUPATIONS: D_ESIGN SCIENCE IN THE NEW PARADIGM AGE

The Gene: Siddhartha Mukherjee. An Intimate History
Are We Smart Enough to Know How Smart Animals Are? : Frans de Waal
The Wasp That Brainwashed the Caterpillar: Matt Simon- Thoughts on Design (Paul Rand)
Originally published as an essay in 1947, Thoughts on Design is still fiercely relevant to today's designers.
Tibor Kalman: Perverse Optimist (Peter Hall and Michael Bierut)
This joint work designed by Pentagram partner Michael Bierut and edited by writer Peter Hall pays tribute to the graphic design of Tibor Kalman.
Design as Art (Bruno Munari) Thinking With Type (Ellen Lupton)
The Visual Display of Quantitative Information (Edward Tufte)
Drawing is Thinking (Milton Glaser)
Graphic Design: A Concise History (Richard Hollis)
Type and Image: The Language of Graphic Design Paperback(Philip B. Meggs) Meggs' History of Graphic Design (Philip B. Meggs, Alston W. Purvis)
Anatomy of Design: Uncovering the Influences and Inspiration in Modern
Graphic Design (Steven Heller and Mirko Ilic) The Design of Everyday Things (Don Norman) Change by Design (Tim Brown)
Designing for Growth (Jeanne Liedtke)
Next Generation Business Strategies for the Base of the Pyramid(Ted London and Stu Hart)
Vision in Motion (Laszlo Moholy-Nagy)
Part of the original Bauhaus school, László Moholy-Nagy illustrates where design, art, and science meet.
World Changing: A User's Guide for the 21st Century (Alex Steffen) Humble Masterpieces: 100 Everyday Marvels of Design (Paola Antonelli) In the Bubble: Designing in a Complex World (John Thackara) Sustainable Design: Explanations in Theory and Practice (Stuart Walker)
Art and Visual Perception: A Psychology of the Creative Eye (Rudolf Arnheim) Weird Ideas that Work, Robert I. Sutton

BOOKS ON CREATIVE THINKING

Serious Creativity, Edward de Bono Cracking Creativity, Michael Michalko The Medici Effect, Frans Johansson
A Technique For Producing Ideas, James Webb Young
Making Ideas Happen, Scott Belsky
Applied Imagination, Alex Osborn
Weird Ideas that Work, Robert I. Sutton
The Art of Innovation, Tom Kelley
Biomimicry; innovation inspired by nature, Janine Benyus
The Power of Positive Deviance, Richard Pascale & Jerry and Monique Sternin

Nir Eyal: Hooked: How to Build Habit-Forming Products
100 Things Every Designer Needs to Know About People, Susan Weinschenk
Designing for the Digital Age by Kim Goodwin
Living with Complexity by Donald A. Norman
The Design of Everyday Things by Donald A. Norman.
Lance Wyman: The Monograph edited by Adrian Shaughnessy
Damn Good Advice (For People with Talent!) by George Lois
Herb Lubalin American Graphic Designer by Adrian Shaughnessy George Nelson: Architect / Writer / Designer / Teacher by Stanley Abercrombie
Saul Bass: A Life in Film and Design Hardcover
Dieter Rams: As Little Design as Possible by Sophie Lovell
Kern and Burn by Tim Hoover
Steve Jobs by Walter Isaacson Isaacson Design Forward by Hartmut Esslinger Design Is the Problem by Nathan Shedroff Obey the Giant by Rick
World without Words by Michael Evamy Evamy shows how simple design can explain so much without words and how culture is moving toward a world without words.
Predictably Irrational by Dan Ariely
The Craft of Words By The Standardistas
The Creative Habit by Twyla Tharp
Thinking, Fast and Slow by Daniel Kahneman Nobel Prize-winning psychologist.
Geek-Art: An Anthology by Thomas Olivri
The Icon Handbook by Jon Hicks
Logo Creed by Bill Gardner
Logo Design Love by David Airey
Monogram logo by Leterme Dowling and Counter-Print Symbol by Angus Hyland and Steven Bateman Articulating Design Decisions by Tom Greever
Insanely Simple: The Obsession That Drives Apple's Success by Ken Segall
Why We Buy: The Science of Shopping by Paco Underhill
How Google Works by Jonathan Rosenberg and Eric Schmidt
Design is a Job by Mike Monteiro This easy read explains how to build your business backbone while feeding your creative talent.
Drawn to Business by Bill Beachy of GoMedia.us
It's Not How Good You Are, It's How Good You Want To Be by Paul Arden
Creativity, Inc. by Ed Catmull and Amy Wallace
Manage Your Day-To-Day by Jocelyn K. Glei and 99U Remote by Jason Fried and David Heinemeier Hansson

NEW PARADIGM OCCUPATIONS: · D_ESIGN SCIENCE IN THE NEW PARADIGM AGE

Seductive Interaction Design: Creating Playful, Fun, and Effective User Experiences by Stephen P. Anderson Don't Make Me Think by Steve KrugIn, About Face by Alan Cooper, Robert Reimann, David Cronin and Christopher Noessel
Interaction Design by Yvonne Rogers, Helen Sharp and Jenny Preece
Product Design for the Web by Randy J. HuntEtsy's
Simple and Usable by Giles Colborne Designing for Emotion by Aarron Walter Designing with the Mind in Mind by Jeff Johnson You're Designing It All Wrong! by Tal Florentin Above the Fold by Brian D. Miller
The Visual Display of Quantitative Information by Edward R. Tufte
The Animator's Survival Kit by Richard Williams
Grid Systems in Graphic Design by Josef Müller-Brockmann
Design, Form, and Chaos by Paul Rand
Data Points by Nathan Yau
Form+Code in Design, Art, and Architecture by CaseyReas

BOOKS ON CREATIVE THINKING(Cont'd)

Graphic Design Before Graphic Designers by David Jury
How To Be a Graphic Designer Without Losing Your Soul by Adrian Shaughnessy
Meggs' History of Graphic Design by Philip B. Meggs and Alston W. Purvis
Drawing Ideas : Mark Baskinger and William
Sascha Michael Trinkaus, CEO of Trinkaus Creative Consultants
90 Degrees by Andrew Kim
Designing Brand Identity by Alina Wheeler
Designing Design by Kenya Hara Designing News by Francesco Franchi Interaction of Color by Josef Albers
Just Enough Research by Erika HallHall presents an easy
The Shape of Design by Frank Chimero
Sass for Web Designers by Dan Cederholm
Universal Principles of Design by William Lidwell, Kritina Holden and Jill
Art as Therapy by Alain de Botton. The Noble Approach by Tod Polson
Scripts: Elegant Lettering from Design's Golden Age by Steven Heller and Louise Fili
Designing With Web Standards by Jeffrey Zeldman
Responsive Web Design by Ethan Marcotte
What They Didn't Teach You In Design School: The Essential Guide to Growing
Your Design Career by Phil Cleaver

Life's a Pitch: How to Sell Yourself and Your Brilliant Ideas by Roger Mavity
Everything I Know by Paul Jarvis
Creativity for Sale by Jason SurfrApp The man behind IWearYourShirt and BuyMyLastName shares a practical guide on how to turn passions into profits.
Execute by Josh Long and Drew Wilson
The Good Creative by Paul Jarvis Steal Like An Artist by Austin Kleon Show Your Work! by Austin Kleon
Where Good Ideas Come From by Steven Johnson Johnson identifies the seven key patterns behind genuine innovation, and traces them across time and disciplines.

MAGAZINES

Computer Arts Magazine The industry-leading title for graphic designers, Computer Arts is the magazine for people who believe design matters.
Off-screen Magazine Off-screen is an independent magazine about people who use the internet and technology to be creative, solve problems, and build successful businesses.
Smashing Magazine and its publications; Smashing Magazine is a website and blog that offers resources, books, and advice to web developers and web designers.
DIS Magazine; The self-described "post-internet lifestyle magazine" has an editorial mission to interrogate and collapse hierarchies.
Dwell Magazine; Dwell is an American magazine devoted to modern architecture and design.

Promoting an International Association and Journal of D$_E$Sign Science is dedicated to research, prototyping and publication of results in the field of form generation, metaphysics, design theory and creativity with applications of the concepts, information technology and manufacturing technology to real world solutions in a holistic methodology known as D$_E$Sign Science.

Original works are expected from artists, industrial and academic contributors. Solutions, inventions and concepts must be presented as solutions to practical problems relevant to needs of industries.

The areas of scope include, but are not limited to: solid modeling, geometric modeling, geometric processing, computer graphics, computational geometry, computer-aided design, computer-aided manufacturing, computer-aided engineering, feature technology, concurrent engineering, collaborative engineering, computer integrated manufacturing, Internet-based CAD/CAM, rapid prototyping, assembly modeling, product data exchange, intelligent CAD, user interaction techniques, human machine and human computer interaction, RFID application, FEM/BEM, mesh generation, virtual reality, scientific visualization, CAPP, NC programming, and topological optimization, Artificial Intelligence and computer science and engineering etc.

ADDENDUM

THOTH WAS SESHAT, GODDESS OF writing, the keeper of books, and patron goddess of libraries and librarians who was alternately his wife or daughter. The *Ogdoad*, *Hehu* or Infinites, '*celestial rulers*' of a cosmic age might have come long before the Egyptian religious system currently recognized. The Ogdoad were concerned with the *preservation and flourishing of the celestial world*, and the '*formation' of the human race*. If we look at this as the creation story, the characters could be very transmutable. They could be GODS, Forces, principles or other phenomena represented in a Spiritual Science tradition.

The characters in our cosmic accounts could very well be the same as the Celestial rulers of the Egyptian era and prior.

There is evidence in sites like Gobekli Tepe that could be the reference to the 'coming long before' of the Infinities. Whether it is before, during or after which will correspond with our time, the process is eternal, and the characters and their languages change. Threads of evidence are pointing to the constant creation model presenting us with parallels that might confirm this hypo or epi-the/i/sis.

The transfiguration of GODS into forces or energies and the reverse, seems to be a spiritual technology in Egypt. Transfiguration— noun: the Transfiguration a complete change of form or appearance into a more beautiful or spiritual state. Ancient Egypt has a history with more of it hidden that's left to the curious to imagine, investigate and interpret to discover the meaning and reason for being and becoming. From the Pre-Dynastic Period (c.6000-3150 BCE) to the Ptolemaic Period (323-30 BCE), the last dynastic era of Egyptian history was influenced by the civilization building that began with the GOD Toth or Hermes Tresmegistus. His wisdom, knowledge and spiritual influence inspired the wisdom tradition, schools and temple cultures. Thoth's Egyptian name was Djehuty (also *dhwty*) meaning "He Who is Like the Ibis". His name would be taken by kings of Egypt. Tuthmoses "Born of Thoth", scribes, and priests is one example.

Thoth is commonly depicted as a man with the head of an ibis or a seated baboon with or without a lunar disc above his head. Were these interpretations fact, spiritual knowledge or magic?

Worshiping Thoth began in Lower Egypt most likely from the Pre-Dynastic Period (c. 6000-3150 BCE) to the Ptolemaic Period (323-30 BCE). Thoth's veneration was among the longest of the Egyptian gods or any deity from any civilization. The Aquarian Gospel tells us of the Transfiguration of Jesus. the hierophant, into 'The Christ'. After intense studies, 'training' and testing by the priests in the temple he becomes a 'Master'. The knowledge Toth imparted to the priest sect became the 'canon' of the wisdom tradition.

Naqada III or King Menes; 3200 to 3000 BC, ruled in the last phase of the Naqada culture. This Protodynastic Period was characterized by an ongoing process of civilization and political unification. Very little is known of the mystery tradition and role that the Pharaonic and temple cultures played in the transfigurations of Egyptian pharaohs into GODS. Were they GODS? Menes founded Memphis as the capital of ancient Egypt in the north, near the apex of the Nile River delta which became the dominant metropolis in ancient Egypt.

Djer was the second or third pharaoh of the first dynasty of Egypt, which dates from approximately 3100 BC. *Uncertainty over the first pharaohs of this dynasty, Menes or Narmer, and Hor-Aha, and possible confusion with the final ruler of the Protodynastic Period, makes the numbering of the First Dynasty problematic.* Thoth is the Egyptian God of *writing, magic, wisdom, and the moon.* He was one of the most important Gods of ancient Egypt. He was *self-created* or born of the *seed of Horus from the forehead of Set*.

What do we find at the forehead that could be the seed? Mystery traditions know this as the third eye. It is connected to the Hypothalamus where the Pineal and Pituitary glands are also considered the *'seat of the soul'*. Horus and Set are essences of consciousness with principles involved in the living dynamic and connections to Source.

As the son of these two deities, who represented order and chaos respectively, he was also the god of equilibrium and balance and associated closely with both the principle of Ma'at (divine balance) and the goddess Ma'at who personified this principle (and who was sometimes seen as his wife). Another of his consorts was the goddess Nehemetawy ('She Who Embraces Those In Need") a protector goddess.

In his form as A'an, Thoth presided over the judgment of the dead with Osiris in the Hall of the Truth and those souls who feared they might not pass through the judgment safely were encouraged to call upon Thoth for help.

A paradigm shift, is a concept identified by Thomas Samuel Kuhn who was an American physicist, historian and philosopher of science. He proposed a fundamental change in basic concepts and experimental practices of scientific discipline in his controversial 1962 book The Structure of Scientific Revolutions. This methodology has become ubiquitous in many creative fields.

In science and philosophy, a paradigm is a distinct set of concepts or thought patterns, including theories, research methods, postulates, and standards for what constitutes legitimate contributions to a field. Sociologists today employ three primary theoretical perspectives: *the symbolic interactionist perspective, the functionalist perspective, and the conflict perspective*. These perspectives offer sociologists theoretical paradigms for explaining how society influences people, and vice versa.

Architects use these principles to Design and build communities, Industrial and Institutional complexes, cities and towns by synthesizing many disciplines into what Richard Buckminster Fuller called Design Science.

This is the discipline I promote to embrace the radical transformations we are experiencing as we prepare for the bright and prosperous future with ascension, not salvation of kind-man. The multitude of not just, 'habits', but desires, thoughts ideas and our beliefs and self-realization are lodged in our subconscious mind. They can facilitate our growth and development. Second, as the paradigms change,

NEW PARADIGM OCCUPATIONS: D$_E$SIGN SCIENCE IN THE NEW PARADIGM AGE

to be in step with our space, time and aesthetic creative energies—through a praxis of acquiring, processing and repetition of Wisdom, Intelligence, knowledge and information to expand our consciousness, we "make the abstract real". Important changes happen when the usual way of thinking about or doing something is replaced by a new and different way. Discoveries and innovation bring paradigm shifts to our understanding of who we are. This gives artists and designers new frameworks for their creative expressions.

Design is the voice of consciousness singing its cosmic melodies, inspiring us to become our best selves, in service to humanity and mother Earth.

DESIGN DEVELOPMENT: D$_E$Sign Science Education and Training for the New Paradigm Age.

The D$_E$Sign Science compendium; volumes one and two with the gallery of color illustrations in eWork Book outlines and offers creative opportunities to artists, designers, architects and other visual disciplines involved in creative research and development related to theoretical innovation, with the applied content and intellectual properties the author presents to enhance their careers and lives.

The purchase of volume one with the eWork Book is required for admission to this exciting journey. The advanced volume two will be available when the work in volume one is satisfactorily completed.

Thank You

Herb G. Bennett

Participants will be requested to submit an application for details and agreements to be reviewed before completing your membership.

Other opportunities are available based on the capabilities, needs assessments upon review of development proposals that are presented and evaluated.

Kindly complete the information on the following page to begin the process.

Herbert G. Bennett RA

Signature: _____

Date: _____ / _____ / _____

Purchaser/   Signature

Address _____

City   State   Zip

Phone No   Cell

Email _____

WELCOME TO A BRIGHT, PROSPEROUS, CREATIVE AND PURPOSEFUL D_ESign Science LIFE AND CAREER.

DEDICATION TO MY MENTOR AND FRIEND:

THE ARTIST THEODORE "TEDDY" GUNN, was born 1931, and raised in Saugerties Upstate New York. His family moved to Harlem in Manhattan New York. During his pioneering career, his cultural leadership was shared with many of New York's most respected arts and cultural institutions.

In his thirty-two-year career with the Bedford Stuyvesant Restoration Corporation, he served as director of the Center for Arts and Culture from 1970 to 1994. As a founding trustee, and acting director, of the arts, he coordinated exhibitions at Harlem's Studio Museum. He was a member of the Metropolitan Museum of Art's Committee for Community Programs.

He was influential in the development of New York's cultural institutions, communities and talent including the Brooklyn Arts and Cultural Association, now BAC, the Brooklyn Masonic Temple, the Washington Heights Arts Show, and The Rotunda Gallery.

He transitioned in August of 2020, leaving the world and august and auspicious legacy that will continue to inspire, nurture and touch the lives of 'his people and communities' he serves. His creativity, honor, compassion and love will sustain us and those we continue to serve through his legacy.

NOTE: The front and back matter of the book will have the covers; front and back, the foreword and dedication in portrait orientation. The rest will follow the landscape formatted interior.

Thank You